CLASSIC COOKING
STEP-BY-STEP

CLASSIC COOKING
STEP-BY-STEP

Moyra Fraser
OVER 750 RECIPES ILLUSTRATED IN FULL COLOR

CRESCENT BOOKS
NEW YORK   AVENEL, NEW JERSEY

CONTENTS

INTRODUCTION

The aim of this book is to make cooking as straightforward and as pleasurable as it possibly can be. The clear step-by-step instructions and the accompanying photographs will help you to achieve impressive results. However, there are also a number of general guidelines that you should follow in order to get the best out of the recipes.

❖ Cook's Notes ❖

❖ All spoon measures are level. All cup measures of dry ingredients are level. To measure flour, scoop it with the cup, then level the surface with the side of a knife.

❖ Make sure you read the line on the cup or pint measure at eye level when measuring liquids.

❖ Do not hold the measuring spoon into which you are pouring liquid over the dish you are making, in case you pour out too much.

❖ Ovens should be preheated to the specified temperature. Broilers should also be preheated. The cooking times given in the recipes assume that this has been done.

❖ Cooking times can vary according to the individual oven. Start checking to see whether the dish is cooked toward the end of the cooking time.

❖ Where a stage is specified in parentheses under freezing instructions, the dish should be frozen at the end of that stage.

❖ Where margarine is required you can use either hard or soft margarine. Otherwise use as specified in the recipe.

❖ Extra large eggs should be used except where otherwise specified.

❖ All-purpose flour should be used unless otherwise specified. Use white or whole wheat flour, but see individual chapters for use in pastry-, bread-, and cake-making.

❖ Brown or white bread crumbs can be used unless one type is specified.

❖ Use freshly ground black pepper unless otherwise specified.

❖ Equivalents ❖

3 tsp	= 1 tbsp
2 tbsp	= 1 fl oz
4 tbsp	= ¼ cup
5 tbsp + 1 tsp	= ⅓ cup
8 tbsp	= ½ cup (4 fl oz)
10 tbsp + 2 tsp	= ⅔ cup
12 tbsp	= ¾ cup
16 tbsp	= 1 cup (8 fl oz)
2 cups	= 1 pint (16 fl oz)
4 cups	= 2 pints = 1 quart
4 quarts	= 1 gallon
16 oz	= 1 lb

Use the following reference charts if you encounter the metric system of measurement in other books. The equivalents given here are not exact, but have been rounded up or down for ease of measurement.

❖ Conversion Charts ❖

❖ Liquid ❖

METRIC ❖	EQUIVALENT ❖
5 ml	1 tsp
15 ml	1 tbsp
30 ml	1 fl oz
60 ml	¼ cup
120 ml	½ cup
185 ml	¾ cup
250 ml	1 cup
500 ml	1 pint (2 cups)
1 liter	1 quart

❖ Solid ❖

METRIC ❖	EQUIVALENT ❖
25 g	1 oz
50 g	2 oz
125 g	4 oz
225 g	8 oz
350 g	12 oz
400 g	14 oz
450 g	1 lb
700 g	1½ lb
900 g	2 lb
1 kg	2.2 lb

❖ Oven Temperature ❖

CENTIGRADE SCALE ❖	FAHRENHEIT SCALE °F ❖
110°C	225°F
130	250
140	275
150	300
170	325
180	350
190	375
200	400
220	425
230	450
240	475

COOKING UTENSILS & EQUIPMENT

A well-equipped kitchen does not mean one that contains every possible gadget and appliance. The most important considerations when choosing cooking utensils and equipment are frequency of use and quality. You should concentrate on buying a small number of high-quality but very practical tools that will stand the test of time rather than a larger number of lower quality items, many of which may never be taken out of the kitchen drawer.

Pots and pans and knives are arguably the most indispensable items used in cooking. And, while they are not strictly essential as all cooking tasks can be performed by hand if necessary, food preparation machines can make such a difference when you are cooking large quantities or involved in a time-consuming task that they should be seriously considered when you are equipping your kitchen.

Following are some general guidelines on how to choose what you need:

❖ Pots and Pans ❖

The key factor here is the material from which a cooking pot or pan is made. This determines how quickly and evenly it conducts heat to the food and how easily it will burn.

❖ ALUMINUM conducts heat evenly. Medium and heavy gauge aluminum are suitable for most types of cooktop but lightweight aluminum is suitable only for gas and has a short life as it tends to distort.

❖ CAST IRON conducts heat well. It is thick, heavy, and good for long, slow cooking at low temperatures. Because cast iron is heavy, it is not suitable if you have problems lifting things and it is also liable to break if dropped on a hard floor surface.

❖ COPPER conducts heat very well and is preferred by many professional chefs. It must be lined with tin, nickel, or aluminum to prevent the copper from reacting with very acid foods. Copper is expensive and needs regular cleaning.

❖ STAINLESS STEEL needs a layer of aluminum or copper bonded onto the base to help it conduct heat well. Pans of stainless steel are expensive, but they are also very durable and will, if looked after properly, last forever.

❖ PORCELAIN, often mislabeled enamel, is frequently applied to various metals (iron, aluminum, or steel) to make them more attractive on the exterior and easier to clean on the interior. Acrylic or polyamide are also used, but these are inferior to porcelain and may discolor.

❖ EARTHENWARE AND CERAMICS are not good conductors of heat although they do tend to retain heat well once hot. They are most suitable for use in the oven and should be set on a heat diffusing mat if used on the cooktop.

Aim for a good range of sizes in building up a collection of pots and pans, so that you can choose the right size for the task in hand. Food will not cook properly if the pan is too big or too small for what is in it.

The following is a guide to what is really essential and what you can acquire when you choose:

❖ Pan Checklist ❖

BASIC SELECTION ❖	ADDITIONAL SELECTION ❖
3 heavy-based saucepans with lids, 1-, 2-, and 3-quart heavy-based frying pan or sauté pan with lid double boiler	steamer omelette or crêpe pan wok preserving kettle fish kettle

❖ Knives ❖

There are few cooking tasks that cannot be achieved with a sharp knife. The material from which a knife is made affects its sharpness and durability.

❖ CARBON STEEL is easy to sharpen. However, it discolors on contact with acidic food and rusts easily. Dry carbon steel knives thoroughly after washing.

❖ STAINLESS STEEL does not discolor or rust easily. However, it blunts quickly and is difficult to sharpen.

❖ HIGH CARBON STAINLESS STEEL has all the advantages. It sharpens well and does not discolor or rust easily. Inevitably, high carbon stainless steel knives are the most expensive.

Knives should be looked after well and the following guidelines will help to keep your knives in good condition:

❖ Always wash and dry them thoroughly after use.

❖ Do not keep knives all together in a drawer. Use a knife block, which will prevent the blades from damaging each other.

❖ Sharpen them regularly.

As with pots and pans, aim to have a basic selection of good knives and acquire others when you can.

❖ Knife Checklist ❖

BASIC SELECTION ❖	ADDITIONAL SELECTION ❖
cook's or utility knife, at least 8-inches long paring knife carving knife and fork heavy butcher knife serrated knife slicing knife	filleting knife boning knife

❖ Food Preparation Machines ❖

The main point to consider when you are buying a machine is just how sophisticated you need it to be. It is easy to be tempted into thinking that you must have the most highly developed model on the market, but do stop to think whether you will really use all those functions, and remember that the machine and any attachments will have to be cleaned and stored somewhere.

Food Processors

A machine that slices vegetables, shreds cheese, blends soups, mixes cakes, chops nuts, purées fruit, kneads bread, and whips cream sounds like the perfect kitchen companion. Most food processors are supplied with a metal blade, a shredder/grater, and a slicer disk as standard. In general, the more you pay, the larger the capacity of the bowl and the more attachments you get. Top-of-the-range models also offer greater power and optional extras such as extra shredders, a fruit press, a mill, an ice-cream maker, a Parmesan disk, and a julienne disk. How much use you make of these clearly depends on the scale and kind of cooking you do. There are, however, a number of essential features that you should look for when buying:

❖ Measurements on the feed tube and bowl.
❖ Variable speeds (although you do not need more than three) and a pulse (a short burst of high speed) for greater control.
❖ Adjustable slicing disks.
❖ Non-slip feet.
❖ Cable storage.
❖ Reversible disks, to save on storage space.
❖ Safety-locking lid.

In addition, there are some particularly useful features offered by more expensive food processors that you may consider paying more for:

❖ Mini chopping bowls for small quantities of food.
❖ Drip-feed lid/feed tube that allows liquids to be added to the bowl while the processor is running (useful when making mayonnaise).
❖ Different feed-tube sizes – a double-feed tube is useful for foods of different sizes and a wide semi-circular feed tube is good for large items such as cabbage.
❖ Integral storage for attachments.
❖ Finger grips on attachments.
❖ Dishwasher-safe attachments.
❖ Liquidizer attachment for fine, smooth purées.
❖ Citrus press or juice extractor.
❖ Blade storage compartment or box.

If you use your food processor a lot it can be worth buying a second bowl to save having to wash it too often during a preparation session.

Blenders

A blender, which may also be an attachment to a food processor, is generally used for puréeing and liquidizing. It purées more finely than a food processor and is especially good for mayonnaise. Blenders are not recommended for dry chopping, however.

There are two types of blender to choose from:
❖ Goblet blenders, in which the cutting blades are at the bottom. Check the height of the blades before you buy as some are too high to cope with one-yolk mayonnaise and small quantities of food. Most goblets carry measurements down the side so you can check the quantity you are working with and add as necessary. A handle on the side of the goblet is useful for lifting it off the base when it contains hot liquid.
❖ Hand-held blenders, which require more effort than goblets but which are very portable.

Mini-choppers

These are useful for chopping small amounts of nuts, herbs, or vegetables and can also blend small amounts of liquid. They cannot compete with full-sized food processors on larger quantities.

Electric Mixers

These are particularly useful for mixing cakes, kneading dough, and beating, as food processors are not very good at incorporating air into mixtures such as egg whites, cream, and sponge cakes. They can be either portable or countertop models.

❖ Portable mixers may come with a bowl and stand and operate without being held. Or they may simply consist of a motorized head into which a selection of blades and beaters can be fitted. There is little advantage in buying the type with a bowl and stand as these then have to be stored somewhere. Beaters alone can be used in a suitable bowl of your own.
❖ Countertop mixers are large and take up a lot of space. They can deal with large quantities of mixtures such as bread dough or fruit cake batter, however, and can be left to operate without supervision.

❖ Other Utensils and Equipment ❖

In spite of the huge range of kitchen tools and equipment on the market, the number of utensils that are needed on a day-to-day basis is relatively small. If you are interested in a particular area of cooking, such as cake decorating or preserving, you may want, or need, to add more specialist tools to your collection to help in specific tasks. The following checklist is intended to act as a general guide to what is essential equipment for the average kitchen:

❖ Basic Selection ❖

saucepans (see above)	pancake turner
knives (see above)	colander
casseroles	strainer
roasting pan	grater
mixing bowls	potato peeler
cake pans	potato ricer
kitchen scales	skewers
measuring cups	rolling pin
measuring spoons	corkscrew
chopping boards	bottle opener
(ideally separate ones for	can opener
different foods, see page 433)	baking sheet
wooden spoons	wire cooling rack
slotted spoon	balloon whisk
ladle	kitchen scissors
spatulas	tongs

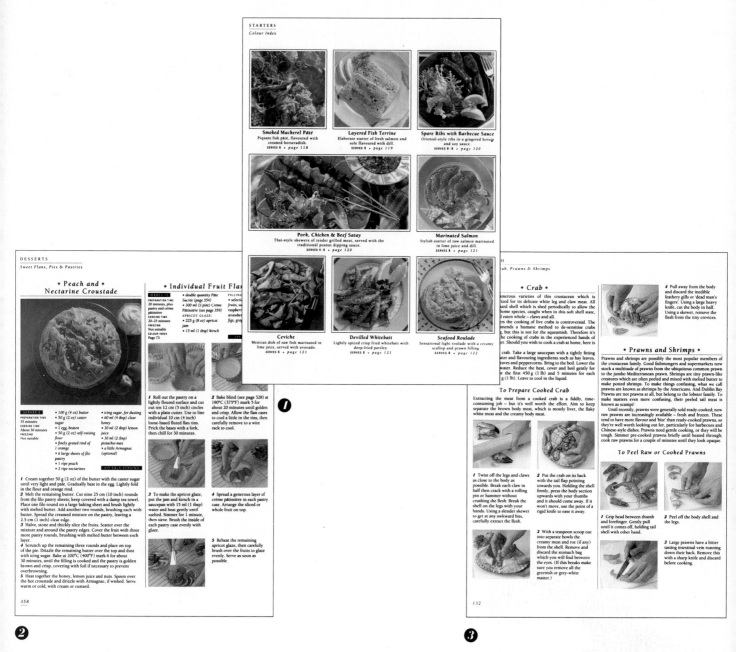

❖ How to Use This Book ❖

❶ Your starting point for choosing recipes and putting together a menu is the Color Index. Here you will find a photograph of every recipe in the book. In addition, you will find the following information:

❖ a brief description of the dish
❖ the number of people it serves
❖ the page on which the recipe appears.

❷ As well as thorough step-by-step instructions, each recipe also provides further useful information:

❖ Preparation and cooking times are listed at the top of each recipe, together with an indication of whether any extra time should be allowed, for example, in the case of marinating or soaking.

❖ Freezing notes indicate the suitability of the dish for freezing.

When the dish can be frozen at the end of a certain stage in the preparation, this stage is given in parentheses.

❖ A reference to a page in the Color Index tells you where to find a photograph of the finished dish if it does not appear with the recipe.

❖ Calorie counts are given per serving or appropriate portion of the dish. Where the calorie count ranges from a higher to a lower figure, this reflects the fact that the dish may serve a larger number of people, in which case the portion size and calorie count are reduced.

❸ At the beginning of each chapter you can find general information on the food in question and on how to choose, prepare, cook, and serve it. Where appropriate, step-by-step photographs illustrate the essential techniques and you can refer back to this section from the recipes if you are unsure about a preparation or cooking method.

COLOR INDEX

Chicken Consommé
Sparkling, clear full-flavored consommé
with classic variations.
SERVES 4 ❖ *page 98*

Cock-a-Leekie Soup
Clear light chicken and leek soup
flavored with prunes.
SERVES 6 ❖ *page 98*

Mushroom Soup
A richly flavored soup served with
crunchy Parmesan croûtons.
SERVES 4 ❖ *page 99*

French Onion Soup
The ever-popular French classic, served with toasted
Gruyère-topped croûtes.
SERVES 4 ❖ *page 99*

Roquefort & Watercress Soup
Deliciously rich, creamy soup, equally
good served hot or chilled.
SERVES 4 ❖ *page 100*

Spinach Soup
Pretty green-flecked soup served hot,
with cream and croutons.
SERVES 4 ❖ *page 100*

Lettuce & Watercress Soup

Refreshing summer soup, ideal for
dieters. Serve hot or chilled.

SERVES 6 ❖ *page 100*

Vegetable Soup with Pasta

Lightly spiced soup flavored with chili
and fresh coriander (cilantro).

SERVES 4 ❖ *page 101*

Green Pea & Chervil Soup

A light, summery soup that acquires
its flavor from empty pea pods.

SERVES 6 ❖ *page 101*

The renow
and shellfis

SER

Carrot & Coriander Soup

A smooth, creamy soup, spiced with
coriander.

SERVES 6 ❖ *page 102*

Chill

A delicious
e

SER

Spiced Leek & Potato Soup

A smooth-textured creamy soup with a
hint of curry flavor.

SERVES 6 ❖ *page 102*

Parsnip & Apple Soup

The characteristic flavor of parsnips is blended with a
hint of tart apple in this velvety-textured soup.

SERVES 6 ❖ *page 102*

C r...

Velvety...
l...
s...

Asparagus with Coriander Hollandaise
A deliciously different way of serving
this prized vegetable.
SERVES 4 ❖ *page 126*

Baked Tomatoes with Cheese
Mozzarella- and goat-cheese stuffed
tomatoes on crisp toast rounds.
SERVES 6 ❖ *page 127*

Deep-Fried Potato Skins
Deep-fried skins, served with two
contrasting tasty dips.
SERVES 2-3 ❖ *page 127*

Comfort...
po...

Warm Salad of Mushrooms
Guaranteed to impress, this warm salad of assorted mushrooms,
tender spinach leaves, and crisp bacon is quick to prepare.
SERVES 6-8 ❖ *page 128*

Filo Purses with Vegetables
Crisp light filo parcels filled with
stir-fried vegetable julienne.
SERVES 6 ❖ *page 128*

Thick,
s...

Salade Tiède
Curly endive in a creamy vinaigrette with
hot crisp bacon and croûtons.
SERVES 4 ❖ *page 128*

Baked Mushroom Croûtes
Mixed wild cultivated mushrooms on
baked slices of French bread.
SERVES 6 ❖ *page 129*

Artichoke & Spinach Salad
Broiled Jerusalem artichokes and young
spinach flavored with lemon.
SERVES 6 ❖ *page 129*

Dressed Crab
An impressive way of serving crab for a
special lunch or supper.
SERVES 2–3 ❖ *page 135*

Avocado with Crab
This tempting appetizer with its rich
blend of flavors is quick to prepare.
SERVES 4 ❖ *page 135*

Grilled Lobster
A simple dish that brings out the fine
delicate taste of lobster.
SERVES 4 ❖ *page 135*

Chili Shrimp with Cashews
Delicious stir-fry of shrimp,
scallions, and cashew nuts.
SERVES 2–3 ❖ *page 136*

Prawns Fried in Garlic
Dublin Bay prawns are the variety used
in this superb dish.
SERVES 2 ❖ *page 136*

Shrimp with Fennel & Rice
Large succulent shrimp, tossed with
fennel, zucchini, and rice.
SERVES 4 ❖ *page 136*

Scallops in Creamy Basil Sauce
Pretty sea scallops served in a wine and
cream sauce with basil.
SERVES 4 ❖ *page 137*

Scallops with Ginger
Tasty spiced seafood dish, with ginger,
chili, and coriander.
SERVES 3 ❖ *page 137*

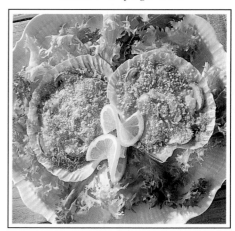

Scallops au Gratin
Sea scallops in a delicate sauce with a
crunchy topping – served in their shells.
SERVES 4 ❖ *page 137*

Mussels & Clams with Tomatoes
Delicious steamed shellfish in a tasty
tomato and garlic broth.
SERVES 2–3 ❖ *page 138*

Mussels with Garlic & Parsley
Baked mussels, coated in garlic and
Parmesan-flavored bread crumbs.
SERVES 4–6 ❖ *page 138*

Monkfish & Mussel Skewers
Brochettes of firm white monkfish,
mussels, and bacon on a salad.
SERVES 4 ❖ *page 138*

Mussels in White Wine
Mussels on the half-shell in a rich
cream and wine sauce.
SERVES 4–6 ❖ *page 139*

Oysters au Gratin
Mouthwatering oysters with bacon and
artichoke hearts.
SERVES 4–6 ❖ *page 139*

Seafood Pilaki
Delicious mixture of monkfish squid, and
mussels in a tomato sauce.
SERVES 8 ❖ *page 140*

Glazed Seafood Platter
Sumptuous mixture of shellfish and fish
with a cheese topping.
SERVES 6 ❖ *page 140*

Mixed Seafood Brochettes
Seafood selection, marinated, then grilled
and served on rice.
SERVES 4 ❖ *page 141*

Italian Seafood Salad
A stunning salad of assorted shellfish
in a lemon dressing.
SERVES 6 ❖ *page 141*

Turbot with Chervil

Delicious turbot steaks served with a
chervil and tomato sauce.

SERVES **4** ❖ *page 146*

Sole with Mousseline Sauce

Delicate fillets of sole in a lemon
cream sauce.

SERVES **8** ❖ *page 146*

Haddock with Parsley & Lemon

Baked haddock served with a smooth
parsley sauce.

SERVES **4** ❖ *page 146*

Monkfish with Lemon & Dill

Firm-fleshed monkfish, marinated and
grilled to perfection.

SERVES **4** ❖ *page 147*

Parchment Baked Fish

Fish steaks baked in parcels with
cucumber and fennel seeds.

SERVES **4** ❖ *page 147*

Rolled Flounder with Pesto

Piquant flounder rolls served on a bed of
colorful vegetables.

SERVES **4** ❖ *page 148*

Sole with Mushrooms

Tasty, nutritious dish, ideal for a
low-calorie supper.

SERVES **4** ❖ *page 148*

Golden Crumbed Flounder

Quick and easy fish dish with a crunchy
crumb and nut topping.

SERVES **4** ❖ *page 148*

Seafood Kebabs

Skewered monkfish, shrimp, and cucumber,
served with a garlic vinaigrette.

SERVES **4** ❖ *page 149*

Monkfish with Mustard Seeds

Nutritious fish in a low-calorie lemon
and mustard yogurt sauce.

SERVES 6 ❖ *page 149*

Sweet & Sour Monkfish Kebabs

Skewers of bacon-wrapped fish,
eggplant, and red onion.

SERVES 4 ❖ *page 150*

Haddock & Sour Cream Gratin

Tasty fish supper, with a creamy
tomato and herb sauce.

SERVES 2 ❖ *page 150*

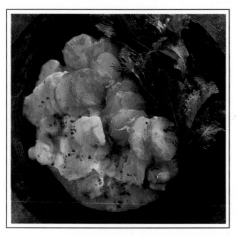

Cod & Crab Gratin

Cod, mushrooms, and crab meat with a
cheesy potato topping

SERVES 4 ❖ *page 150*

Sweet & Sour Fish

Stir-fried fish with green beans, red bell
pepper and mushrooms.

SERVES 4 ❖ *page 151*

Trout in Riesling

Succulent trout braised in wine
on a bed of leeks.

SERVES 4 ❖ *page 152*

Lemon & Mustard Mackerel

Broiled mackerel flavored with a tangy
lemon and mustard butter.

SERVES 6 ❖ *page 152*

Salmon Steaks in Citrus Dressing

Grilled salmon enhanced with lime,
orange, and a hint of cardamom.

SERVES 4 ❖ *page 152*

Salmon & Thyme Parcels

Deliciously moist salmon steaks baked
in paper with herbs.

SERVES 4 ❖ *page 153*

Salmon Steaks with Hollandaise
Simply baked salmon portions with
a rich Hollandaise sauce.
SERVES 8 ❖ *page 153*

Dill-Glazed Salmon
This poached whole salmon makes an impressive centerpiece
for a special occasion. It is served cold, with a lemon mayonnaise.
SERVES 8 ❖ *page 154*

Sea Trout with Herb Sauce
Delicate cold sea trout, served with
a watercress and herb sauce.
SERVES 4 ❖ *page 154*

Salmon en Croûte
Delicious whole salmon with a spinach
filling, encased in melting puff pastry.
SERVES 8 ❖ *page 155*

Spinach & Seafood Turnovers
A tasty mélange of cod, shrimp, and
spinach in puff pastry.
SERVES 4 ❖ *page 155*

Crispy Layered Fish Pie
Light, crisp filo pastry enveloping
a haddock and rice filling.
SERVES 6 ❖ *page 156*

Golden Topped Fish Pie
Mixed seafood in a creamy sauce
with a crisp potato topping.
SERVES 4 ❖ *page 156*

Smoked Haddock Soufflé
Light hot soufflé flavored with
watercress and Parmesan.
SERVES 4 ❖ *page 157*

Spiced Fish Stir-Fry
Sea scallops and monkfish stir-fried with
spices and colorful vegetables.
SERVES 4 ❖ *page 158*

Curried Fish with Lemon
Fillets of sole in a creamy curried sauce
with ginger and coconut.
SERVES 6 ❖ *page 158*

Italian Fish Stew
A variety of fish and shellfish cooked with
saffron, garlic, and tomatoes.
SERVES 8 ❖ *page 161*

Fritto Misto
Assorted seafood deep-fried until
crisp and golden.
SERVES 8 ❖ *page 159*

Greek-Style Fish Casserole
A quick fish dish, flavored with
marjoram and garlic.
SERVES 4 ❖ *page 159*

Smoked Haddock Casserole
Rich, creamy mixture of shrimp,
haddock, and vegetables.
SERVES 6 ❖ *page 160*

Paella
Colorful Spanish dish of mixed
seafood, rice, and bell peppers.
SERVES 4 ❖ *page 160*

Fish Cakes with Herbs
Tasty fish and potato cakes, coated
with bread crumbs.
SERVES 4 ❖ *page 158*

Kedgeree
Flavorful mixture of smoked haddock,
rice, and hard-boiled egg.
SERVES 4 ❖ *page 161*

Roast Beef & Yorkshire Pudding
Succulent roast with gravy and
individual Yorkshire puddings.
SERVES 4–8 ❖ *page 168*

Beef Tenderloin with Mushrooms
Tenderloin stuffed with mushrooms and
bell peppers, with a tasty sauce.
SERVES 8 ❖ *page 168*

Beef en Croûte
Tenderloin roast flavored with pâté and
mushrooms, in puff pastry.
SERVES 8 ❖ *page 169*

Boeuf Bourguignon
Rich beef casserole with baby onions and
mushrooms in red wine.
SERVES 8 ❖ *page 170*

Peppered Rib of Beef
Boned and rolled rib, flavored with
herbs, garlic, and coriander.
SERVES 6 ❖ *page 170*

Boiled Beef & Carrots
Corned brisket simmered with
vegetables and aromatics.
SERVES 6 ❖ *page 170*

Spiced Beef Casserole
Slow-cooked beef and mushroom casserole
flavored with horseradish and ginger.
SERVES 6 ❖ *page 171*

Italian Braised Beef
Beef casseroled in wine, with artichoke
hearts, mushrooms, and olives.
SERVES 6 ❖ *page 171*

Oxtail & Lentil Casserole
Hearty, nourishing winter dish with
root vegetables and lentils.
SERVES 6 ❖ *page 172*

Beef Casserole with Kumquats
Chuck steak cooked with celery,
leeks, and kumquat slices.
SERVES 4 ❖ *page 172*

Beef Hotch-Potch
Chuck steak cooked with root
vegetables, with a crisp potato topping.
SERVES 4 ❖ *page 173*

Steak & Kidney Pie
Tender cubes of chuck steak and
kidney under a piecrust.
SERVES 4 ❖ *page 173*

Steak au Poivre
Sirloin steaks encrusted with
peppercorns in a brandy cream sauce.
SERVES 4 ❖ *page 174*

Grilled Steaks with Madeira
Grilled filet mignons served with a
Madeira-flavored demi-glace.
SERVES 4 ❖ *page 174*

Peppered Beef Sauté
Sautéed strips of sirloin and
red onion in a creamy sauce.
SERVES 2–3 ❖ *page 174*

Steak & Stilton Parcels
Stilton-toped steaks encased in crisp,
light filo pastry.
SERVES 4 ❖ *page 175*

Steak & Kidney Kebabs
Skewers of sirloin steak, kidneys,
mushrooms, and baby onions.
SERVES 4 ❖ *page 175*

Stir-Fried Beef & Vegetables
Steak stir-fried with baby corn,
snow peas, and broccoli.
SERVES 4 ❖ *page 176*

Chili Beef with Noodles
Stir-fried beef with red bell pepper,
broccoli, and thin noodles.
SERVES 4 ❖ *page 176*

Hamburgers
Moist oaty burgers flavored with herbs,
served in buns.
SERVES 4 ❖ *page 176*

Beef & Potato Moussaka
Ground beef, eggplant chunks, and
tomato, with a cheesy potato topping.
SERVES 4 ❖ *page 177*

Chile Tacos
Spicy beef and kidney beans in taco
shells, topped with cheese.
SERVES 4 ❖ *page 177*

Italian-Style Veal Kebabs
Tender strips of veal wrapped in Parma
ham and grilled on skewers.
SERVES 4 ❖ *page 178*

Basil & Citrus Scaloppine
Meltingly tender veal liberally flavored
with basil, orange, and lemon.
SERVES 4 ❖ *page 178*

Veal Goulash
Sustaining casserole, spiced with paprika
and topped with sour cream.
SERVES 8 ❖ *page 179*

Calf's Liver with Grapes
An unusual but delicious combination,
served with a Madeira sauce.
SERVES 4 ❖ *page 179*

Liver with Sage & Apple
Tender calf's liver sautéed with leeks,
apple slices, and sage.
SERVES 4 ❖ *page 179*

Crown Roast of Lamb
Celebration roast of 2 racks of lamb,
with a tasty apricot stuffing.
SERVES 6 ❖ *page 180*

Thyme Roasted Loin of Lamb
Boned loins rolled around a spinach,
thyme, and mushroom stuffing.
SERVES 6 ❖ *page 180*

Garlic & Rosemary Rack of Lamb
Spectacular roast liberally flavored
with garlic and herbs.
SERVES 4 ❖ *page 181*

Lamb with Peppers & Eggplants
Roast half leg with red bell peppers,
eggplants, and oregano.
SERVES 4 ❖ *page 181*

Roast Lamb Tenderloin with Garlic
Stuffed boned rack of lamb with a
piquant mustard sauce.
SERVES 4 ❖ *page 182*

Lamb & Zucchini Pilaf
Lean lamb with zucchini,
dried apricots, and brown rice.
SERVES 4 ❖ *page 182*

Lamb Casserole with Almonds
Creamy lamb casserole with ground
almonds, cumin, and ginger.
SERVES 8 ❖ *page 182*

Country Lamb Casserole
Lamb cooked with rutabaga, carrots,
celery, and pearl barley.
SERVES 6 ❖ *page 183*

Irish Stew
Lamb rib chops layered with potatoes,
onions, and herbs.
SERVES 4 ❖ *page 183*

Grilled Lamb Chops with Mint
Sirloin chops marinated in wine vinegar,
honey, and mint, then grilled.
SERVES 4 ❖ *page 184*

Lamb Chops with Apricots
Tender chops braised with
dried apricots and cinnamon.
SERVES 4 ❖ *page 186*

Lamb Noisettes with Mushrooms
Boned chops cooked with button
mushrooms and onions in white wine.
SERVES 4 ❖ *page 186*

Lamb Kebabs in a Spicy Dressing
Skewers of lamb, zucchini, corn, and
tomatoes in a yogurt dressing.
SERVES 4 ❖ *page 184*

Lamb & Pepper Stir-Fry
Stir-fried lamb with bell peppers,
carrots, snow peas, and zucchini.
SERVES 4 ❖ *page 185*

Spiced Lamb Meatballs
Bite-sized meatballs spiced with
chili and cumin.
SERVES 4 ❖ *page 185*

Oat-Coated Lamb Scaloppine
Pounded leg steaks flavored with
mustard, in crisp oat coating.
SERVES 4 ❖ *page 186*

Grilled Lamb with Zucchini
Loin chops spiked with rosemary,
grilled with zucchini.
SERVES 4 ❖ *page 184*

Cinnamon-Spiced Lamb
Slices of lamb cooked with ginger,
cinnamon, and nutmeg.
SERVES 4 ❖ *page 187*

Lamb Chops & Leeks with Lentils
Loin chops braised on a bed of leeks
and red lentils.
SERVES 4 ❖ *page 187*

Spiced Lamb with Spinach
Spicy casserole of lamb with turnips
and spinach.
SERVES 6 ❖ *page 187*

Spiced Lamb Scaloppine
Tender slices of leg marinated
in a spicy paste, then baked.
SERVES 4 ❖ *page 188*

Shepherd's Pie
Ideal family meal, ground lamb and
vegetables baked with a potato topping.
SERVES 4 ❖ *page 188*

Lamb & Eggplant Bake
Topped with golden, cheesy gnocchi,
this is simply delicious.
SERVES 6 ❖ *page 189*

Minted Lamb Burgers
Flavorsome burgers, cooked with
cucumber and scallions.
SERVES 4 ❖ *page 198*

Pan-Fried Liver with Tomatoes
Wafer-thin slices of lamb's liver
marinated and cooked in Marsala.
SERVES 4 ❖ *page 190*

Kidneys Provençale
Delicate lamb's kidneys cooked with
tomatoes, zucchini, and basil.
SERVES 4 ❖ *page 190*

Pork Loin with a Fruit Crust
Roast loin of pork encrusted with
a mixture of dried fruits.
SERVES 4 ❖ *page 191*

Roast Pork Loin with Rosemary
Succulent roast with a Dijon mustard
and rosemary glaze.
SERVES 6–8 ❖ *page 191*

Lemon-Roasted Pork with Garlic
Tender roast tenderloin with a lemon,
basil, and garlic stuffing.
SERVES 6 ❖ *page 192*

Pork with Celeriac Stuffing
Pork tenderloin with a tasty bacon,
celeriac, and bulgur wheat stuffing.
SERVES 6 ❖ *page 192*

Quick Pork Cassoulet
Pork blade steaks and kidney beans
in a spicy tomato stock.
SERVES 4 ❖ *page 192*

Pork & Herb Bean Pot
Slow-cooked casserole of pork, garlic
sausage, and pinto or black-eye peas.
SERVES 8 ❖ *page 193*

Pork with Prunes
Thin pork chops cooked in white wine
with plump prunes.
SERVES 4 ❖ *page 194*

Pork & Pasta Sauté
Quick, easy sauté of pork tenderloin,
vegetables, and pasta.
SERVES 4 ❖ *page 194*

Stir-Fried Pork with Baby Corn
Tasty stir-fry of pork, baby corn, carrots,
and sugar-snap peas.
SERVES 4 ❖ *page 195*

Pork in Wine & Coriander
Pan-fried tenderloin with green bell
pepper and ground coriander.
SERVES 4 ❖ *page 195*

Toad in the Hole
Fresh pork sausages baked in a
popover-type batter.
SERVES 4 ❖ *page 196*

Golden Grilled Pork Steaks
Boned loin chops, marinated and served
with a tangy citrus sauce.
SERVES 4 ❖ *page 196*

Sausages with Lentils
Coarse-ground fresh pork sausages cooked
with brown lentils and parsnips.
SERVES 4 ❖ *page 196*

Sausage & Bean Casserole
Herby sausages with chick peas and
kidney beans in tomato stock.
SERVES 6 ❖ *page 197*

Sausage & Potato Skewers
Tasty kebabs of fresh Italian sausages
and new potatoes.
SERVES 4–6 ❖ *page 197*

Glazed Baked Ham
Smoked boneless ham with a delicious
honey and orange glaze.
SERVES 8 ❖ *page 198*

Ham with a Crunchy Glaze
Fully cooked ham baked with an almond
and sesame seed coating.
SERVES 8 ❖ *page 198*

Smoked Pork Chops in Cider Sauce
Chops baked with mustard, served
with a hard cider sauce.
SERVES 4 ❖ *page 199*

Pork Shoulder with Parsley Sauce
Smoked pork butt simmered with
vegetables, served with parsley sauce.
SERVES 6–8 ❖ *page 199*

Pot Roast Chicken with Peppers
Whole chicken cooked with bell peppers
and garlic in wine and stock.
SERVES 4 ❖ *page 207*

Traditional Roast Chicken
Succulent chicken with a tasty parsley and lemon stuffing,
served with roast potatoes and seasonal vegetables.
SERVES 4–6 ❖ *page 206*

Saffron Chicken with Spinach
Spinach-stuffed chicken supremes, served
with a creamy saffron sauce.
SERVES 6 ❖ *page 207*

Chicken & Gorgonzola Parcels
Gorgonzola-stuffed chicken breasts
wrapped in sage and Parma ham.
SERVES 4 ❖ *page 208*

Chicken Breasts with Pesto
Low-calorie dish of baked chicken filled
with soft cheese and pesto.
SERVES 4 ❖ *page 208*

Chicken Casserole with Apricots
Chicken cooked with bacon rolls,
apricots, and thyme in Marsala wine.
SERVES 4 ❖ *page 208*

Chicken Parmigiana
Chicken baked with eggplant, tomato, mozzarella, and Parmesan.
SERVES 6 ❖ *page 209*

Chicken with Lemon & Sage
Braised chicken breasts with sage, garlic, and lemon.
SERVES 4 ❖ *page 210*

Chicken & Artichoke Pie
Chicken and artichoke hearts in a cheesy sauce, topped with filo pastry.
SERVES 4 ❖ *page 210*

Chicken with Spicy Tomato Sauce
Chicken thighs flavored with cumin, coriander, chili, and tomatoes.
SERVES 4 ❖ *page 210*

Chicken with Mushrooms & Cognac
Chicken cooked in white wine and enriched with cream and egg yolks.
SERVES 4 ❖ *page 211*

Spicy Chicken with Cashews
Chicken thighs coated with nuts, garlic, and ginger, in a yogurt sauce.
SERVES 4 ❖ *page 211*

Coq au Vin
Famous French casserole in red wine, served with bread croûtes.
SERVES 8 ❖ *page 212*

Chicken with Corn & Peppers
Chicken thighs with corn, green bell pepper, and brown rice.
SERVES 4 ❖ *page 212*

Chicken Curry with Coconut
Creamy curry, flavored with ginger, creamed coconut, and cashews.
SERVES 8 ❖ *page 213*

Spring Chicken Fricassée

Chicken breasts flavored with garlic
cream cheese, with baby vegetables.

SERVES **4** ❖ *page 214*

Sesame Chicken Stir-Fry

Chicken strips stir-fried with broccoli,
baby corn, and peanuts.

SERVES **4** ❖ *page 214*

Chicken with Oyster Sauce

Stir-fried chicken with flat
mushrooms and snow peas.

SERVES **4** ❖ *page 215*

Stir-Fried Chicken & Zucchini

Tasty stir-fry of chicken, red bell pepper
and zucchini strips.

SERVES **4** ❖ *page 215*

Chicken with Nuts & Mushrooms

Chicken sautéed with walnuts,
mushrooms, and cucumber.

SERVES **4** ❖ *page 216*

Chicken with Tarragon

Breasts of chicken braised in wine,
enhanced with juniper and tarragon.

SERVES **4** ❖ *page 216*

Chicken Chow Mein

Chicken and shrimp with bean sprouts
and noodles in Chinese sauce.

SERVES **4** ❖ *page 216*

Chicken & Avocado Stroganoff

Chicken, mushrooms, and avocado
chunks in a mustardy yogurt sauce.

SERVES **4** ❖ *page 217*

Honey-Barbecued Drumsticks

Barbecued or broiled drumsticks in a
soy, citrus, and honey marinade.

SERVES **8** ❖ *page 217*

Baked Artichokes

Tender young purplish globe artichokes
baked in extra-virgin olive oil.

SERVES **6** ❖ *page 256*

Jerusalem Artichoke & Chive Bake

Light, tasty casserole enriched with eggs
and topped with shredded cheese.

SERVES **4** ❖ *page 256*

Asparagus with Beurre Blanc

Perfectly cooked asparagus spears, accompanied by a classic herb-
flavored butter sauce. Serve as an elegant accompaniement or first course.

SERVES **6** ❖ *page 257*

Spiced Eggplant with Yogurt

Tender-cooked eggplant, flavored with
chili, coriander, and mustard seeds.

SERVES **4-6** ❖ *page 258*

Broccoli Stir-Fry

Broccoli florets cooked in a soy sauce
mixture, with garlic and sesame seeds.

SERVES **6** ❖ *page 258*

Sautéed Eggplants & Zucchini

"Bâtons" of eggplant and zucchini
flavored with toasted sesame seeds.

SERVES **8** ❖ *page 257*

Fava Beans with Artichokes
Young fava beans with artichoke
hearts, raw cured ham, and saffron
SERVES 6 ◆ *page 258*

Green Beans with Tomatoes & Herbs
Green beans with fresh tomatoes, basil,
parsley, garlic, and onion.
SERVES 6 ◆ *page 259*

Chestnut & Brussels Sprout Sauté
Whole chestnuts cooked with onion
wedges, celery, and Brussels sprouts.
SERVES 8 ◆ *page 259*

Green Beans with Feta
Fine green beans tossed with crumbly
feta cheese and sun-dried tomatoes.
SERVES 4 ◆ *page 259*

Cauliflower with Olives & Capers
Cauliflower florets with anchovy fillets,
black olives, capers, and parsley.
SERVES 6 ◆ *page 260*

Sautéed Greens
Coarsely shredded hearty greens sautéed
with garlic and topped with pine nuts.
SERVES 6 ◆ *page 260*

Cabbage with Juniper Berries
Shredded cabbage cooked with onion,
garlic, and juniper berries.
SERVES 4 ◆ *page 261*

Braised Red Cabbage with Pine Nuts
Red cabbage flavored with ginger,
balsamic vinegar, and toasted pine nuts.
SERVES 8 ◆ *page 260*

Chinese Braised Vegetables
Colorful assortment of vegetables,
flavored with ginger, garlic, and soy sauce.
SERVES 8 ◆ *page 261*

Glazed Carrots with Lemon
Fine carrot slices, flavored with lemon,
garlic, butter, and a little sugar.
SERVES 4 ❖ *page 262*

Zucchini with Sesame Seeds
Stir-fried zucchini with scallions, garlic,
and toasted sesame seeds.
SERVES 6 ❖ *page 262*

Celery Gratin
Celery in sour cream with a crisp bread
crumb and cheese topping.
SERVES 6 ❖ *page 263*

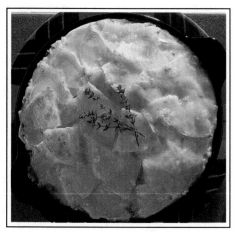

Celeriac with Gruyère
Celery root baked in cream with garlic
and topped with Gruyère.
SERVES 6 ❖ *page 263*

Fennel with Beans & Snow Peas
Fennel slices stir-fried with green beans
and snow peas, flavored with lemon.
SERVES 6 ❖ *page 263*

Stir-Fried Mixed Vegetables
Carrot ribbons stir-fried with beans, Napa
cabbage, scallions, and snow peas.
SERVES 4 ❖ *page 261*

Squash with Tomato & Onion
Summer squash cubes braised with
onions, herbs, and fresh tomatoes.
SERVES 4–6 ❖ *page 264*

Citrus Leeks with Sugar-Snaps
Leeks and sugar-snap peas tossed in a
tangy citrus dressing.
SERVES 6 ❖ *page 264*

Baby Carrots in Spiced Dressing
Tender, young carrots with sliced
almonds, cumin, coriander, and chives.
SERVES 4 ❖ *page 262*

Baked Mushrooms with Parsley
Flavorful flat mushrooms enhanced with
garlic and parsley.
SERVES 4–6 ❖ *page 264*

Mushrooms Sautéed with Thyme & Garlic
A mouthwatering mixture of mushrooms with thyme, garlic,
and a hint of lemon, in a mustardy crème fraîche sauce.
SERVES 4–6 ❖ *page 265*

Spinach & Mushroom Bhaji
A delicious spicy accompaniment from
India to serve with curries.
SERVES 8 ❖ *page 265*

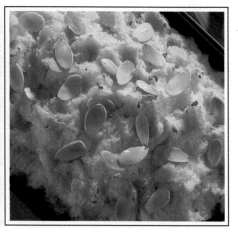

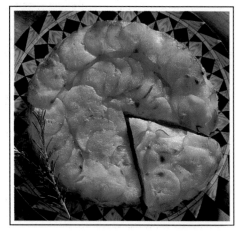

Parsnip & Ginger Bake
A delicious baked purée of parsnips, enriched
with cream, eggs, and sliced almonds.
SERVES 4 ❖ *page 266*

Golden Parsnip Galette
Finely sliced parsnips layered with garlic
and baked until golden and tender.
SERVES 4–6 ❖ *page 266*

Roast Potatoes with Garlic
Potatoes roasted with whole garlic
cloves until crisp and golden.
SERVES 8 ❖ *page 266*

Gratin of Potatoes
Irresistible creamy potato gratin with a
crunchy bread crumb topping.
SERVES 6-8 ♦ *page 266*

Hasselback Potatoes
Fanned whole roast potatoes coated
with sesame seeds.
SERVES 8 ♦ *page 267*

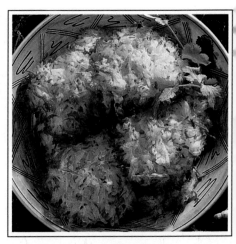

Coriander Rosti
Shredded potato cakes flavored with
onions and coriander (cilantro).
SERVES 6-8 ♦ *page 267*

Rutabaga & Orange Purée
A tasty purée, ideal served with a roast
or hearty casserole.
SERVES 4 ♦ *page 268*

Sweet Potatoes Dauphinoise
Sweet potato slices layered with garlic
and nutmeg, baked in cream.
SERVES 6 ♦ *page 268*

Glazed Shallots
Tender shallots braised in butter and
tossed in chopped parsley.
SERVES 4 ♦ *page 268*

Ratatouille
An authentic Provençale ratatouille,
liberally flavored with herbs.
SERVES 6 ♦ *page 269*

Turnips Stir-Fried with Leeks
Fine slices of turnip with leeks, bacon,
and a hint of lemon.
SERVES 3-4 ♦ *page 269*

Herb-Glazed Tomatoes
Beefsteak tomatoes baked with cream,
lemon juice, and basil.
SERVES 8 ♦ *page 269*

Crab Salad
Delicious crab meat tossed in a lemon dressing and served on a
bed of cucumber, tomatoes, pasta shells, and shredded lettuce.
SERVES 2 ❖ *page 274*

Tuna-Bean Salad
Flaked tuna with red onion rings and
cannellini beans in a tangy dressing.
SERVES 4–6 ❖ *page 275*

Warm Seafood Salad
Sea scallops, shrimp, artichokes, and
bacon on a bed of salad leaves.
SERVES 2 ❖ *page 276*

Salad Niçoise
Superb Mediterranean main-dish salad of
tuna, anchovies, eggs, olives, and vegetables.
SERVES 4 ❖ *page 275*

Chicken & Spiced Wheat Salad
Spiced bulgur wheat, topped with
chicken, scallions, and cherry tomatoes.
SERVES 6 ❖ *page 277*

Chicken & Pasta Salad
Tricolor pasta tossed in a pesto dressing
with chicken, ham, fennel, and tomatoes.
SERVES 4 ❖ *page 276*

Coronation Chicken
Bite-sized chicken pieces tossed in a
creamy curried mayonnaise.
SERVES 4 ❖ *page 276*

Oriental Chicken Salad
Marinated chicken breasts on a bed of
salad, with a citrus-soy dressing.
SERVES 4 ❖ *page 277*

53

Duck Salad

Crisp-cooked duck breast slices in a
ginger dressing on a bed of salad leaves.
SERVES 6 ❖ *page 278*

Peasant Salad

Hearty, colorful vegetarian salad,
which makes a meal in itself.
SERVES 8 ❖ *page 278*

Greek Salad

Refreshing salad of cucumber, tomatoes,
olives, and feta cheese.
SERVES 4–6 ❖ *page 278*

Grilled Vegetable Salad

Delicious salad of grilled/Mediterranean
vegetables in a balsamic vinaigrette.
SERVES 4–6 ❖ *page 279*

Mixed Leaf Salad

Crisp salad leaves, alfalfa sprouts, and
pine nuts in a light dressing.
SERVES 4 ❖ *page 280*

Summer Leafy Herb Salad

Assorted salad leaves and herbs,
enhanced with edible flowers.
SERVES 8 ❖ *page 280*

Green Bean & Fennel Salad

Beans, fennel, and cucumber tossed with
avocado slices and olives.
SERVES 8 ❖ *page 281*

Cauliflower, Broccoli, & Pepper Salad

Crisp, colorful salad in a tahini and lemon
dressing, with sesame seeds.
SERVES 6 ❖ *page 281*

Summer Salad Bowl

Versatile salad, which can be adapted
according to availability of ingredients.
SERVES 6 ❖ *page 280*

Spinach, Watercress, & Bacon Salad
Tender young spinach leaves and
watercress with crisp snippets of bacon.
SERVES 4 ❖ *page 281*

Snow Pea & Mushroom Salad
Snow peas and button mushrooms tossed
in a herb mayonnaise dressing.
SERVES 4 ❖ *page 282*

Watercress, Croûton, & Feta Salad
Simple, crunchy salad that can be
assembled in minutes.
SERVES 4–6 ❖ *page 283*

Pepper, Snow Pea, & Corn Salad
A quick and easy salad in a tangy
lemon dressing.
SERVES 6 ❖ *page 282*

Grilled Pepper Salad
Vividly colorful bell pepper and chili
salad with a ginger and onion dressing.
SERVES 4 ❖ *page 283*

Tomato & Basil Salad
Simple, classic summer salad enhnaced
with a garlic vinaigrette.
SERVES 6 ❖ *page 284*

Fennel, Pear, & Parmesan Salad
Wafer-thin fennel slices with pears
and finely pared Parmesan.
SERVES 6 ❖ *page 282*

Avocado & Cucumber Salad
Slices of avocado and cucumber with
crushed coriander seeds.
SERVES 8 ❖ *page 282*

Flageolet & Artichoke Salad
Tasty combination of beans, artichoke
hearts, olives, and parsley.
SERVES 6 ❖ *page 284*

Tomato & Artichoke Salad
Tomato wedges and artichoke hearts in
a garlic and lemon dressing.
SERVES 4 ❖ *page 284*

Three Bean Salad
Colorful mixed bean and pepper salad
with coriander and a spicy dressing.
SERVES 6 ❖ *page 285*

Spinach & Baby Corn Salad
Light spinach salad with alfalfa,
Belgian endive, and baby corn.
SERVES 6–8 ❖ *page 284*

Bulgur Wheat Salad
Tasty salad with crisp vegetables, liberally
flavored with herbs and hazelnuts.
SERVES 6 ❖ *page 285*

Mustardy Potato Salad
Small tender potatoes tossed in a piquant
creamy dressing.
SERVES 4 ❖ *page 286*

Pasta Salad
Small pasta, zucchini julienne, and thin
asparagus with feta and Swiss cheese.
SERVES 6 ❖ *page 286*

Spiced Potato Salad
New potatoes tossed with coriander
(cilantro) in a spiced yogurt dressing.
SERVES 6 ❖ *page 287*

Wild Rice & Thyme Salad
Pretty rice salad with fava beans, green
beans, and mushrooms.
SERVES 6–8 ❖ *page 287*

Roasted New Potato Salad
Rosemary-flavored potatoes in a tasty
dressing with bacon and mushrooms.
SERVES 6 ❖ *page 286*

Jerusalem Artichoke Gratin
Crisp-topped gratin of Jerusalem
artichokes, leeks, peas, and baby onions.
SERVES 4 ◆ *page 291*

Mixed Lentil Casserole
A nutritious combination of lentils, carrots, leeks, daikon,
and button mushrooms, flavored with ginger, garlic, and coriander (cilantro).
SERVES 6 ◆ *page 292*

Vegetable Bake with Cheese
Root vegetables baked with a Cheddar
cheese topping.
SERVES 6 ◆ *page 291*

Root Vegetable & Tahini Stew
Chunky vegetable stew with an
unusual flavor.
SERVES 4 ◆ *page 293*

Winter Vegetable Casserole
A sustaining root vegetable mixture,
enriched with a little cream.
SERVES 6 ◆ *page 292*

Red Kidney Bean Pot
Tasty combination of kidney beans and
vegetables with a crunchy topping.
SERVES 4–6 ◆ *page 293*

Vegetable Chile
Spicy vegetarian chile, delicious topped
with sour cream or yogurt.
SERVES 8 ❖ *page 294*

Bean Goulash
Based on the Hungarian classic, this
version uses a mixture of different beans.
SERVES 6 ❖ *page 294*

Vegetable Couscous
Steamed couscous topped with a spicy
mixture of vegetables.
SERVES 4 ❖ *page 295*

Vegetable Curry
A versatile curry that can be varied
according to the vegetables available.
SERVES 4–6 ❖ *page 296*

Vegetable Korma
Traditional southern Indian dish,
enriched with cream and ground almonds.
SERVES 4–6 ❖ *page 296*

Boston Baked Beans
Navy beans cooked in a dark, rich
sauce, flavored with molasses.
SERVES 6–8 ❖ *page 295*

Spinach Dhal
Spicy dish, best served as part of
an Indian-style meal.
SERVES 6 ❖ *page 297*

Savory Nut Burgers
Broiled nut burgers, flavored with
onion, parsley, and soy sauce.
SERVES 8 ❖ *page 297*

Hot Spiced Chick Peas
A quick and easy supper dish. Serve with
rice, baked potatoes, or bread.
SERVES 4 ❖ *page 295*

Vegetable Tempura
Japanese-style crisp vegetables, quickly
fried in a light batter.
SERVES 4 ❖ *page 298*

Stir-Fried Vegetables
Any combination of vegetables can be
used for this tasty stir-fry.
SERVES 4–6 ❖ *page 298*

Glazed Vegetable Pastries
Crisp filo baskets filled with baby
vegetables, topped with a creamy dressing.
SERVES 4 or 8 ❖ *page 299*

Curried Tofu Burgers
Moist low-calorie burgers, with
coriander, nuts, and garlic.
SERVES 4 ❖ *page 297*

Quorn Kebabs with Tomato Salsa
Grilled Quorn and corn kebabs, served
with a tomato and chili salsa.
SERVES 4 ❖ *page 300*

Vegetable Kebabs with Tofu Sauce
Skewers of zucchini, baby corn, mushrooms,
and tomatoes, with a tasty sauce.
SERVES 2–4 ❖ *page 299*

Potato Gnocchi
Classic Italian dish, traditionally served
with pesto and Parmesan.
SERVES 4 ❖ *page 301*

Eggplant & Tomato Gratin
Eggplant slices baked with tomato,
herbs, and mozzarella.
SERVES 4–6 ❖ *page 300*

Peppers with Goat Cheese & Lentils
Broiled bell peppers with a tasty cheese,
lentil, and olive stuffing.
SERVES 4 ❖ *page 301*

Tian de Courgettes

A simple supper dish of rice and
zucchini baked with a cheese topping.

SERVES 3–4 ❖ *page 302*

Vegetable & Nut Roast

Any type of chopped nuts can be used for
this loaf, which can be served hot or cold.

SERVES 4–6 ❖ *page 303*

Eggplant Cannelloni

Eggplant slices rolled around a tasty
ricotta filling, baked in a tomato sauce.

SERVES 6 ❖ *page 302*

Lentil Loaf

A soft-textured mildly flavored loaf, best
served with a crisp salad.

SERVES 4–6 ❖ *page 303*

Stuffed Bell Peppers

Red bell peppers baked with a mushroom,
rice, and pine nut stuffing.

SERVES 6 ❖ *page 304*

Imam Bayildi

Traditional Turkish dish of stuffed eggplant,
served warm or cold with crusty bread.

SERVES 6 ❖ *page 304*

Chile-Stuffed Potatoes

Baked potatoes with a spicy
chile filling.

SERVES 4 ❖ *page 305*

Bulgur-Stuffed Tomatoes

Beefsteak tomatoes with a tasty bulgur
wheat, nut, olive, and pesto stuffing.

SERVES 4 ❖ *page 305*

Catalan Red Peppers

Cold bell peppers stuffed with a mixture of wild
and white rice, tomatoes, olives, and capers.

SERVES 4 ❖ *page 305*

Seafood Spaghetti
Spaghetti with a superb mixture of mussels, shrimp, sea scallops,
and leeks in a delicious creamy saffron and wine sauce.
SERVES 4–6 ❖ *page 311*

Spaghetti alla Carbonara
Spaghetti tossed in a creamy egg and
bacon sauce, with parsley.
SERVES 4 ❖ *page 310*

Spaghetti with Garlic
Simple, yet intensely flavored pasta, with
garlic, chili, and herbs.
SERVES 4–6 ❖ *page 311*

Pasta with Bacon Sauce
Pasta tossed in a tasty bacon, olive, and
tomato sauce with plenty of herbs.
SERVES 4 ❖ *page 310*

Tagliatelle with Tomato Sauce
Pasta topped with a tasty sun-dried tomato
sauce, Parmesan, and crème fraîche.
SERVES 4 ❖ *page 312*

Fettucine with Gorgonzola Sauce
A very rich creamy dish, flavored with
Gorgonzola and basil.
SERVES 4–6 ❖ *page 312*

Linguine with Clams & Smoked Salmon
An elegant first course of fine noodles
tossed with seafood.
SERVES 6 ❖ *page 312*

Pasta with Spicy Sausage & Tomato
Substantial pasta dish flavored with a fresh tomato sauce
and kabanos sausages.
SERVES 6 ❖ *page 313*

Pappardelle with Parma Ham
Broad noodles with asparagus, leeks,
Parma ham, and a creamy Parmesan sauce.
SERVES 4 ❖ *page 313*

Cappelletti with Mushroom Sauce
Pasta in a deliciously rich sauce,
enhanced with dried porcini mushrooms.
SERVES 4 ❖ *page 313*

Spring Vegetable Pasta
Penne with a colorful assortment of
vegetables in a creamy herb sauce.
SERVES 4–6 ❖ *page 314*

Pasta, Veal, & Rosemary Gratin
Giant pasta shells baked with a tasty veal
stuffing and a cheese topping.
SERVES 6 ❖ *page 315*

Pasta with Mushroom & Leek Sauce
Creamy pasta dish flavored with bacon, mushrooms, and leeks.
SERVES 4 ❖ *page 314*

Lasagne
Traditional recipe featuring layers of pasta, Bolognese sauce, and Béchamel, with a Parmesan crust.
SERVES 4-6 ❖ *page 316*

Pasta & Eggplant Gratin
Mediterranean-style bake with zucchini, eggplant, and tomatoes.
SERVES 4 ❖ *page 315*

Shrimp & Leek Pasta Shells
Giant pasta shells filled with leeks, shrimp, and cottage cheese.
SERVES 4 ❖ *page 317*

Spinach & Ricotta Cannelloni
Sheets of lasagne rolled around a tasty filling, then baked in a tomato sauce.
SERVES 4-6 ❖ *page 316*

Vegetable Lasagne
Vegetarian lasagne well flavored with Mediterranean vegetables and herbs.
SERVES 6 ❖ *page 317*

Fragrant Saffron Pilaf
Basmati rice flavored with cloves, cardamom, cinnamon,
and saffron, cooked with button mushrooms.
SERVES 6 ❖ *page 321*

Special Fried Rice
Tasty combination of stir-fried rice,
shrimp, and vegetables.
SERVES 4 ❖ *page 320*

Egg-Fried Rice
Fried rice flavored with vegetables,
nuts, and scrambled eggs.
SERVES 6 ❖ *page 320*

Fragrant Coconut Rice
Lemon grass lends a unique flavor to
this rice accompaniment.
SERVES 4–6 ❖ *page 320*

Mixed Rice Pilaf
Wild and brown rice mixture, with toasted
pine nuts and chopped parsley.
SERVES 6 ❖ *page 321*

Thai Fried Rice
Thai-style rice with scallions,
spiced with hot red chili.
SERVES 4 ❖ *page 322*

Asparagus Risotto

Traditional creamy risotto, with fine
asparagus and grated Parmesan.

SERVES 4 ❖ *page 322*

Mushroom Risotto

Tasty combination of mushrooms,
broccoli, green beans, and rice.

SERVES 4 ❖ *page 323*

Buttered Saffron Couscous

Steamed couscous flavored with saffron,
pine nuts, and parsley.

SERVES 6 ❖ *page 324*

Basmati Pilaf

The perfect complement to authentic Indian curries, this delicious pilaf
is flavored with an assortment of spices, pistachio nuts, and raisins.

SERVES 4 ❖ *page 322*

Lemon Couscous with Mushrooms

Instant couscous flavored with lemon and
topped with flat mushrooms.

SERVES 2 ❖ *page 324*

Hot Noodles with Sesame Dressing

Chinese egg noodles tossed in a spicy
dressing with sesame seeds.

SERVES 6 ❖ *page 324*

Singapore Noodles

Serve this tasty mixture of stir-fried
vegetables and noodles as a light meal.

SERVES 4 ❖ *page 325*

Toasted Polenta

Broiled polenta, ideal as an accompaniment
to casseroles or grilled meat.

SERVES 6 ❖ *page 325*

Vegetable Potpie
Assorted vegetables in a cheesy sauce
topped with Parmesan-flavored pastry.
SERVES 4–6 ❖ *page 331*

Quiche Lorraine
Classic quiche with a creamy cheese,
bacon, and parsley filling.
SERVES 4 ❖ *page 332*

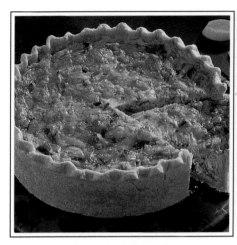

Rich Leek Quiche
Rich, moist, quiche with plenty of
leeks, cream, and cheese.
SERVES 6–8 ❖ *page 332*

Tarte Provençale
This delicious quiche combines all the classic flavors of Provence –
eggplant, green bell pepper, tomatoes, garlic, olives, and herbs.
SERVES 6–8 ❖ *page 333*

Spinach and Garlic Quiche
Rich quiche flavored with spinach, garlic,
ground almonds, and pine nuts.
SERVES 4–6 ❖ *page 332*

Mediterranean Quiches
Individual quiches filled with sun-dried
tomatoes, feta, onions, and basil.
SERVES 6 ❖ *page 334*

Goat Cheese & Watercress Quiche
Delicious quiche with a creamy filling,
best served with a salad.
SERVES 4–6 ❖ *page 334*

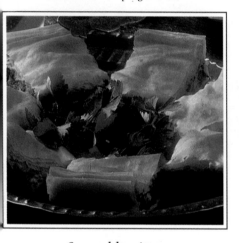

Spanakhopitas
Squares of filo pastry with a tasty spinach
and feta cheese filling.
SERVES 4–6 ❖ *page 335*

Sweet Pepper & Basil Quiche
Broiled red bell peppers and herbs in
a creamy cheese mixture.
SERVES 4 ❖ *page 333*

Sole & Spinach Quiche
An unusual filling of rolled sole
fillets and spinach.
SERVES 4–6 ❖ *page 334*

Smoked Salmon Quiche
Olive pastry shell with a deliciously
rich smoked salmon filling.
SERVES 6 ❖ *page 335*

English Game Pie
Impressive hot water crust pie encasing
a mixture of game, herbs, and dried fruit.
SERVES 8–10 ❖ *page 336*

Sausage Rolls
Homemade sausage rolls – ideal for
parties and picnics.
MAKES 28 ❖ *page 338*

Gougère
Crisp, light cream-puff pastry with a
colorful filling of stir-fried vegetables.
SERVES 4 ❖ *page 338*

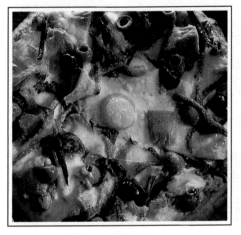

Pizza Niçoise
Tasty pizza topped with tuna, anchovies,
olives, and mozzarella.
SERVES 4 ❖ *page 340*

Mushroom & Pepper Vol-au-Vents
Individual patty shells filled with a mixture of
mushrooms, bell peppers, and shallots in a creamy sauce.
MAKES 8 ❖ *page 337*

Wild Mushroom & Hollandaise Pizza
Luxurious topping of assorted wild
mushrooms in a rich hollandaise sauce.
SERVES 4 ❖ *page 340*

Smoked Salmon & Avocado Pizza
Special pizza with a creamy salmon,
avocado, and dill topping.
SERVES 4 ❖ *page 341*

Chorizo, Feta, & Eggplant Pizza
Ready-made pizza bases with a quick and
easy Mediterranean-style topping.
SERVES 2 ❖ *page 341*

Peaches in Spiced Wine
Luscious ripe peaches soaked in wine
flavored with cinnamon and cloves.
SERVES 6 ✦ *page 344*

Pears in Red Wine
Whole pears, gently simmered in wine
flavored with cloves, until tender.
SERVES 4 ✦ *page 345*

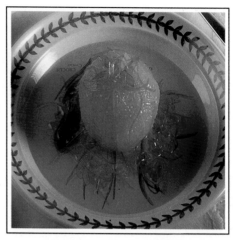

Oranges in Caramel
Classic dessert with a crunchy
caramel topping.
SERVES 6 ✦ *page 344*

Fragrant Fruit Salad
Refreshing mixture of litchis, pineapple,
mangoes, and kiwi fruit.
SERVES 8 ✦ *page 345*

Red Fruit Terrine
Ripe red fruit and delicate mint leaves
set in a splendid wine gelatin.
SERVES 6 ✦ *page 346*

Soft Fruit in Summer Sauce
Mouthwatering summer fruits in a red
sauce, lightly flavored with Kirsch.
SERVES 8 ✦ *page 345*

Strawberry & Champagne Gelatin
Full-flavored frais du bois set in a delicate pink
champagne gelatin.
SERVES 6 ✦ *page 346*

Summer Pudding
Case of fruit-syrup-soaked
bread, filled with fruit.
SERVES 8 ✦ *page 346*

Steamed Fruit Pudding
Delicious sponge pudding with a fruit topping, plus
variations for all kinds of steamed puddings.
SERVES 4 ❖ *page 349*

Baked Stuffed Apples
Tender apples baked with a
mincemeat filling.
SERVES 4 ❖ *page 348*

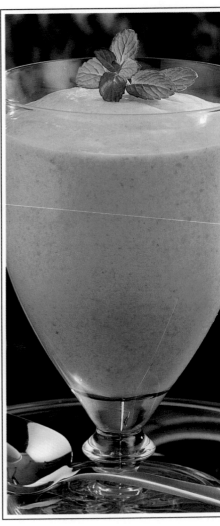

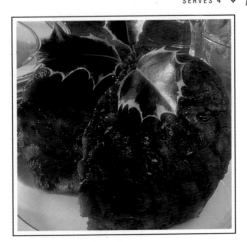

Christmas or Plum Pudding
Traditional rich English pudding,
served with brandy butter.
SERVES 10 ❖ *page 350*

Cinnamon Fruit Wafers
Wafer-thin cake rounds layered with
spiced cream and poached fruits.
SERVES 8 ❖ *page 348*

Gooseberry Fool
Soft, creamy dessert, best served with
crisp cookies for a contrast in texture.
SERVES 4–6 ❖ *page 347*

Bread & Butter Pudding

Traditional favorite, laden with fruit
and flavored with cinnamon.

SERVES 6 ❖ *page 352*

St Clement's Pudding

During baking this pudding separates into
a custard layer with a cakelike topping.

SERVES 4 ❖ *page 351*

Old-Fashioned Rice Pudding

An all-time winter favorite, popular
with adults and children alike.

SERVES 4–6 ❖ *page 351*

Queen of Puddings

An old English pudding, with
a light meringue topping.

SERVES 4 ❖ *page 351*

Lemon Caramel Rice

Light, creamy textured pudding with a
caramelized lemon topping.

SERVES 4 ❖ *page 351*

Bakewell Tart

A tart with an almond filling,
equally good hot or cold.

SERVES 6 ❖ *page 355*

Rich Pear Pudding

An impressive tart with a rich almond
filling, studded with pear halves.

SERVES 10–12 ❖ *page 352*

Blueberry Crisp

An irresistible warming crisp, with a
crunchy oat and nut topping.

SERVES 6–8 ❖ *page 353*

Rhubarb & Orange Streusel Cake

An orange-flavored cake, topped with
rhubarb and a crunchy streusel topping.

SERVES 8 ❖ *page 353*

Apple Pie

An irresistible apple pie, flavored with brown sugar,
raisins, nutmeg, cinnamon, and orange rind.

SERVES 6 ❖ *page 355*

Pineapple Tarte Tatin

A delicious adaptation of the classic
French upside-down tart.

SERVES 6 ❖ *page 356*

Pear Tart

Luscious tart with a pear purée filling,
topped with pear slices.

SERVES 6 ❖ *page 357*

Mille Feuilles

Featherlight layers of puff pastry, interleaved with spiced plums and cream.

SERVES 4 ❖ *page 357*

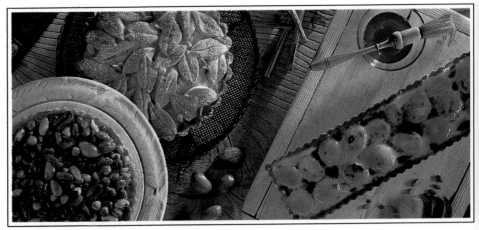

Glazed Nut Tart; Spiced Apple Tart; Apricot & Cardamom Tart

Attractive glazed tarts with tempting fillings – good
enough to rival the best bakery goods.

SERVES 6-8 ❖ *page 355–7*

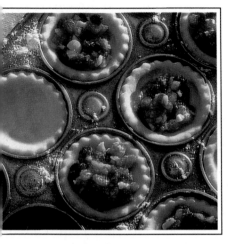

Little Mince Pies
Individual holiday mince pies,
with a sugar glaze.
MAKES 18 ❖ *page 354*

Peach & Nectarine Croustade
Crisp filo pastry encasing a creamy filling,
with peach and nectarine slices.
SERVES 8 ❖ *page 358*

Cream Puffs
Crisp light choux puffs, filled with cream
in a rich chocolate sauce.
SERVES 4 ❖ *page 359*

Baked Cheesecake with Red Fruit Sauce
Creamy, velvety smooth baked cheesecake with a crisp
base and topping, served with a fruit sauce.
SERVES 8 ❖ *page 360*

Individual Fruit Tarts
Attractive glazed fresh fruit tarts with a
crème patissière filling.
MAKES 10 ❖ *page 358*

Hot Chocolate Cheesecake
Tempting rich cheesecake, served
warm from the oven.
SERVES 8–10 ❖ *page 360*

Raspberry Cheesecake
Chilled raspberry yogurt cheesecake,
rippled with raspberry purée.
SERVES 10–12 ❖ *page 361*

Lemon Cheesecake
Light chilled cheesecake, with a
refreshing citrus tang.
SERVES 8 ❖ *page 361*

Meringue Basket
This impressive basket is the ideal way to
serve fruits in season.
SERVES 6–8 ❖ *page 363*

Meringues with Chocolate Sauce
Meringue shells with a Grand Marnier cream
filling, topped with a rich dark sauce.
SERVES 8 ❖ *page 362*

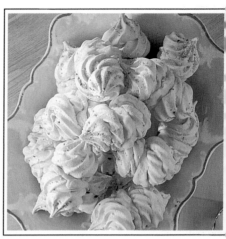

Brown Sugar & Hazelnut Meringues
Golden meringue shells with a delicious
flavor, filled with cream or ice cream.
MAKES 18 ❖ *page 362*

Snow Eggs
Light fluffy poached meringues, floating
on a smooth coffee custard.
SERVES 6 ❖ *page 363*

Pavlova
Colorful assortment of fruits nestling in
cream on a luscious deep meringue.
SERVES 8 ❖ *page 364*

Lemon Meringue Pie
Ever-popular dessert with a tangy lemon
filling and meringue topping.
SERVES 6–8 ❖ *page 364*

Hazelnut Meringue Cake
Nutty meringue layers with raspberries
and whipped cream.
SERVES 6–8 ❖ *page 365*

Chocolate-Chestnut Vacherin
Layers of hazelnut meringue interleaved with a deliciously
rich mixture of chestnut purée, chocolate, and cream.
SERVES 10 ❖ *page 365*

Hot Chocolate Soufflé
An impressive soufflé with a hint of
cinnamon in its rich flavor.
SERVES 4 ❖ *page 366*

Kirsch & Almond Soufflés
Delicious individual soufflés, with a
hidden fresh plum filling.
SERVES 6 ❖ *page 366*

Summer Fruit Mousse
Superb soft fruit mousse, which can be
adapted according to available fruit.
SERVES 6-8 ❖ *page 368*

Chocolate-Orange Soufflé
A velvety smooth, rich dessert topped
with whipped cream and grated chocolate.
SERVES 6-8 ❖ *page 368*

Lemon Mousse
Mouthwatering and refreshing dessert
with a sharp tang of citrus.
SERVES 4-6 ❖ *page 368*

Chilled Lemon Soufflé
Topped with slices of star fruit, this light creamy
soufflé has a crunchy pistachio-caramel side coating.
SERVES 6-8 ❖ *page 367*

Quick Cheese & Apple Bread
Non-yeast bread flavored with sharp
Cheddar, apple, and peanuts.
8 SLICES ❖ *page 421*

Schiacciata
Flat pizza-type bread liberally coated with rosemary
and extra-virgin olive oil.
12 SLICES ❖ *page 420*

Mini Hot Cross Buns
Tempting moist, spicy fruit rolls
traditionally made around Eastertime.
MAKES 25 ❖ *page 422*

Stollen
Irresistible fruity yeast bread from
Germany, with a marzipan filling.
SERVES 10 ❖ *page 422*

Brioche
Rich yeast bread, shaped in a
characteristic fluted mold.
SERVES 10 ❖ *page 421*

Chelsea Buns
Sweet yeast rolls with a spicy fruit and
nut filling, and a shiny glaze.
MAKES 4 ❖ *page 423*

Savarin
Ring-shaped French yeast bread with a red currant
jelly glaze, filled with strawberries.
SERVES 6 ❖ *page 423*

Gooseberry Jam; Strawberry Preserve
Full-flavored spreads to make during
the early summer months.
page 426; page 427

Raspberry Jam
Excellent homemade jam with an intense
flavor and a superb texture.
page 426

Blackberry Jam
Ideal recipe for using this short-season
fruit to optimum effect.
page 426

Strawberry Jam
Mouthwatering jam made from this
popular summer fruit.
page 427

Apricot Jam
Vividly colored jam, with a fine flavor
and a good texture.
page 427

Apple & Mint Jelly
Clear herb-flavored jelly, best served
with roast lamb or pork.
page 428

Rosehip Jelly
A delicious jelly made from the ripe dark
red fruits of the wild rose.
page 428

Lime Marmalade
Tangy marmalade, made with whole
slices of thin-skinned limes.
page 428

Seville Orange Marmalade
The traditional marmalade, made from
bitter Seville oranges.
page 429

Lemon Curd
Luscious, smooth, rich spread with a
refreshing, tangy flavor.
page 429

Mincemeat
A rich fruity, spicy mincemeat with more
than a dash of alcohol.
page 430

Pickled Pears with Ginger
Delicious accompaniment to cold meats.
Ideal as an unusual gift.
page 98

Brandied Cherries
Plump fresh cherries preserved in a cinnamon- and brandy-
flavored syrup; best served with thick yogurt or cream.
page 430

Mustard-Vegetable Relish
A colorful medley of vegetables in a
sweet-sour mustardy sauce.
page 431

Pickled Summer Vegetables
This tasty pickle is the perfect
companion to bread and cheese.
page 431

Mango Chutney; Squash & Tomato Chutney
Dark, fruity chutneys – ideal served with
cold meats or cheese.
page 432

Green Tomato Chutney
A delicious way of using unripened
homegrown tomatoes.
page 432

RECIPES

STOCKS & SAUCES

Flavorful stocks form the basis of good soups, sauces, stews, and a host of other savory dishes. Sauces – on the other hand – provide the finishing touch to many dishes, complementing and enhancing their flavor.

❖ Stocks ❖

Homemade stocks lend a superb flavor, so it's well worth making your own stock from leftover bones, poultry carcasses, and fresh vegetables. You will also find that most fish merchants are only too happy to let you have fish bones, while many butchers will supply meat bones and chicken carcasses. Make up a good quantity of stock and freeze any that is not required, in manageable quantities. To save freezer space, boil the stock to reduce the volume; cool, then freeze in ice cube trays.

The characteristics of a good stock are a fine flavor and clarity. Guard against over-seasoning, as boiling concentrates the flavor and saltiness. Fat and impurities will make a stock cloudy, so these should always be removed. For successful stock-making follow these guidelines:
❖ Don't cover your stock pot completely; the stock needs to reduce by boiling and evaporation.
❖ Skim frequently to remove scum and fat.
❖ Use a conical strainer for straining if possible. Let the stock drip through; if you squeeze the vegetables in the strainer you will lose clarity.
❖ Let the stock cool, then refrigerate until the fat forms a solid layer on the surface; remove.
❖ Use fish stock on the day it is made, or within 2 days. Meat and chicken stocks can be kept in the refrigerator up to 4 days, but they should be boiled each day.

If you don't have time to make your own stock, use one of the ready-made bouillons. The range of bouillons products available has increased and improved in recent years and you can now buy a wide range of flavors. Most are inclined to be strong and salty, so use sparingly. Some products, including a range of stocks sold fresh in cartons, have no added salt, sugar, or artificial additives.

❖ Sauces ❖

Sauces are intended to enhance the foods with which they are served; they should never be so over-powering as to disguise the intrinsic flavors of a dish. A great deal of mystique is attached to sauce-making, but all that is required is a little time and your undivided attention. Once the basic techniques have been mastered, you can create your own variations.

Roux-based sauces are the most common type. For a white sauce, the butter and flour mixture – known as the roux – is cooked, but not colored. Béchamel is the classic white sauce. For a brown sauce, such as Espagnole, the roux is cooked until it is brown.

The classic emulsified sauces, including Hollandaise and Béarnaise, are more difficult to make than roux-based sauces because of their tendency to separate. They are therefore prepared in a double boiler over low heat.

Other sauces included in this chapter are tomato sauces; curry and barbecue sauces; and dessert sauces. Salad dressings are to be found in the Salads chapter, while recipes for classic pasta sauces are in the Pasta chapter. Whatever type of sauce you are making, consider the texture and consistency, as well as the flavor. These characteristics are all-important to a successful sauce.

❖ Beef Stock ❖

MAKES 3½ CUPS	• 1 lb beef shank, cut into pieces	• 1 onion, peeled and sliced
PREPARATION TIME 15–40 minutes	• 1 lb marrow bones or veal shanks, chopped	• 1 carrot, peeled and sliced
COOKING TIME 4–5 hours	• 1 bouquet garni	• 1 celery stalk, sliced
FREEZING Suitable		• ½ tsp salt

1 To give a good flavor and color, brown the meat and bones in the oven before using them. Place in a roasting pan and roast in a preheated 425°F oven until well browned, 30–40 minutes.
2 Put the bones and meat in a saucepan with 7 cups water, the bouquet garni, vegetables, and salt. Bring to a boil and remove any scum.
3 Partially cover and simmer 4–5 hours.
4 Strain the stock and, when cold, remove any trace of fat from the surface using a large spoon.

PRESSURE COOKER METHOD: Follow steps 1 and 2 as above, using the pressure cooker instead of a saucepan, but reduce the amount of liquid to 6 cups. Bring to HIGH (15 lb) pressure and cook 1–1¼ hours. Reduce pressure at room temperature. After cooking, finish as above.

Variation
Replace the beef shank with fresh or cooked meat bones.

❖ Chicken Stock ❖

MAKES 5 CUPS	• 1 chicken carcass, bones, and trimmings from a roast chicken	• 1 celery stalk, sliced
PREPARATION TIME 15 minutes		• 1 bouquet garni
COOKING TIME 2–3 hours	• 1 onion, peeled and sliced	• 1 bay leaf
FREEZING Suitable	• 1 carrot, peeled and sliced	• salt

1 Break up the chicken carcass and put in a large saucepan with any skin and meat attached, plus other bones and trimmings.
2 Add 7 cups water, the onion, carrot, celery, bouquet garni, bay leaf, and a little salt. Bring to a boil, then skim.
3 Partially cover and simmer 2–3 hours.
4 Strain the stock and, when cold, remove all traces of fat.

PRESSURE COOKER METHOD: Follow steps 1 and 2 as above, using the pressure cooker instead of a saucepan but reduce the amount of liquid to 6 cups. Bring to HIGH (15 lb) pressure and cook 45 minutes to 1 hour. After cooking, finish as above.

❖ Fish Stock ❖

MAKES 3½ CUPS	• 1–1½ lb fish bones and trimmings	• 1 bouquet garni
PREPARATION TIME 10 minutes	• salt	• 1 onion, peeled and sliced
COOKING TIME 20 minutes		
FREEZING Suitable		

1 Put the fish bones and trimmings into a saucepan, cover with 3½ cups water, and add a little salt. Bring to a boil, then skim.
2 Reduce the heat and add the bouquet garni and onion. Cover and simmer 20 minutes.
3 Strain and let cool. Use the same day, or store in the refrigerator not more than 2 days.

❖ Court Bouillon ❖

MAKES 5 CUPS	• 1 carrot, peeled and sliced	• 6 peppercorns
PREPARATION TIME 5 minutes	• 1 onion, peeled and sliced	• ½ cup white wine vinegar
COOKING TIME 30 minutes	• 1 bouquet garni (thyme, parsley, bay leaf)	• ½ tsp salt
FREEZING Not suitable		

1 Place all the ingredients in a saucepan. Add 5 cups water. Bring to a boil, lower the heat, and simmer gently 30 minutes. Strain if required before use.

NOTE: A court bouillon is a flavoring liquid used for cooking delicately flavored fish.

❖ Vegetable Stock ❖

MAKES 5 CUPS	• 2 tbsp oil	• 4 celery stalks, chopped
PREPARATION TIME 15 minutes	• 1 onion, peeled and minced	• vegetable trimmings, such as celery tops, cabbage leaves, mushroom peelings, tomato skins
COOKING TIME 1¼ hours	• 1 carrot, peeled and diced	
FREEZING Suitable	• 2 oz turnip, peeled and diced	• 1 bouquet garni
	• 2 oz parsnip, peeled and diced	• 6 black peppercorns
		• salt

1 Heat the oil in a saucepan, add the onion, and fry gently until soft and lightly colored, about 5 minutes.
2 Add the other vegetables to the pan with the trimmings and 7 cups water. Add the bouquet garni and peppercorns. Season with a little salt.
3 Bring to a boil, partially cover, and simmer 1½ hours, skimming occasionally.
4 Strain the stock and let cool. Cover and store in the refrigerator. Use within 1–2 days.

❖ Brown Onion Stock ❖

MAKES 3½ CUPS	• 2 tbsp vegetable oil	• a few sage leaves, thyme stems, and parsley stems or 2 tsp dried mixed herbs
PREPARATION TIME 15 minutes	• 2 large onions, peeled and roughly chopped	
COOKING TIME 45 minutes	• 2 garlic cloves, peeled and halved	
FREEZING Suitable	• 2 celery stalks, chopped	• 2 bay leaves
	• 2 carrots, peeled and chopped	• 1 tsp yeast extract (optional)
		• salt

1 Heat the oil in a large heavy-based saucepan. Add the onions and cook, stirring all the time, until they turn a dark golden brown, about 10 minutes. Be careful not to let the onions burn.
2 Add the remaining vegetables, the herbs, and yeast extract, if using. Cook over a high heat until the vegetables are lightly browned, 4–5 minutes.
3 Add 5 cups water to the pan and bring to a boil. Season with a little salt, lower the heat, and simmer gently 30 minutes.
4 Strain through a fine sieve into a measure or bowl. The stock is now ready to use, or it can be returned to a clean saucepan and boiled rapidly to reduce the quantity and intensify the flavor. Cool and store in the refrigerator up to 2–3 days.

NOTE: Caramelizing the onions before adding the other ingredients produces a stock with a strong, slightly sweet flavor and a good brown color.

❖ Béchamel Sauce ❖

MAKES 1¼ CUPS
PREPARATION TIME
5 minutes, plus
standing
COOKING TIME
5 minutes
FREEZING
Suitable

- 1¼ cups milk
- 1 slice of onion
- 1 bay leaf
- 6 peppercorns
- 1 blade of mace

- 1 tbsp butter or margarine
- 1½ tbsp flour
- salt and pepper
- freshly grated nutmeg

180 CALS/⅓ CUP

1 Pour the milk into a sauce-pan. Add the onion, bay leaf, peppercorns, and mace. Bring to scalding point, remove from heat, cover, and let infuse 10–30 minutes. Strain.

2 To make the roux, melt the butter in a saucepan. Stir in the flour and cook, stirring, 1 minute.

3 Remove from the heat and gradually pour on the warm milk, whisking constantly. Season lightly with salt, pepper, and nutmeg.

4 Return to the heat and bring to a boil, whisking constantly until the sauce thickens and is smooth. Simmer 2–3 minutes.

Variations

THICK BÉCHAMEL SAUCE: Increase the butter to 2 tbsp and the flour to 3 tbsp. This thick sauce is used to bind mixtures.

SIMPLE WHITE SAUCE: Omit the infusing stage, simply stirring the cold milk into the roux.

CHEESE (MORNAY) SAUCE: Off the heat, stir in ½ cup shredded sharp Cheddar or Gruyère cheese and a large pinch of mustard powder.

PARSLEY SAUCE: Add about 2 tbsp chopped parsley.

ONION (SOUBISE) SAUCE: Mince 1 onion, then sauté in a little butter until softened, 10–15 minutes. Stir into the Béchamel. Purée in a blender or food processor, if desired.

MUSHROOM SAUCE: Thinly slice 3 oz mushrooms; sweat gently in a little butter until tender. Stir into the Béchamel.

❖ Espagnole Sauce ❖

MAKES 1¼ CUPS
PREPARATION TIME
20 minutes
COOKING TIME
1¼ hours
FREEZING
Suitable

- 1 tbsp butter or margarine
- 1 thick slice bacon, chopped
- 1 shallot, peeled and chopped
- ¼ cup chopped mushroom stems
- 1 small carrot, peeled and chopped
- 2–3 tbsp flour

- 2 cups brown beef stock
- 1 bouquet garni
- 2 tbsp tomato paste
- salt and pepper
- 1 tbsp sherry wine (optional)

250 CALS/⅓ CUP

1 Melt the butter in a saucepan, add the bacon, and fry 2–3 minutes. Add the vegetables and fry until lightly browned, 3–5 minutes longer. Stir in the flour, mix well, and continue cooking until it turns brown.
2 Remove from the heat and gradually add the stock, stirring after each addition.
3 Bring to a boil, stirring constantly, and continue to cook, stirring, until the sauce thickens. Add the bouquet garni, tomato paste, and salt and pepper. Reduce the heat and let simmer very gently 1 hour, skimming occasionally.
4 Strain the sauce, reheat, and skim the surface. Adjust the seasoning and add the sherry, if using, just before serving.

NOTE: This classic brown sauce is traditionally served with red meat and game. This quantity is sufficient to serve 4.

❖ Demi-Glace Sauce ❖

MAKES 1¼ CUPS
PREPARATION TIME
20 minutes
COOKING TIME
About 1 hour
FREEZING
Suitable

- 1 small onion, peeled
- 1 small carrot, peeled
- ½ celery stalk
- 2 tbsp oil
- 1 tbsp flour
- 1 tsp tomato paste
- 1 tbsp mushroom peelings

- 2½ cups brown beef stock
- 1 bouquet garni
- salt and pepper

270 CALS/⅓ CUP

1 Mince the onion, carrot, and celery. Heat the oil in a heavy-based saucepan. Add the minced vegetables. Reduce the heat and cook until the vegetables begin to crinkle and shrink, about 8 minutes; do not let them color.
2 Mix in the flour and cook over low heat, stirring occasionally, until it turns brown; this may take as long as 15 minutes.
3 Off the heat, stir in the tomato paste, mushroom peelings, and three-quarters of the cold stock. Add the herbs and seasoning. Bring to a boil, stirring. Partially cover the pan and simmer gently about 35–40 minutes, skimming occasionally.
4 Strain the sauce into a clean pan. Boil and add one-third of the remaining cold stock. Bring the sauce to a boil and remove the scum from the surface. Repeat twice more with the remaining cold stock. Adjust the seasoning as necessary. The sauce should be thin and syrupy.

NOTE: An ideal accompaniment to steaks; this quantity serves 4.

❖ Tomato Sauce ❖

SERVES 4	• 1 lb ripe tomatoes	• ⅔ cup dry white wine
PREPARATION TIME 20 minutes	• 1 onion, peeled	or vegetable stock
COOKING TIME 25–30 minutes	• 2 oz carrot, peeled	• salt and pepper
FREEZING Suitable	• 4 oz celery	

- 1 tbsp olive oil
- 1 large garlic clove, minced
- 1 tbsp chopped mixed herbs, such as parsley, thyme, basil, and marjoram, or 1 tsp dried mixed herbs
- 1 bay leaf
- 1 tbsp tomato paste

65 CALS/SERVING

1 Peel the tomatoes and chop finely, discarding the seeds.

2 Mince the onion, carrot, and celery. Heat the oil in a saucepan and sauté the onion, carrot, and celery with the garlic and mixed herbs until softened, 4–5 minutes.

3 Stir in the tomatoes, bay leaf, tomato paste, wine or stock, and seasoning. Bring to a boil, cover, and simmer until the vegetables are tender, 15–20 minutes.

4 Uncover the sauce and continue to simmer 4–5 minutes longer to reduce and thicken slightly. Adjust the seasoning and discard the bay leaf. The sauce is now ready to use, or if preferred it can be puréed in a blender or food processor for a smooth texture.

NOTE: It is essential to use full-flavored tomatoes for this fresh sauce. Serve with pasta, hamburgers, or other grilled or broiled meats; or use as a pizza topping.

❖ Quick Tomato Sauce ❖

SERVES 4	• 16-oz can chopped	• ⅔ cup dry white wine
PREPARATION TIME 5 minutes	tomatoes	or vegetable stock
COOKING TIME 15–20 minutes	• 1 tbsp chopped mixed herbs, such as parsley,	• salt and pepper
FREEZING Suitable	thyme, basil, and	• 1 large garlic clove, minced

- marjoram, or 1 tsp dried mixed herbs
- 1 tbsp tomato paste
- pinch of sugar

50 CALS/SERVING

1 Place all the ingredients in a saucepan. Bring to a boil, then simmer, uncovered, until the mixture has reduced and thickened, 15–20 minutes.

2 Adjust the seasoning. Serve as above.

❖ Tomato Coulis ❖

SERVES 4–6	• 1 lb tomatoes	• pinch of sugar
PREPARATION TIME 15 minutes, plus standing	• salt and pepper	
FREEZING Not suitable	• 2 tbsp chopped herbs, such as basil or chervil (optional)	

25–20 CALS/SERVING

1 Peel the tomatoes: Immerse in a bowl of boiling water 15–30 seconds, then remove with a slotted spoon and peel off the skins. Alternatively spear on a fork and turn over a gas flame until blistered, then peel.

2 Quarter the tomatoes, seed, then finely chop the flesh and place in a nylon strainer. Let drain 10–15 minutes, then transfer to a bowl.

3 Season lightly with salt and pepper and stir in the herbs if using, with the sugar. Chill before serving.

NOTE: This uncooked fresh tomato sauce is delicious served with vegetable and fish terrines.

❖ Curry Sauce ❖

MAKES 2¼ CUPS	• 2 tbsp oil	• salt and pepper
PREPARATION TIME 5 minutes	• 1 large onion, peeled and chopped	• ⅔ cup thick plain yogurt
COOKING TIME 40 minutes	• 1 garlic clove, minced	
FREEZING Not suitable	• 2 tsp ground coriander	

- 1 tsp fenugreek seeds
- 1 tsp ground cumin
- 2 tsp turmeric
- ¼ cup split red lentils
- 2 cups vegetable stock

165 CALS/SERVING

1 Heat the oil in a heavy-based saucepan. Add the onion and garlic and fry until softened, about 5 minutes. Add the spices and fry 2 minutes, stirring.

2 Add the lentils and stock, bring to a boil, then reduce the heat, cover, and simmer until the lentils are very soft, about 30 minutes. Season with salt and pepper. Stir in the yogurt and reheat gently before serving.

NOTE: This is ideal served with vegetables, beans, and hard-boiled eggs. The quantities are sufficient to serve 4–6.

❖ Barbecue Sauce ❖

SERVES 4	• 4 tbsp butter or	• 2 tbsp Worcestershire
PREPARATION TIME 5 minutes	margarine	sauce
COOKING TIME 20 minutes	• 1 large onion, peeled and chopped	• 2 tbsp vinegar
FREEZING Suitable	• 1 tsp tomato paste	

- 2 tbsp light brown sugar
- 2 tsp mustard powder

150 CALS/SERVING

1 Melt the butter in a saucepan, add the onion, and fry until soft, about 5 minutes. Stir in the tomato paste and continue cooking 3 minutes longer.

2 Mix together the remaining ingredients with ⅔ cup water until smooth, then stir into the onion mixture. Bring to a boil and boil, uncovered, 10 minutes longer.

NOTE: This is an excellent accompaniment for barbecued chicken, burgers, chops, and sausages.

❖ Hollandaise Sauce ❖

SERVES 4

PREPARATION TIME
20 minutes
COOKING TIME
2–3 minutes
FREEZING
Not suitable

- 3 tbsp white wine vinegar
- 6 peppercorns
- 1 small bay leaf
- 1 blade of mace
- 6–8 tbsp butter, at room temperature
- 2 egg yolks
- salt

215 CALS/SERVING

1 Place the vinegar, peppercorns, bay leaf, and mace in a small pan and boil rapidly until reduced to only 2 tsp; strain. Soften the butter until it is creamy.

2 In a small heatproof bowl or the top of a double boiler, whisk the egg yolks with a pinch of salt and the flavored vinegar until thoroughly combined.

3 Set the bowl over a pan of gently simmering water on low heat and whisk until the mixture is thick enough to leave a trail when the whisk is lifted, about 3 minutes.

4 Gradually add the butter, a little at a time, whisking constantly. When 6 tbsp has been added, season lightly with salt. If still too sharp, add a little more butter.

5 The sauce should be lightly piquant and have a smooth pouring consistency. If too thick, add a little water or vinegar. Serve warm.

NOTE: Hollandaise is traditionally served with asparagus, but it makes an excellent accompaniment to many vegetables.

It is a sauce that curdles easily. If this begins to happen, add an ice cube and whisk well; the sauce should re-form.

❖ Beurre Blanc Sauce ❖

SERVES 4–6

PREPARATION TIME
20 minutes
COOKING TIME
12–15 minutes
FREEZING
Not suitable

- 2 oz shallots, peeled
- ⅔ cup white wine vinegar
- 1¼ cups dry white wine
- 2½ sticks (1¼ cups) unsalted butter, chilled and diced
- 3 tbsp heavy whipping cream
- 2 tsp chopped chervil, tarragon, or dill
- salt and pepper

515–345 CALS/SERVING

1 Mince the shallots. Place in a saucepan with the vinegar and wine. Bring to a boil and boil, uncovered, until the liquid is reduced to about 6 tbsp, 10–12 minutes.
2 Strain the liquid into a small saucepan. Over very low heat, whisk in the butter a piece at a time, making sure each piece is thoroughly incorporated before adding the next.
3 When all the butter has been added, whisk in the cream, herbs, and seasoning to taste. Serve warm.

NOTE: This sharp buttery sauce is ideal for serving with poached or steamed fish.

❖ Béarnaise Sauce ❖

SERVES 4

PREPARATION TIME
20 minutes
COOKING TIME
2–3 minutes
FREEZING
Not suitable

- 1 shallot, peeled and minced
- 4 tsp chopped tarragon
- 2 tsp chopped chervil
- 6 tbsp dry white wine
- 6 tbsp tarragon vinegar
- pinch of crushed white peppercorns
- pinch of salt
- 3 egg yolks
- 2 sticks (1 cup) butter, melted
- freshly ground pepper

480 CALS/SERVING

1 Put the shallot, 1 tsp of the tarragon, ½ tsp of the chervil, the white wine, and tarragon vinegar in a saucepan. Add the peppercorns and salt and boil until reduced by two-thirds. Let cool.
2 Transfer the mixture to a small heatproof bowl set over a saucepan of gently simmering water, or to a double boiler. Add the egg yolks and whisk over very low heat about 3 minutes to form an emulsion.
3 Gradually add the tepid melted butter, whisking well after each addition. Strain the sauce through a cheesecloth-lined strainer or a fine sieve.
4 Adjust the seasoning and stir in the remaining tarragon and chervil. Serve warm.

NOTE: Béarnaise is an enriched version of Hollandaise sauce, with a more pungent flavor. It is traditionally served as an accompaniment to grilled or broiled meats.

❖ Crème Anglaise ❖

This "real" stirred egg custard is the classic accompaniment to many hot and cold desserts.

SERVES 4
PREPARATION TIME
20 minutes, plus standing
COOKING TIME
10 minutes
FREEZING
Not suitable

- ½ vanilla bean or few drops of vanilla extract
- 1¼ cups milk
- 3 egg yolks
- 4 tsp sugar

115 CALS/SERVING

1 If using a vanilla bean, split open and scrape out the seeds into a heavy-based saucepan. Add the vanilla bean and the milk. Bring slowly to a boil, take off the heat, cover, and let infuse 30 minutes. Remove the vanilla bean.
2 Place the egg yolks and sugar in a bowl. Using a balloon whisk, electric mixer, or wooden spoon, beat the egg yolks and sugar together until they lighten in color and thicken slightly.
3 Pour the infused milk onto the mixture, whisking or stirring until evenly mixed. Add vanilla extract to the milk at this stage, if using. Rinse the saucepan, then return the mixture to the pan.
4 Place the saucepan over low heat and cook the custard, stirring all the time, until it thickens slightly and begins to coat the back of the spoon, about 10 minutes. Do not boil or the custard will curdle. (Watch for the froth: When it begins to disappear on the surface, the custard is starting to thicken.)
5 Immediately strain the custard into a cold bowl to stop it cooking further. Whisk to reduce the temperature. To serve warm, pour into a pitcher. To serve cold, place damp wax paper on the surface of the hot custard to prevent a skin forming, let cool, then chill.

NOTE: To rescue a custard that is beginning to separate and curdle, immediately strain it into a cold bowl, add a few ice cubes, and whisk vigorously to reduce the temperature – it should smooth out again quite quickly.

If you are nervous of curdling the custard, beat 1 tsp cornstarch with the egg yolks in step 2; this helps thicken the custard. Make sure you taste it after cooking to ensure that the taste of cornstarch has disappeared; if necessary, stir over low heat for a little longer, but do not boil.

Variations

CHOCOLATE: Omit the vanilla bean. Break up 2 oz semisweet chocolate and add to the milk. Bring slowly to a boil, whisking until smooth. Finish as above, using 1 tbsp sugar only.

ORANGE, LEMON, OR MINT: Omit the vanilla bean. Add the pared rind of ½ lemon or ½ orange, or a handful of mint leaves, to the milk and bring to a boil. Complete as above, straining the milk onto the whisked egg yolks and sugar.

NUTMEG: Omit the vanilla bean. Prepare the custard as above, adding a dash of freshly grated nutmeg, and 1–2 tbsp sherry wine, if desired, at the end.

EXTRA CREAMY CUSTARD: Replace half or all of the milk with light whipping cream, or half light and half heavy whipping cream.

❖ Chocolate Custard Sauce ❖

SERVES 4
PREPARATION TIME
5 minutes
COOKING TIME
5 minutes
FREEZING
Not suitable

- 1 tbsp unsweetened cocoa powder
- 1½ tbsp cornstarch
- about 1½ tbsp sugar, or to taste
- 1¼ cups milk

110 CALS/SERVING

1 Blend the cocoa powder, cornstarch, and sugar to a smooth paste with a little of the milk.
2 In a heavy-based, preferably nonstick saucepan, heat the remaining milk until almost boiling. Pour onto the cornstarch mixture, stirring all the time.
3 Return the mixture to the saucepan and bring to a boil, stirring constantly. Continue cooking for 2 minutes after the sauce has boiled. Add a little extra sugar to taste, if desired. Serve hot, with steamed and baked puddings, pies, and tarts.

Variation

COFFEE CUSTARD: Replace the cocoa powder with instant coffee granules.

❖ Chocolate Fudge Sauce ❖

SERVES 4–6
PREPARATION TIME
5 minutes
COOKING TIME
7 minutes
FREEZING
Suitable

- ⅓ cup light whipping cream
- ⅓ cup unsweetened cocoa powder
- 9 tbsp sugar
- ½ cup light corn syrup
- 2 tbsp butter or margarine
- pinch of salt
- ½ tsp vanilla extract
- 1 tbsp rum or brandy (optional)

365–245 CALS/SERVING

1 Combine all the ingredients, except the vanilla extract and rum, in a saucepan over low heat, and mix well. Slowly bring to a boil, stirring occasionally. Boil 5 minutes, then add the vanilla extract, and rum if using.
2 Let cool slightly before serving, with ice cream.

❖ Raspberry Coulis ❖

SERVES 4
PREPARATION TIME
10 minutes
FREEZING
Suitable

- 1 pint raspberries
- confectioners' sugar, to taste
- dash of liqueur, such as Kirsch or framboise (optional)

50 CALS/SERVING

1 Purée the raspberries in a blender or food processor, then push through a nylon strainer to remove the seeds. If the raspberries are very ripe, simply press them through a strainer.
2 Add sugar to taste, then stir in a little liqueur, if using. Serve cold, with ices, sorbets, mousses, or cakes.

Variations

Replace the raspberries with strawberries, red currants, black currants, mango, papaya, apricots, or kiwi fruit.

SOUPS

Plenty of it, piping hot or thoroughly chilled and packed with the goodness of endless combinations of vegetables, meat, fish, beans, rice – that's the secret of a good soup. Infinitely superior to canned and packaged varieties, homemade soups are well worth making. Homemade stock lends a depth and quality of flavor that's hard to match with cubes or canned bouillon. It's the most important ingredient in consommé, bisques, and French onion soup; for these, substitutes just will not do. Robust soups thick with legumes or vegetables, or spicy soups, can be made successfully with commercial stock, but season with caution as they tend to be salty. The quality of commercial bouillons has improved dramatically in recent years, and it's worth experimenting until you find the brand you prefer. Canned chicken or beef consommé is a good alternative, too.

Serving quantities vary according to the type of soup and ensuing courses. For a first course allow about 8–10 fl oz. If serving soup as a main course allow about 12–14 fl oz, although similarly this will depend on how substantial the soup is.

Freezing Soups

Most soups freeze well. It makes sense to add less liquid than the recipe states to reduce bulk – make a note of how much you need to add when reheating. Freeze soup in large shallow containers for speediest thawing, not forgetting to leave some headroom to allow for expansion. Even with the help of a microwave, soups seem to take forever to thaw. They're best thawed overnight at cool room temperature; attempts to speed up defrosting by mashing inevitably ruin the texture of chunky soups. Don't add cream, yogurt, fromage blanc, or eggs before freezing because they will curdle when the soup is reheated.

Garnishes

Choose a garnish that's appropriate to the soup and the occasion. Wholesome, chunky soups need nothing more than a sprinkling of roughly chopped herbs or a few shavings of Parmesan. Smooth purées or creamy soups are enhanced by a sprinkling of crispy bacon, toasted nuts, or decorative vegetable shapes (cut with petit-four cutters). Sophisticated soups call for a swirl of cream, a delicate herb sprig, or perhaps a sprinkling of fleurons. These small decorative shapes are cut from puff pastry, glazed with egg, and baked until golden; sprinkle with poppy seeds, Parmesan, or herbs for extra interest.

Croûtons are irresistible, adding texture and flavour. Cut slightly stale bread into cubes and fry in butter or olive oil. Add crushed garlic for extra flavor or toss croûtons in chopped herbs. For theme parties, cut appropriate shapes using cookie cutters. Croûtons are best served separately for guests to add at the table since they go soft very quickly once added to the soup.

A julienne of colorful vegetables can transform plain soups. Cut matchstick-thin strips from carrots, zucchini, or bell peppers and blanch in salted water. Drain thoroughly and float on the soup just before serving. You can prepare a julienne of finely pared lemon, lime, or orange rind in much the same way (omitting the salt from the water); apply to soups sparingly.

Herb-filled ice cubes add color and interest to chilled soups. Choose herbs that complement the flavor of the soup.

Likewise, a chiffonade of salad leaves adds a summery freshness to chilled soup. Shred arugula, baby spinach, or delicate lettuce leaves. Add a tiny pile to each bowl just before serving.

Accompaniments

Whether you're serving soup as a first course or a meal in itself, warm bread is the obvious but perfect accompaniment. If possible bake your own bread (see pages 414–424). Potted Herb Bread (page 419) is good with chunky vegetable soups, while something lighter and more delicate like small rolls are better with subtly flavored soups. Poppadums are delicious with spiced or curried soups.

If you don't have the time to bake a loaf from scratch, take advantage of the wonderful range of delicious breads now available in the stores. Partly baked loaves and rolls are particularly useful, or you can liven up an uninteresting loaf with a flavored butter. Garlic is the most popular choice, but following the same principle try flavoring the butter with grated lemon rind; chopped fresh herbs; chopped hot chili peppers; a little curry paste, pesto sauce, or wholegrain mustard.

CONSOMMÉ

A consommé is a rich, clear soup made by reducing chicken, beef, or veal stock until it is concentrated in flavor and clarifying it by cooking with egg whites. A consommé may be served as a soup, with other flavorings added if desired, or it may be used as the basis of another dish. If a consommé is garnished it takes its name from the garnish (see below). To ensure the garnish does not cloud the soup, it should be added to the hot consommé just before serving.

❖ Chicken Consommé ❖

3 Gradually pour in the stock, whisking all the time, then bring to a boil, still whisking. Immediately boiling point is reached, stop whisking, lower the heat, and simmer very gently 1 hour.

4 Carefully make a hole in the scum on the surface of the liquid and ladle the liquid out into a strainer lined with cheesecloth over a large bowl. Reheat the consommé, check seasoning, and flavor with a little wine if desired.

Variations

BEEF CONSOMMÉ: Use well-flavored fat-free beef stock and lean ground steak in place of chicken.

CONSOMMÉ WITH HERBS: Flavor the consommé with 2–3 tbsp chopped tarragon, parsley, chives, or mint.

CONSOMMÉ JULIENNE: Cut small quantities of vegetables such as carrot, turnip, and celery into thin strips and cook separately; rinse, drain, and add to the soup before serving.

JELLIED CONSOMMÉ: Cold consommé should be lightly jellied. Let the consommé cool, then chill until set. Chop roughly and serve in individual dishes.

SERVES 4		
PREPARATION TIME 30 minutes COOKING TIME 1¼ hours FREEZING Suitable	• 7 cups well-flavored fat-free chicken stock • 2 leeks • 2 celery stalks • 2 carrots, peeled • 2 shallots, peeled • 12 oz chicken meat, ground	• 2 egg whites, lightly whisked • 2 egg shells, crushed • salt and pepper • dash of sherry or Madeira wine (optional)

56 CALS/SERVING

❖ Cock-a-Leekie Soup ❖

SERVES 6		
PREPARATION TIME 15 minutes COOKING TIME 1 hour 10 minutes FREEZING Not suitable COLOR INDEX Page 14	• 1 tbsp butter or margarine • 10–12 oz chicken (1 large or 2 small portions) • 12 oz leeks • 5 cups chicken stock • 1 bouquet garni	• salt and pepper • 6 prunes, pitted • parsley sprigs, for garnish

95 CALS/SERVING

1 Melt the butter in a large saucepan and fry the chicken quickly until golden on all sides.
2 Quarter the white part of the leeks lengthwise and chop into 1-inch pieces; reserve the green parts. Add the white parts to the pan and fry until soft, about 5 minutes.
3 Add the stock, bouquet garni, and salt and pepper to taste. Bring to a boil and simmer until the chicken is tender, about 30 minutes.
4 Shred the reserved green parts of the leeks, then add to the pan with the prunes. Simmer 30 minutes longer.
5 To serve, remove the chicken and cut the meat into large pieces, discarding the skin and bones. Place the meat in a warmed soup tureen and pour in the soup. Serve hot, garnished with parsley.

1 Heat the stock gently in a large pan. Meanwhile, thinly slice the leeks, celery, and carrots. Dice the shallots.

2 Mix the chicken and vegetables together in a large saucepan, then mix in the egg whites and shells.

❖ French Onion Soup ❖

PREPARATION TIME
20 minutes
COOKING TIME
50–55 minutes
FREEZING
Not suitable

- 3 onions, peeled
- 4 tbsp butter or margarine
- 1 tbsp flour
- 3½ cups beef stock
- salt and pepper
- 1 bay leaf
- ½ medium French loaf
- ¾ cup shredded Gruyère cheese

245 CALS/SERVING

1 Slice the onions thinly. Melt the butter in a saucepan, add the onions, and cook gently until dark golden brown, 15–20 minutes.

2 Stir in the flour and cook, stirring, 1 minute. Stir in the stock, seasoning, and bay leaf. Bring to a boil, cover, and simmer 30 minutes.

3 Cut the loaf diagonally into ½-inch slices and toast lightly on both sides. Place two slices in each ovenproof soup bowl. Ladle the hot soup over the bread, discarding the bay leaf.

4 Sprinkle liberally with the cheese to form a thick layer over the bread. Place under a hot broiler until the cheese is melted and bubbling. Serve immediately.

❖ Mushroom Soup ❖ with Parmesan Croûtons

PREPARATION TIME
20 minutes, plus soaking
COOKING TIME
1 hour
FREEZING
Suitable

- 1 oz dried mushrooms (porcini/cèpes)
- 4 shallots, peeled
- 3 tbsp olive oil
- 2 garlic cloves, minced
- 2 lb common or brown mushrooms
- 3½ cups vegetable stock
- salt and pepper
- 1½ tbsp wholegrain mustard

PARMESAN CROÛTONS:
- 3 slices white bread, crusts removed
- oil for shallow frying
- ¼ cup freshly grated Parmesan cheese
TO SERVE:
- ¼ cup heavy whipping cream

275 CALS/SERVING

1 Soak the dried mushrooms in enough water to cover for 30 minutes. Drain, reserving half of the liquid. Rinse well under running water. Chop roughly and set aside.

2 Chop the shallots. Heat the olive oil in a large saucepan. Add the shallots and garlic and fry gently until softened. Add the soaked mushrooms and cook 5 minutes. Roughly chop the common mushrooms and add to the pan. Cook, stirring, about 10 minutes.

3 Pour in the stock, season and bring to a boil. Cover and simmer gently until the dried mushrooms are tender, about 45 minutes.

4 Meanwhile make the croûtons. Cut the bread into small cubes. Heat a 1-inch depth of oil in a deep frying pan. When a piece of bread dropped into the oil sizzles, it will be hot enough. Fry the bread cubes in the oil until golden. Remove with a slotted spoon and drain on paper towels. While still warm, toss the croûtons in Parmesan cheese.

5 Purée the soup in a blender or food processor, in two batches if necessary, until smooth. Return to the pan. Stir in the mustard and reserved mushroom liquid; check seasoning. Serve hot with a little cream swirled in and accompanied by the croûtons.

A P P E T I Z E R S

The perfect appetizer is something attractive and delicious, which sets the tone of the meal and tempts guests' appetites for the food that is to follow. There's no point in planning a spectacular main course and dessert and then serving an uninteresting first course. It is at the beginning of the meal that appetites are keenest and most appreciative, so choose carefully. Get a casual supper for friends off to a relaxed start by serving a tasty dip with crudités, Deep-Fried Potato Skins (page 127), or a selection of tidbits. Smart formal affairs call for something rather more elegant like a Layered Fish Terrine (page 119) or Avocado with Raspberry Vinegar (page 126).

Choosing an Appetizer

Aim to achieve a balance and contrast of flavors, textures, and colors throughout the meal. If you're serving a substantial main course – a hearty stew or a roast with all the trimmings – then a small portion of a fruit- or vegetable-based appetizer is adequate. In fact the "wet and dry" rule is as good as any when choosing your courses. That is, a "wet" course such as a soup or dip should precede a "dry" course such as grilled or broiled meat or fish. Aim, too, for balance in "weight" of the courses. A chunky soup, followed by a deep-dish meat pie and a cobbler may be traditional country fare, but is far too filling for most appetites.

Pay attention to the variety and balance of flavors throughout the courses, and avoid repetition both of ingredients and "heavy" cooking methods such as deep-frying. A delicate pastry tartlet or a filo parcel starts any meal in style but precludes a tart or pie for dessert. If fish is the main course then obviously fish is inappropriate as an appetizer. A salad or meat course would be better instead. If you're planning a "themed" meal, then the first course should hint at what is to come.

Bear in mind how health-conscious many people are today and avoid putting together a meal that consists of several rich cream- or butter-based courses. If your main course is heavy and filling, serve a very light and refreshing appetizer. Most people are cutting down on their meat consumption, so don't plan a menu with meat in both the first and second courses.

Consider, too, the time of year. Food in season will always be the cheapest, freshest, and most appropriate. Homegrown asparagus makes a short appearance in the summer so it's a shame not to take advantage of this. Try serving it lightly steamed with coriander hollandaise (see page 126).

Plan the menu so that you leave plenty of time to be with your guests. For very large numbers, cold appetizers such as pâtés, terrines, mousses, or salads that can be laid out on the table in advance are easiest. Warm salads and hot soufflés are best for smaller affairs or where the main course requires little last-minute attention.

For informal supper parties or speedy pre-theater suppers you may find it more convenient to serve a selection of canapés or tidbits with cocktails rather than a sit-down first course. These can be prepared beforehand, warmed if necessary, and handed around as guests arrive.

For impromptu after-work suppers or when preparation time and energy are limited, simple hors d'oeuvres are best. Smoked salmon with brown bread and lemon; Parma ham with figs; salami with olives; grilled vegetables drizzled with olive oil; tomato, basil, and mozzarella salad – these unpretentious combinations never fail.

Having made your choice, it really is worth adding a garnish, no matter how simple. A wedge of lemon or lime adds color to fish and seafood appetizers, while a sprinkling of chopped fresh herbs brings most foods to life.

Party Food

Included in this chapter are plenty of ideas for delicious tidbits to serve at cocktail parties. These little nibbles are notoriously time-consuming to prepare, but we've cut corners to enable you to prepare party food in half the time it usually takes. For quick and easy canapés, try Whole Wheat Blinis, savory Mini Croissants, and Asian Parcels (page 112).

Other ideas for party nibbles include Spiced Cashews, Toasted Seed and Nut Mix, and Olives with Garlic and Lemon (page 114). You can also dress up sausage rolls by glazing with egg, then sprinkling with shredded cheese or sesame seeds before baking. Or try tossing cooked chicken nuggets in Parmesan and serving with a Herbed Cheese Dip (page 115). A colorful platter of crudités and a selection of dips always look attractive. Allow 8–10 "bites" per head, with nuts, olives, dips, and "dunks" as extras.

❖ Salmon Mousse ❖

SERVES 8

PREPARATION TIME
30 minutes, plus
chilling
COOKING TIME
10–15 minutes
FREEZING
Not suitable
COLOR INDEX
Page 19

- 12 oz tail-end piece salmon or sea trout fillet
- 1 small onion, peeled and sliced
- 1 medium carrot, peeled and sliced
- 2 bay leaves
- 4 black peppercorns
- salt and pepper
- ⅓ cup white wine
- 1 envelope unflavoured gelatin
- 1¼ cups milk

- 2 tbsp butter or margarine
- 2 tbsp flour
- ⅓ cup lemon mayonnaise (page 273)
- ⅔ cup light whipping cream
- 1 egg white

FOR GARNISH:
- English cucumber slices
- dill sprigs

295 CALS/SERVING

5 Fold the mayonnaise into the salmon mixture. Whip the cream until soft peaks form, then fold into the mousse; adjust the seasoning. Beat the egg white until stiff and fold lightly into the mousse until no traces of egg white are visible.

6 Spoon the mousse into an oiled 6-inch diameter soufflé dish, smooth the surface, cover, and refrigerate at least 2 hours, until set. Leave at room temperature for 30 minutes before serving. Garnish with English cucumber slices and dill sprigs.

1 Place the salmon in a small shallow pan. Add half the onion and carrot slices, 1 bay leaf, 2 peppercorns, and a large pinch of salt. Spoon over the wine and add ⅓ cup water. Bring slowly to a boil, then cover and simmer gently until the fish flakes easily when tested with a knife, 10–15 minutes.

2 Flake the fish, discarding the skin, and place in a bowl. Boil the cooking liquid until reduced by half, strain and reserve. Sprinkle the gelatin over 3 tbsp water in a bowl and let soak 5 minutes until sponge-like. Bring the milk to a boil with the remaining onion, carrot, bay leaf, and peppercorns. Remove from heat and let infuse 10 minutes; strain.

❖ Smoked Mackerel Pâté ❖

SERVES 6

PREPARATION TIME
15 minutes
FREEZING
Suitable

- 10 oz smoked mackerel fillets
- 4 tbsp butter or margarine, softened
- 3 tbsp cream-style horseradish

- 2 tbsp light whipping cream
- pepper

195 CALS/SERVING

3 Melt the butter in a pan, stir in the flour, and cook, stirring, 1 minute. Remove from the heat and gradually stir in the strained milk. Bring to a boil slowly and cook, stirring, until the sauce thickens. Pour into a bowl, add gelatin, and stir until dissolved. Let cool.

4 Stir the fish into the cooled sauce with the reserved cooking juices. Spoon into a blender or food processor and work a few seconds only; the fish should retain a little of its texture. Transfer to a large bowl.

1 Remove the skin from the smoked mackerel and tweezer out any small bones. Flake into a bowl.
2 Add the butter, creamed horseradish, and cream. Mash with a fork until evenly blended. Season with pepper; salt is not usually needed.
3 Spoon the mixture into a serving dish, cover tightly, and refrigerate until required. Leave the pâté at room temperature for 30 minutes before serving. Serve with toast or rye wafers.

NOTE: Make sure the type of smoked mackerel you buy for this recipe does not need further cooking.

❖ Layered Fish Terrine ❖

SERVES 8

PREPARATION TIME
30 minutes, plus
chilling
COOKING TIME
45 minutes
FREEZING
Not suitable

- 1½ lb whiting, sole, or hake fillets, skinned and chilled
- 3 egg whites, chilled
- salt and white pepper
- 1 tbsp lemon juice
- 2 tbsp chopped dill
- 2 tbsp chopped tarragon
- 1¼ cups heavy whipping cream, chilled
- 2 tbsp butter
- 1 lb tail-end piece salmon fillet, skinned

- 1 tbsp green peppercorns in brine, drained
- dill, for garnish

380 CALS/SERVING

1 Remove any bones from the white fish, then cut into pieces. Work in a blender or food processor until finely ground.

2 Add the egg whites and pepper; process until evenly mixed. Turn into a bowl, cover, and chill 30 minutes.

3 Add the lemon juice, dill, and tarragon; process, slowly adding the cream. Add salt to taste, cover, and chill at least 30 minutes.

4 Meanwhile liberally grease a 1½-quart terrine or loaf pan with the butter; line the bottom with wax paper.

5 Cut the salmon into chunky strips, about ½-inch square and the length of the loaf pan or terrine. Cover and chill in the refrigerator until required.

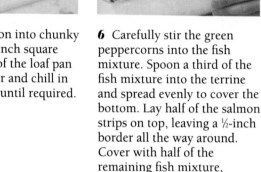

6 Carefully stir the green peppercorns into the fish mixture. Spoon a third of the fish mixture into the terrine and spread evenly to cover the bottom. Lay half of the salmon strips on top, leaving a ½-inch border all the way around. Cover with half of the remaining fish mixture, leveling it carefully.

7 Repeat the salmon layer, using the remaining salmon strips. Finally, cover with the remaining fish mixture and smooth the top.

8 Cover the terrine with buttered foil. Set in a roasting pan and pour in enough boiling water to come halfway up the sides of the terrine. Bake in a preheated 350°F oven until a skewer inserted into the center comes out clean, about 45 minutes.

9 Transfer the terrine to a wire rack and let cool, then cover with plastic wrap and chill in the refrigerator for at least 4 hours.

10 When ready to serve unmold the terrine onto a plate and wipe with paper towels to remove any butter or liquid. Cut into thick slices and serve garnished with dill.

❖ Pork Satay ❖

3 To make the satay sauce, heat the oil in a saucepan and add the garlic, curry, and chili powders. Cook, stirring, 1–2 minutes. Add the peanut butter, sugar, and lemon rind, with 1¼ cups water. Bring to a simmer and cook, stirring, until the sauce is thick, 4–5 minutes.

4 Thread the pork onto 8 or 12 bamboo skewers. Grill the satay or cook under a hot broiler, turning occasionally, until well browned and tender 4–5 minutes on each side. Serve on a bed of salad leaves, accompanied by the satay sauce, garnished with chopped peanuts and coriander.

Variations

CHICKEN AND BEEF SATAY: Replace the pork tenderloin with chicken breast or beef tenderloin (filet mignon), or serve an assortment of satays as an appetizer.

❖ Spareribs ❖ in Barbecue Sauce

SERVES 4–6

PREPARATION TIME
15 minutes, plus marinating
COOKING TIME
15–20 minutes
FREEZING
Not suitable

- 1 lb pork tenderloin
- 2 oz onion, peeled
- 3 tbsp dark soy sauce
- 1 tsp dark brown sugar

SATAY SAUCE:
- 1 tbsp oil
- 1 garlic clove, minced
- 1 tsp curry powder
- 2 tsp mild chili powder
- 1 cup crunchy peanut butter
- 1 tbsp dark brown sugar
- finely grated rind of 1 lemon

FOR SERVING:
- salad leaves
FOR GARNISH:
- chopped peanuts
- chopped coriander (cilantro)

580–385 CALS/SERVING

SERVES 6–8

PREPARATION TIME
10 minutes, plus marinating
COOKING TIME
About 1 hour
FREEZING
Suitable
COLOR INDEX
Page 20

- 3–3½ lb spareribs
- 1 oz piece fresh gingerroot
- ¼ cup hoisin sauce
- 3 tbsp soy sauce
- 3 tbsp dry sherry wine
- ¼ cup thin honey
- 1 tbsp vinegar
- 1 large garlic clove, minced
- salt and pepper

665–500 CALS/SERVING

1 Trim the spareribs of any excess fat and cut down between the bones to separate into individual ribs. Place in a single layer in a large, shallow, non-metallic dish.
2 Peel and mince the ginger; mix with the remaining ingredients and 2½ cups water. Pour over the spareribs; cover tightly and refrigerate several hours, turning occasionally.
3 Transfer the spareribs and marinade to a large flameproof casserole or Dutch oven. Bring to a boil, cover, and simmer until the ribs are quite tender, about 1 hour.
4 Uncover and cook steadily until the liquid has reduced to about a quarter of its original volume. Adjust the seasoning. Serve each portion of ribs with some of the sauce.

NOTE: Look out for spareribs with plenty of meat attached. This may seem a large quantity for 6–8 people, but much of the weight is bone. To be at their best, spareribs must be really tender, with the meat almost falling off the bone.

1 Cut the pork into ½-inch pieces. Mince the onion.

2 In a shallow dish, mix together the minced onion, soy sauce, and 1 tsp brown sugar. Toss the pork in the soy sauce mixture, cover, and let marinate at least 1 hour.

❖ Marinated Salmon ❖

SERVES 8

PREPARATION TIME
15 minutes, plus
marinating
FREEZING
Suitable

- 2 tbsp sea salt
- 2 tbsp caster sugar
- 2 tsp crushed black peppercorns
- ¼ cup chopped dill
- ½ cup fresh lime juice
- 3–4 lb salmon or sea trout, filleted (with skin intact)

335 CALS/SERVING

1 Mix all the ingredients except the salmon together in a small bowl. Spoon a quarter of the mixture over the bottom of a non-metallic dish.

2 Lay one salmon fillet, skin-side down, in the dish. Spoon over half of the remaining marinade. Cover with the second fillet, skin-side up. Pour over the remaining marinade.

3 Cover with wax paper, then plastic wrap. Weigh down with a 2-lb weight (cans of food) in a cool place for 2 days, turning occasionally.

4 To serve the salmon, drain well and trim off any hard edges. Cut into wafer-thin slices on the bias. Serve with lime slices and brown bread.

❖ Ceviche ❖

SERVES 6

PREPARATION TIME
20 minutes, plus
marinating
FREEZING
Not suitable
COLOR INDEX
Page 20

- 1½ lb haddock fillets
- 1 hot red chili pepper
- 1 tbsp coriander seeds
- 1 tsp black peppercorns
- juice of 6 limes
- 1 tsp salt
- 8 oz English cucumber
- 2 small avocados
- 1 bunch scallions
- few drops of hot pepper sauce
- 3 tbsp chopped coriander (cilantro)
- pepper

140 CALS/SERVING

1 Cut the haddock fillets diagonally into ½-inch thick strips and place in a bowl.

2 Seed and chop the chili, wearing rubber gloves to avoid skin irritation. Crush the coriander seeds and black peppercorns to a fine powder, using a pestle and mortar. Strain to remove the seed husks, then mix with the lime juice, salt, and chili. Pour over the haddock. Cover and chill at least 24 hours, lightly stirring from time to time.

3 To serve, drain the fish, discarding the marinade. Thinly slice the cucumber. Halve, pit, and peel the avocados, then slice thickly. Shred the scallions. Mix the cucumber, avocado and scallions with the fish. Add the pepper sauce and chopped coriander and season with pepper to taste. Serve chilled.

NOTE: Don't be put off by the thought of raw fish – the lime juice "cooks" the haddock. Ceviche can be made using any firm white fish, as long as it is really fresh.

❖ Deviled Whitebait with Fried Parsley ❖

SERVES 8

PREPARATION TIME
10 minutes
COOKING TIME
10 minutes
FREEZING
Not suitable
COLOR INDEX
Page 20

- ½ cup flour
- ½ tsp curry powder
- ½ tsp ground ginger
- ½ tsp cayenne pepper
- salt
- 2½ lb whitebait (smelts)
- oil for deep-frying
- 1 oz parsley sprigs
- sea salt
- lemon wedges, for serving

975 CALS/SERVING

1 Sift the flour, curry powder, ginger, cayenne, and salt together into a large plastic bag. Put a quarter of the whitebait into the bag and shake well to coat in the flour mixture. Lift the fish out and shake in a strainer to remove excess flour. Repeat with the remaining whitebait.

2 Heat the oil in a deep-fat fryer to 375°F. Put a single layer of whitebait into the frying basket and lower it into the oil. Fry, shaking the basket occasionally, until the whitebait make a rustling sound as they are shaken, 2–3 minutes. Tip out onto a warmed plate lined with paper towels. Fry the remaining whitebait in the same way.

3 Allow the oil temperature to reduce to about 365°F. Deep-fry the parsley a few seconds until it stops sizzling. Drain on paper towels, then sprinkle with sea salt.

4 Divide the whitebait among warmed serving plates. Scatter over the parsley and garnish with lemon wedges.

❖ Seafood Roulade ❖

SERVES 8	• *12 oz cooked shrimp in shells*	• *½ cup flour*
PREPARATION TIME 35 minutes	• *⅞ cup dry white wine*	• *4 eggs, separated*
COOKING TIME 12 minutes	• *onion slices and a bay leaf, for flavoring*	• *2 tbsp light whipping cream*
FREEZING Not suitable	• *8 oz shelled sea scallops*	• *2 tsp chopped dill*
	• *8 oz haddock fillet*	• *dill sprigs, for garnish*
	• *⅞ cup milk*	
	• *salt and pepper*	
	• *6 tbsp butter or margarine*	**250 CALS/SERVING**

3 Place the haddock in a small saucepan with the milk and seasoning. Bring to a boil, cover, and simmer until the fish is tender, about 8 minutes. Strain and reserve the liquor; there should be about ⅞ cup. Flake the fish, discarding skin and bone.

4 Melt 4 tbsp butter in a saucepan. Stir in 6½ tbsp flour followed by the reserved milk. Bring to a boil and cook 1 minute, stirring all the time to make a very thick sauce. Le[t] cool slightly, then mix in the flaked haddock and the egg yolks. Adjust seasoning.

5 Beat the egg whites until stiff but not dry. Stir one large spoonful into the haddock mixture, then lightly fold in the remainder and pour gently into the paper case. Push the mixture out carefully to fill the case to the edges. Bake in a preheated 400°F oven until lightly browned and just firm to touch, about 12 minutes. Remove paper clips.

6 Meanwhile, add the scallop[s] to the fish stock and simmer 1–2 minutes. Take off the heat. Melt 2 tbsp butter in a saucepan and stir in 1½ tbsp flour, followed by the stock mixture. Bring to a boil, stirring, and cook 1 minute. Take off the heat and mix in the shrimp, cream, and dill. Adjust the seasoning and keep warm in a water bath.

1 First prepare the paper case. Cut a sheet of strong parchment paper into a rectangle measuring 16 × 12 inches. Fold up 1 inch around the edges, then snip in at the corners and secure with paper clips or staples. Place on a baking sheet and brush the paper case generously with melted butter.

2 To prepare the fish stock, remove the shells from the shrimp, reserving the flesh, and place in a small saucepan with the wine, ⅞ cup water, and the flavoring ingredients. Bring to a boil and simmer 10 minutes. Strain the stock into a food processor, add the scallop coral (if available), and blend until smooth. Strain into a jug. Cut the white scallop flesh into small pieces and reserve.

7 Flip the cooked roulade onto a large sheet of damp wax paper. Carefully ease off the paper case. Make a shallow cut along one short edge – this helps to start rolling.

8 Spread thinly with the sauce and fish mixture and roll up from the short edge. Serve immediately, accompanied by the remaining sauce.

❖ Smoked Salmon ❖ and Cream Cheese Rolls

SERVES 8

PREPARATION TIME
25 minutes, plus
chilling
FREEZING
Not suitable
COLOR INDEX
Page 21

- 10 oz cream cheese, at room temperature
- 2 tbsp mayonnaise
- finely grated rind of 1 lime or lemon
- 8 oz cooked peeled shrimp (thawed and thoroughly dried if frozen)
- 1 envelope unflavored gelatin
- 2 tbsp lime or lemon juice
- 8 large thin slices smoked salmon
- 4–5 tbsp finely chopped dill
- pepper

FOR GARNISH:
- lime or lemon twists
- dill sprigs

`355 CALS/SERVING`

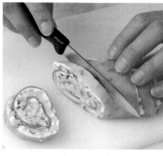

5 Carefully roll up the salmon slices from a short end, then place seam-side down on a plate. Cover with plastic wrap and refrigerate at least 2 hours, until firm.

6 To serve, cut each salmon roll on the diagonal into 8 neat slices, then arrange the slices, slightly overlapping, on individual plates. Garnish with lime or lemon twists and dill. Serve at room temperature, with crusty white or whole wheat rolls.

1 Put the cream cheese in a bowl with the mayonnaise and lime or lemon rind and beat until evenly mixed. Chop the shrimp finely.

2 Sprinkle the gelatin over ¼ cup cold water in a small heatproof bowl. Let soak about 5 minutes until spongy, then set the bowl in a saucepan of gently simmering water until the gelatin has dissolved. Remove and let cool a few minutes.

3 Stir the dissolved gelatin into the cream-cheese mixture until evenly blended, then stir in the lime or lemon juice. Cover the bowl and chill until the mixture is just firm enough to hold its shape, about 30 minutes.

4 Divide the cream cheese mixture evenly among the salmon slices and spread it out, then scatter over the chopped dill. Sprinkle the chopped shrimp over the dill and press down gently with your fingertips. Grind black pepper over the top.

❖ Shrimp Cocktails ❖

SERVES 4

PREPARATION TIME
10 minutes
FREEZING
Not suitable

- ¼ cup mayonnaise
- ¼ cup light whipping cream
- 2 tsp tomato paste
- 2 tsp lemon juice
- dash of Worcestershire sauce
- dash of dry sherry wine
- salt and pepper
- 8 oz cooked peeled shrimp
- few lettuce leaves, shredded
- lemon slices, for garnish

`200 CALS/SERVING`

1 In a small bowl, mix together the mayonnaise, cream, tomato paste, lemon juice, Worcestershire sauce, and sherry. Season to taste. Add the shrimp and stir well to coat.
2 Place the shredded lettuce in four glasses and top with the fish mixture.
3 Garnish each shrimp cocktail with lemon slices. Serve with thinly sliced brown bread.

SHELLFISH

Fresh, perfectly cooked shellfish is prized the world over for its delicate flavor and stunning appearance. There's nothing that quite compares with a plateful of juicy shrimp; a bowl of steaming mussels; or a magnificent platter of "fruits de mer." Shellfish can be divided into three types: crustaceans, mollusks, and cephalopods. Crustaceans include the prized lobster, crabs, shrimp, and freshwater crayfish. They have hard external skeletons that are segmented to allow for movement. Mollusks live inside one or two hard shells (valves). The bivalves include oysters, mussels, clams, and scallops. Cephalopods, namely squid, octopus and cuttlefish, belong to the mollusk family but have no shells.

All shellfish is highly perishable, so freshness should be the main consideration. Get to know a good local fish merchant – look for a market with a fast turnover and a clean, well-presented display. Avoid anywhere that has lots of fish left at the end of the day.

Choosing Shellfish

Look for tightly closed, undamaged shells. Lobsters and crabs should feel heavy for their size. Fresh shellfish has a clean, unnoticeable smell – don't buy if it has a strong smell of any kind. Shrimp develop a strong chlorine-like smell if past their best.

When buying frozen shellfish, choose firm, thoroughly frozen, and undamaged packages. Buy more than the recipe calls for to allow for weight loss after thawing. Cook quickly once thawed.

Refrigerate shellfish as soon as possible after purchase. It will deteriorate rapidly if stored in warm conditions. All shellfish really should be eaten on the day of purchase, particularly oysters, mussels, and shrimp, but if this is impractical, it can be stored in the refrigerator up to 1 day. Frozen shellfish will deteriorate and lose its flavor after 2–3 months.

❖ Lobster ❖

There is much controversy surrounding the cooking of live lobsters. Animal welfare groups recommend putting them in a freezer for 2 hours, to render them unconscious before cooking. But for many cooks there is still something inhumane about this. If you have the choice it is preferable to get your fish man to cook the lobster for you. If you haven't, here is our method:

Note the lobster's weight. Take a large saucepan with a tightly fitting lid; fill with water and add flavorings such as onion, carrot, celery, bouquet garni, and peppercorns. Bring the water to a rapid boil, then holding the lobster by its back lower it in. Cover, reduce the heat, and boil gently, allowing 10 minutes for the first 1 lb and 5 minutes for each additional 1 lb. Let cool in the liquid.

Some classic lobster dishes call for raw, cut-up pieces of lobster. This is another job that's best left to your fish man.

To Prepare Cooked Lobster

1 Twist off the claws and pincers. Crack open the large claws using the back of a heavy knife, being careful not to crush the meat inside. Reserve the smaller claws to use as a garnish.

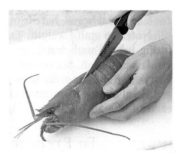

2 Put the lobster, back upward, on a flat surface and using a sharp knife split the lobster cleanly in two, piercing through the "cross" at the center of the head.

3 Remove and discard the intestine that runs through the center of the tail, the stomach (which lies near the head), and the spongy-looking gills or "dead man's fingers," which are inedible.

4 Using a teaspoon, scoop out the edible soft gray liver (tomalley) and red roe (if any). Carefully lift the tail meat from the shell, pulling it out neatly and in one piece if you can. Cut into thick slices (or as directed in the recipe).

5 Using a skewer, carefully remove the meat from each rear leg, in a whole piece.

❖ Mussels and ❖ Clams with Tomatoes

SERVES 2–3

PREPARATION TIME
10 minutes
COOKING TIME
10 minutes
FREEZING
Not suitable
COLOR INDEX
Page 24

- 1 small onion, peeled
- 8 oz ripe tomatoes
- 2 tbsp butter
- 1–2 large garlic cloves, minced
- ⅔ cup dry white wine
- finely grated rind of 1 lemon
- 2 tbsp chopped parsley
- 2¼ lb mussels, scrubbed
- 1 lb small hard-shell clams, cleaned
- pepper

`560–375 CALS/SERVING`

1 Mince the onion. Chop the tomatoes roughly. Melt the butter in a saucepan and cook the garlic and onion until soft. Add the wine, tomatoes, lemon rind, and half the parsley. Bring to a boil.
2 Add the mussels and clams to the pan, cover, and cook over high heat until the mussels and clams are open, about 5 minutes, shaking the pan frequently. Discard any mussels or clams that have not opened.
3 Season with pepper to taste. Transfer to large bowls or soup plates and sprinkle with the remaining parsley. Serve at once.

NOTE: If you cannot obtain fresh mussels, use extra clams instead.

❖ Mussels with ❖ Garlic and Parsley

SERVES 4–6

PREPARATION TIME
20 minutes
COOKING TIME
15 minutes
FREEZING
Not suitable

- 2½–3 lb mussels, scrubbed
- ⅔ cup fresh white bread crumbs
- ⅔ cup chopped parsley
- 2 garlic cloves, minced
- pepper
- 7 tbsp olive oil
- 2 tbsp freshly grated Parmesan cheese
- lemon wedges, for serving

`435–290 CALS/SERVING`

1 Place the mussels in a large saucepan containing ½ inch boiling water. Cover and cook over high heat until the mussels are open, about 5 minutes, shaking the pan frequently. Discard any mussels that do not open.

2 Discard the empty half-shell from each mussel. Strain the cooking liquid through a strainer lined with paper towels and reserve. Place the mussels in their half-shells on two baking sheets.

3 Mix together the bread crumbs, parsley, garlic, and plenty of pepper. Add the oil and ¼ cup of the strained cooking liquid. Mix well, then adjust the seasoning.

4 With your fingers, pick up good pinch of the bread-crumb mixture and press it down on each mussel, covering it well and filling the shell. Sprinkle with the Parmesan and bake in a preheated 450°F oven for 10 minutes, reversing the baking sheets halfway through cooking. Serve with lemon wedges and French bread.

❖ Monkfish and Mussel Skewers ❖

SERVES 4

PREPARATION TIME
20 minutes
COOKING TIME
10 minutes
FREEZING
Not suitable
COLOR INDEX
Page 24

- 12 thick bacon slices
- 1½ lb monkfish fillet, skinned
- 24 shelled mussels
- 2 tbsp butter or margarine
- ¼ cup chopped parsley
- finely grated rind and juice of 1 large lemon
- 4 garlic cloves, minced
- pepper
- shredded lettuce, for serving
- lemon slices, for garnish

`415 CALS/SERVING`

1 Halve the bacon slices and roll up neatly. Cut the monkfish into 1-inch cubes. Thread the cubed fish, mussels, and bacon alternately onto 12 oiled skewers.

2 Melt the butter in a saucepan, remove from the heat, then add the parsley, lemon rind and juice, and garlic. Season with pepper; the mussels and bacon should provide sufficient salt.
3 Place the skewers on an oiled wire rack and brush with the parsley mixture. Cook under the broiler, about 4 inches from the heat, 10 minutes, turning frequently and brushing with the parsley mixture with each turn.
4 Arrange the hot skewers on a serving platter lined with shredded lettuce. Garnish with lemon slices and serve immediately.

❖ Mussels in White Wine ❖

SERVES 4–6

PREPARATION TIME
15 minutes
COOKING TIME
5 minutes
FREEZING
Not suitable

- *1 shallot, peeled*
- *1 oz celery*
- *½ cup dry white wine*
- *3 lb mussels, cleaned*
- *1 tbsp chopped parsley*
- *½ cup heavy whipping cream*
- *pepper*

225–150 CALS/SERVING

1 Mince the shallot and celery. Put into a saucepan with the wine and bring to a boil. Add the mussels and cover the pan with a close-fitting lid. Cook over high heat, shaking the pan frequently, until the mussel shells are open, about 5 minutes.
2 Remove from the heat and discard any mussels that have not opened. Discard the one loose shell from each mussel. Put the mussels on their half-shell into a warmed dish or individual cocottes. Keep warm.
3 Strain the cooking liquid through a strainer lined with paper towels. Return to the pan and add the parsley, cream, and pepper to taste. Bring just to boiling point, then pour over the mussels.
4 Serve immediately, as a first course or light meal accompanied by warm crusty bread.

❖ Oysters au Gratin ❖

SERVES 4–6

PREPARATION TIME
20 minutes
COOKING TIME
10 minutes
FREEZING
Not suitable

- *2 oz slab bacon*
- *3 oz celery*
- *½ 16-oz can artichoke hearts, drained*
- *12 large oysters*
- *7 oz mozzarella cheese, thinly sliced*

220–150 CALS/SERVING

1 Mince the bacon, celery, and artichokes. In a small pan, fry the bacon until the fat begins to run. Add the celery and artichokes; cook, stirring, 2 minutes. Cool.

2 Scrub the oyster shells well. Open the oysters by inserting an oyster knife into the hinge linking the shells and cutting through the muscle. Prise shells apart; discard flatter ones.

3 Spoon a little of the bacon and artichoke mixture over each oyster.

4 Top with cheese. Cook under the broiler, 4 inches from the heat, 10 minutes. Serve as an appetizer or light meal.

FISH

No wonder fish is regaining popularity. It is a rich source of protein, vitamins, and minerals, and it's relatively low in calories, too.

As more and more exotic species find their way to our markets, the choice of fresh fish has never been better. Most fish merchants are only too willing to clean and fillet fish and to act as cooking advisors, too. They will suggest which fish to try as alternatives to your favorites and how to cook them to get the best results.

In general, fish requires little cooking; its delicate flavor and texture is easily spoiled. Freezing doesn't do most cooked fish dishes any good either; sauces dry up and the fish itself becomes mushy, so we rarely recommend doing this. Frozen raw fish keeps well 2–3 months, after which it begins to lose its flavor. Ideally, buy and cook fresh fish on the same day, but if this is impossible, remove it from the original wrappings, rinse, and dry, then rewrap and store in the refrigerator up to 1 day.

Choosing Fish

Really fresh fish is unmistakable. It will look bright and fresh with vivid markings, clean shiny scales, bright eyes, and bright red gills. The flesh should be soft and spring back when pressed – ask your fish merchant for permission before you check this!

Fillets and steaks should look translucent rather than opaque. Avoid fillets and steaks if they look dry and shriveled. If buying fish pre-packed from a supermarket, check the use-before date. If buying frozen fish choose solidly frozen fillets in undamaged packages. With the exception of skate and shark, fresh fish does not smell "fishy."

❖ Preparing Fish ❖

Most fish merchants will willingly and expertly prepare fresh fish for you. There's no point in attempting to do this at home if you find the prospect daunting or unpleasant. However, it is quite simple if you remember that for preparation purposes, fish is divided into two basic categories: flatfish such as flounder, sole, brill; and round fish such as mackerel, cod, trout, whiting.

All fish, with the exception of smelts, must have their scales and insides removed before cooking. Scaling is definitely a job for the fish man. If there are a few scales still attached when you get the fish home, simply scrape them off using the blunt side of a large knife, working from tail to head.

Before cleaning, remove the fins with kitchen scissors to make the fish look neater. If you're going to bone the fish, remove the dorsal fin completely by cutting down each side of the fin into the bony structure that connects the fin to the flesh. The fin can then be pulled away along with the underlying bones. Trim the tail and cut off the head behind the gills, if desired.

Cleaning Fish

The easiest way to clean a fish is through the belly. If cleaning a round fish, cut along the belly as far as you can and pull out the innards. Rinse thoroughly to remove all traces of blood. To clean a flatfish, make a small incision below the gills and pull the innards out.

If you wish to preserve the shape of the fish or keep it whole for stuffing, you will need to clean the fish through the gills. To do this, push your finger through the gills to open them out, then keeping the gills open with one hand, grip the innards with the other hand, and pull them out in one piece. Reach into the body cavity to make sure that you have removed everything. Rinse thoroughly.

Skinning Fish

Once cleaned, fish can be broiled, barbecued, baked, steamed, or fried, but many recipes call for skinned fish fillets. If you're intending to cook whole flatfish, remove the dark skin only; the white skin will help keep the fish in one piece during cooking. Flatfish that are to be filleted should be skinned completely. Round fish and very large flatfish, such as turbot, are easier to skin after filleting or cooking.

To Skin Flatfish

1 Lay the fish on a board, dark-side uppermost, and make an incision across the skin where the tail joins the body. Starting at the cut, use the point of the knife to lift a flap of skin until you can get a firm grip.

2 Salt your fingers. Grasping the flap of skin with your salted fingers (the salt should help you to grip) and holding down the tail in the other hand, pull the skin away. It should come away cleanly in one piece. Turn the fish over and remove the white skin in the same way, if desired.

❖ Boning and Filleting ❖

In order to fillet fish at home, you must have a proper sharp filleting knife with a long flexible blade that will glide over the bones as you cut. If your knife is blunt or too short you will inevitably end up leaving a lot of flesh attached to the bones. You will get four fillets from a flatfish, which should be skinned before filleting. Round fish yield two fillets and are skinned after filleting. Cook fillets as soon as they have been prepared, or wrap in plastic wrap to prevent them drying out and store in the refrigerator until required.

To Fillet Flatfish

1 Lay the fish on a board with its tail pointing toward you and its eyes facing up. Cut down the center of the fish from the head to the tail along the backbone.

2 Starting at the head end, insert the blade of the knife between the flesh and the bones. Aiming to skim the blade over the bones, cut down along the flesh. When the head end of the fillet is detached, lift it and continue cutting until the whole fillet is removed.

3 Repeat this procedure to remove the second fillet.

4 Turn the fish over and cut two more fillets from the other side. If there is any orange roe, save it for stock. When all the fillets are removed you should be left with a clean skeleton (which can also go in the stockpot) and four neat fillets.

To Fillet Round Fish

1 Lay the fish on its side with the tail pointing toward you. Cut along the backbone from the head to the tail, cutting right through to the backbone.

2 Cut through behind the gills to separate the fillet from the head. Starting at head end, insert knife between fillet and bones. Aiming to skim the knife over the bones, cut the fillet to detach completely.

3 Holding the fish by the exposed bones and with the tail still toward you, cut the remaining fillet from the ribs. Check fillets in case any bones are still attached; remove with tweezers or your fingers.

4 To skin fillets, lay skin-side down with the tail end toward you. Make a cut at the tail end so the fillet can be lifted slightly from the skin. With salted fingers press on exposed skin to keep it on the board. Insert the knife at a slight angle beneath the fillet and cut away from you to separate the fillet.

Boning Whole Round Fish

Small round fish like herrings are often cooked whole because they are troublesome to fillet. Sometimes you may need to bone a large round fish if you are cooking it whole.

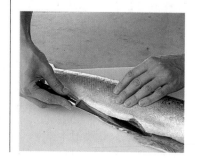

1 Scale and clean the fish in the usual way (see page 143). Cut off the head and tail or leave them on if preferred. Extend the cut along the belly (used for cleaning) so that it goes right to the tail.

2 Open the fish out, then lay it on its side on a board. Carefully cut the rib bones free from the flesh on the upperside.

3 Turn the fish over and repeat on the other side, working through to the backbone, being careful not to cut through the flesh.

4 With a pair of kitchen scissors, cut through the backbone as close to the head as possible. Hold the backbone at the head end and carefully pull it free. Snip it at the tail end so that it can be removed completely.

5 Check the flesh for any remaining bones, removing any small bones with tweezers.

NOTE: If it is a small fish, simply open it out, then lay it on a board cut-side down. Press firmly along the backbone with your fingers to loosen it. Turn the fish over and you should now be able to pull the backbone away with the ribs attached. Remove any fine bones that don't come away, using tweezers.

❖ Cooking Fish ❖

Because white fish is lacking in fat, it is easily dried out during cooking. If you're cooking fish by a "dry" method such as grilling, it's important to baste frequently with butter, oil, or a marinade. For moist methods of cooking like poaching it's vital to cook the fish gently; if the cooking liquid boils vigorously the fish will disintegrate during cooking.

Bear in mind that the subtle flavor is easily masked or overpowered by strong flavors, so choose accompanying sauces carefully. Similarly, choose a cooking method that's appropriate to the fish. Chunky steaks of firm or oily fish or sturdy whole fish can withstand fierce treatments that would ruin less robust fillets. Here are a few basic methods of cooking; refer to individual recipes for more detailed instructions.

Deep-frying

Coat the prepared fish with seasoned flour, batter, or egg and bread crumbs. Half fill a deep saucepan or deep-fat fryer with vegetable oil and heat to 375°F. Fry the fish, a few pieces at a time, until golden brown. The cooking time will depend on the density and size of the fish. Obviously tiny whitebait (smelts) will cook very quickly, while larger fish will take several minutes. The most accurate way to determine doneness is to cut a piece open and try it. Drain thoroughly on paper towels.

Shallow-frying

Coat the fish in seasoned flour or egg and bread crumbs and fry in vegetable oil or a mixture of vegetable oil and butter. Test whether the fish is cooked as above. Drain as above.

Fillets or steaks, brushed with olive oil, will cook on a hot oiled griddle in a matter of minutes.

Broiling and Grilling

Before you start cooking, line the broiler pan with foil to prevent lingering fish smells. If cooking whole fish or thick fillets with skin on, slash the skin so that the heat can penetrate. Brush generously with melted butter, oil, or a marinade, season with salt and pepper, and cook under a preheated hot broiler until the flesh looks opaque. Turn large fillets or fish occasionally. Cut into the fish at the thickest point to check for doneness.

Barbecued fish is cooked in much the same way. Choose robust tuna, monkfish, mackerel, shark, or sardines in preference to delicate fish like sole. To make turning easier and to help prevent the fish breaking up, put it in a fish rack or thread it onto skewers. Brush frequently with marinade or oil.

Baking

Put the fish in a shallow dish with a few herbs, seasoning, and a splash of wine, fish stock, or milk. Cover and bake in a preheated 350°F oven. Alternatively, bake "en papillote" – wrapped in a foil or parchment paper parcel – at the same temperature. Whole fish will take about 30–40 minutes, while fillets and steaks will take anything from 15–25 minutes depending on their size.

Poaching

Heat a well-flavored court bouillon or fish stock or some dry white wine or milk flavored with aromatics such as parsley, onion, bay, celery, and a few peppercorns. Add the fish and simmer very gently until the fish is just opaque. Don't let the liquid boil or the fish will break up.

Steaming

Season thoroughly before cooking and sprinkle with a few herbs, a squeeze of lemon juice, or a pat of butter. Wrap in foil and steam over boiling water until the fish is opaque. This will take about 10 minutes but will depend on the thickness of the fillets. Delicate thin sole fillets will cook very quickly.

Fillets of uniform thickness can also be cooked in the microwave oven, flavored as above.

❖ Turbot with ❖
Chervil and Tomato Sauce

SERVES 4

PREPARATION TIME
20 minutes
COOKING TIME
10–12 minutes
FREEZING
Not suitable
COLOR INDEX
Page 25

- 1¼ cups milk
- 1 onion slice
- 1 mace blade
- 4–6 black peppercorns
- 2 tomatoes
- 2 tbsp butter
- 1½ tbsp flour
- salt and pepper
- 1 tsp tomato paste
- 1 large bunch chervil
- 4 turbot steaks, about 6 oz each
- lemon juice, to taste

280 CALS/SERVING

1 Put the milk in a small pan with the onion, mace, and peppercorns. Bring to a boil and remove from heat. Let infuse 10 minutes; strain.

2 Immerse the tomatoes in boiling water 15–30 seconds, then remove and peel away the skins. Cut the flesh into strips, discarding seeds.

3 Melt 1 tbsp butter in a small pan. Stir in the flour and cook 1 minute. Off the heat, gradually stir in the strained milk. Season.

4 Bring to a boil, stirring constantly. Simmer gently a few minutes. Whisk in the tomato paste and about ¼ cup chopped chervil.

5 Meanwhile, melt the remaining butter. Halve the turbot steaks, brush with melted butter, and broil about 5–6 minutes each side.

6 Add the tomato strips to the sauce. Reheat gently, stirring in lemon juice to taste. Garnish the turbot with chervil and serve with the sauce.

❖ Sole ❖
with Mousseline Sauce

SERVES 6

PREPARATION TIME
15 minutes
COOKING TIME
4–6 minutes
FREEZING
Not suitable
COLOR INDEX
Page 25

- 2 egg yolks
- 2 tsp lemon juice
- salt and pepper
- 4 tbsp unsalted butter, softened
- 12 sole fillets
- melted butter, for brushing
- ¼ cup light whipping cream

260 CALS/SERVING

1 To make the mousseline sauce, place the egg yolks in a small bowl. Add 1 tsp of the lemon juice, salt and pepper, and a pat of the softened unsalted butter. Place the bowl in a water bath over low heat and whisk well until the mixture is quite thick.

2 Remove the bowl from the water bath and whisk in the rest of the softened butter, a small piece at a time. Add the remainder of the lemon juice. Keep the sauce warm by returning the bowl to the water bath over low heat.

3 Brush the sole fillets with melted butter and broil 2–3 minutes on each side.

4 Lightly whip the cream and fold into the sauce. Serve the sole fillets immediately, with the mousseline sauce spooned over.

❖ Haddock with ❖
Parsley and Lemon

SERVES 4

PREPARATION TIME
15 minutes
COOKING TIME
20–25 minutes
FREEZING
Not suitable

- 1 lb haddock fillet, skinned
- 3 tbsp lemon juice
- 6 tbsp chopped parsley
- salt and pepper
- 4 tbsp butter or margarine
- 3 tbsp flour
- 1¼ cups milk

260 CALS/SERVING

1 Divide the fish into about 8 equal pieces and place in a shallow baking dish. Sprinkle with the lemon juice and half of the parsley. Season with salt and pepper. Add ¼ cup water, then cover tightly.

2 Bake the fish in a preheated 350°F oven until it starts flaking apart, 20–25 minutes.

3 Meanwhile, melt the butter in a small pan. Stir in the flour and cook 1 minute. Gradually stir in the milk and bring to a boil, stirring. Cook, stirring, until thickened and smooth, 1–2 minutes. Stir in the remaining parsley.

4 Using a slotted spatula, lift the fish onto a serving platter, draining slightly; cover and keep warm. Add the cooking juices to the sauce and reheat gently without boiling. Adjust the seasoning.

5 Spoon some of the sauce over the fish to serve, and accompany with creamed potatoes and glazed carrots. Serve the remaining sauce separately.

❖ Grilled Monkfish ❖ with Lemon and Dill

SERVES 4

PREPARATION TIME
10 minutes, plus marinating

COOKING TIME
12 minutes

FREEZING
Not suitable

- 1½ lb monkfish tail, or other firm white fish
- 3 tbsp lemon juice
- 1 tbsp chopped dill or ½ tsp dried dill
- 2 garlic cloves, sliced
- 3 tbsp olive oil
- salt and pepper
- lemon slices, for garnish

`200 CALS/SERVING`

1 Remove all membrane from the fish and cut out the backbone to give two long fillets. Cut these in half to give four "steaks." Place in a non-metallic dish.

2 Whisk the lemon juice with the dill, garlic, and olive oil; season well. Pour over the fish, cover, and let marinate in a cool place at least 4 hours, turning occasionally.

3 Drain the fish, arrange on the rack, and grill or broil about 6 minutes on each side, basting regularly with the marinade. Serve immediately, garnished with lemon slices and accompanied by green beans and fennel.

❖ Parchment Baked Fish ❖

SERVES 4

PREPARATION TIME
15 minutes, plus soaking

COOKING TIME
15 minutes

FREEZING
Not suitable

- ¼ cup dry white wine
- 4 oz English cucumber, thinly sliced
- 4 fish steaks (cod, halibut, turbot, or salmon), about 5 oz each
- 1 tsp fennel seeds
- 2 tbsp butter or margarine
- salt and pepper
- fennel sprigs, for garnish

`170 CALS/SERVING`

1 Cut 4 pieces of parchment paper, each about 11 inches square, and crumple them together into a small bowl. Pour over the wine and let soak 1 hour; push down into the wine occasionally.

2 Separate and open out the parchment sheets. Arrange a circle of cucumber rounds in the center of each sheet. Place a fish steak on top. Sprinkle with fennel seeds and dot with a small piece of butter. Season with salt and pepper. Drizzle over any remaining wine.

3 Lift up opposite sides of the parchment and fold together. Twist and tuck under the two shorter ends. Place the parcels on a baking sheet. Bake in a preheated 400°F oven for about 15 minutes. Serve at once, garnished with fennel.

❖ Sweet and Sour ❖ Monkfish Kebabs

SERVES 4

PREPARATION TIME
25 minutes, plus
marinating
COOKING TIME
10–12 minutes
FREEZING
Not suitable
COLOR INDEX
Page 26

- 1 lb monkfish fillet, skinned
- 12 thick bacon slices
- 1 small eggplant, about 4 oz, thinly sliced
- 2 small red onions, peeled
- 2 lemons or limes, sliced
- 1 tbsp lemon juice
- 2 tbsp clear honey
- 1 tbsp soy sauce
- 1 tbsp tomato paste
- salt and pepper
- curly endive, for garnish

355 CALS/SERVING

1 Cut the monkfish into 1-inch cubes. Stretch the bacon slices with the back of a knife and cut in half. Wrap a piece of bacon around each fish cube.

2 Blanch the eggplant slices in boiling water, drain, and dry on paper towels. Quarter the onions, then separate each quarter into two, to give thinner pieces.

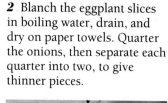

3 Thread the fish, onions, eggplant, and lemon or lime slices onto 8 bamboo skewers. Place the kebabs side by side in a non-metallic dish.

4 Whisk together the lemon juice, honey, soy sauce, tomato paste, and seasoning. Spoon over the kebabs.

5 Cover and let marinate in the refrigerator at least 12 hours, turning once. Brush the kebabs with a little of the marinade and broil or grill, turning occasionally, until all ingredients are tender, 10–12 minutes. Serve the kebabs garnished with endive.

❖ Haddock and ❖ Sour Cream Gratin

SERVES 2

PREPARATION TIME
10 minutes
COOKING TIME
10 minutes
FREEZING
Not suitable
COLOR INDEX
Page 26

- 12 oz haddock fillet
- 1 tbsp of butter
- 2 medium firm tomatoes
- ⅔ cup sour cream
- 1 tbsp chopped chives
- 1 tbsp chopped parsley
- ¼ cup shredded Gruyère cheese
- salt and pepper

380 CALS/SERVING

1 Skin the haddock if necessary and chop roughly. Choose a shallow flameproof serving dish just large enough to take the fish in a single layer. Put the butter in the dish and place under a hot broiler to melt.

2 Add the fish to the dish and turn in the butter. Broil 10 minutes, turning occasionally, until cooked.

3 Chop the tomatoes and mix with the sour cream, herbs, shredded cheese, and seasoning. Spoon over the fish and cook under the broiler until bubbling. Serve immediately, with boiled new potatoes and spinach.

❖ Cod and Crab Gratin ❖

SERVES 4

PREPARATION TIME
15 minutes
COOKING TIME
15 minutes
FREEZING
Not suitable

- 1½ lb medium new potatoes
- 1 lb cod fillet
- 1¼ cups milk
- salt and pepper
- 8 oz small button mushrooms
- 2 tbsp butter or margarine
- 3 tbsp flour
- 1oz each white and dark crab meat
- 2 tsp Dijon mustard
- ¾ cup shredded sharp Cheddar cheese

445 CALS/SERVING

1 Scrub the potatoes and boil in their skins until tender. Drain, then slice thickly.

2 Meanwhile, skin the cod fillet and cut the flesh into 1-inch pieces.

3 Place the fish in a saucepan with the milk and seasoning. Bring to a boil, cover, and simmer 5 minutes. Add the mushrooms, re-cover, and simmer until the fish is tender, about 5 minutes longer. Strain off and reserve the milk. Place the fish and mushrooms in a shallow flameproof dish, cover, and keep warm.

4 Melt the butter in a small saucepan. Stir in the flour and cook 1 minute. Off the heat, gradually stir in the reserved milk. Cook, stirring, until thickened and smooth, 2–3 minutes. Stir in the crab meat, mustard, and seasoning and heat through gently.

5 Pour the sauce over the cod and mushrooms, stirring gently to mix. Level the surface with a knife.

6 Top with thick slices of potato and scatter over the shredded cheese. Broil until golden and bubbling. Serve immediately, accompanied by a crisp green salad.

❖ Sweet and Sour Fish ❖

SERVES 4

PREPARATION TIME
10 minutes
COOKING TIME
10–12 minutes
FREEZING
Not suitable

- 4 cod fillets, about 5 oz each, skinned
- 1 tbsp soy sauce
- 2 tbsp lemon juice
- 2 tsp white wine vinegar
- 1 tbsp clear honey
- 2 tsp tomato ketchup
- 1 garlic clove, minced
- ¼ tsp paprika
- 1 red bell pepper
- 4 oz scallions
- 4 oz button mushrooms
- 1 tbsp oil
- 4 oz frozen green beans
- pepper

200 CALS/SERVING

1 Divide each cod fillet in half lengthwise. Roll up neatly with the skinned side inside.
2 Mix together the soy sauce, lemon juice, vinegar, honey, tomato ketchup, garlic, and paprika. Place in a large sauté pan, add the fish, and baste with the sauce. Bring to a very gentle simmer, cover, and cook until tender, 10–12 minutes.
3 Meanwhile halve the pepper, remove the core and seeds, and cut into strips. Slice the scallions; halve the mushrooms.
4 Heat the oil in another sauté pan and stir-fry the vegetables over high heat until just tender, 3–4 minutes. Season well with pepper.
5 Serve the fish with the sauce spooned over and accompanied by the stir-fried vegetables.

Variation

If you like fresh gingerroot, grate a little into the pan as you stir-fry the vegetables.

MEAT

The current desire for a healthier, lower-fat diet means that our consumption of meat is decreasing. Thankfully, meat producers are gradually responding to this and producing new leaner cuts. The increased demand for fast food means that they're also developing new tender cuts that cook quickly. In fact, meat is highly nutritious, and for a lot of people it's still their major source of protein, B vitamins, and iron. If you are worried about your fat consumption, or on a diet, choose the lean cuts without too much visible fat. Alternatively, make a small amount of meat go further by serving it with lots of vegetables or by mixing it with legumes in casseroles and stews.

Choosing Meat

Meat should look and smell fresh. As for color, a lurid red doesn't necessarily indicate freshness. Instead look for a good clear color; the color of meat will darken naturally on exposure to the air. A grayish tinge is certainly a bad sign. Any fat should be creamy white; if it's yellow the meat is probably past its prime, unless it comes from a breed where yellower fat is common. Look for a smooth outer layer of fat, if appropriate to the cut, and a fair amount of "marbled" fat distributed throughout the meat; this will keep it moist during cooking and add flavor.

Always look for a neat, generally well trimmed piece of meat. Splinters of bone and ragged edges indicate poor butchery. Cuts should be trimmed of sinew. Roasts and steaks should be of uniform thickness so that they cook evenly. Variety meats should look fresh and moist, and should not smell.

A good butcher is invaluable; a market run by helpful knowledgeable staff inevitably means that they care about their meat and will have treated it properly. It is also likely that they will be able to advise you about cooking times and methods as well as prepare roasts, steaks, and the like to your specific requirements.

Storing Meat

All meat should be stored loosely wrapped in the coldest part of the refrigerator. It's advisable to remove meat from its original wrapping and place it, freshly wrapped, on a plate to prevent any blood dripping through the refrigerator shelves. Always store raw meat well away from cooked foods.

Variety meats, ground meat, and small cuts of veal are best eaten on the day of purchase. Larger roasts, chops, and steaks will keep 2–3 days. Lean cuts will keep for longer than fatty cuts since the fat turns rancid first. "Off" or bad meat will have an unpleasant smell, slimy surface, and possibly even a greenish tinge. Because of the possibility of food poisoning it's not worth taking a risk with meat that you suspect of being past its best.

Marinades

A good marinade will make all the difference to the taste and texture of a piece of meat. Usually based on oil or wine or something acidic, like fruit juice or yogurt, it will tenderize tough cuts and lend a subtle aroma and flavor. Oil- and wine-based marinades tend to soak into the meat, adding moisture to dry cuts, while yogurt will tenderize and form a soft crust on the food as it cooks. Aromatics like lemon rind, bay leaves, thyme, garlic, and onion add fragrance as well as flavor.

Put the food in a shallow non-metallic dish and pour over the marinade. Leave in a cool place at least 1 hour but preferably overnight. When ready to cook, brush or drain off excess marinade and cook as directed in the recipe. If you're cooking on a barbecue or under the broiler, baste the meat frequently with the marinade as it cooks. Any remaining marinade can be brought to a boil in a small pan, strained if necessary, and served poured over accompanying vegetables or salad leaves. The exception to this is any yogurt-based marinade, which would curdle.

❖ Cooking Methods ❖

To get the most from a cut of meat it is vital to cook it appropriately. Lean, fine-grained cuts respond well to quick cooking, while tougher cuts with more connective tissue need long, slow cooking to make them tender.

Roasting

Only good-quality tender cuts are suitable for roasting. Opinions differ about roasting times and temperatures because there is a great deal of variation in the way people like their meat cooked. We found that high temperature roasting, at 450°F, was only suitable for really top-quality cuts, such as beef tenderloin.

However you decide to cook your roast, it's important to bring it to room temperature before cooking. Put the meat, fat-side up, on a roasting rack and smear with mustard or stud with slivers of garlic. Baste all roasts frequently during cooking to keep them moist; if the meat is very lean add moisture in the form of drippings or oil. Refer to the chart overleaf for roasting times.

To determine accurately whether the meat is cooked, insert a meat thermometer into the thickest part to ascertain the internal temperature. Alternatively and much less accurately, push a skewer right into the middle of the roast. If the juices run clear the meat is thoroughly cooked; if they run pink, the meat is medium; if bloody, it's rare.

❖ Roast Beef ❖ and Yorkshire Pudding

SERVES 4–8

PREPARATION TIME
20 minutes
COOKING TIME
Depends on size of roast
FREEZING
Not suitable
COLOR INDEX
Page 29

- 3- to 4½-lb beef roast such as rib, sirloin tip, or top round (see note)
- 2 tbsp beef drippings (optional)
- salt and pepper
- 1 tsp mustard powder (optional)
  YORKSHIRE PUDDING:
- ¾ cup flour
- pinch of salt
- 1 egg
- 1¼ cups milk
  GRAVY:
- 2 tsp flour
- 1¼ cups beef stock

1135–575 CALS/SERVING

1 Weigh the meat and calculate the cooking time (see page 164). Put the meat into a shallow roasting pan, preferably on a roasting rack, with the thickest layer of fat uppermost and the cut sides exposed to the heat. Add drippings if the meat is lean. Season the meat with pepper and mustard powder, if desired.
2 Roast in a preheated 350°F oven for the calculated time, basting occasionally with the juices from the pan. Forty-five minutes before the end of the cooking time, cover the roast with foil and place on the bottom shelf of the oven, then increase the oven temperature to 425°F.
3 To make the Yorkshire pudding, mix the flour and salt in a bowl, then make a well in the center and break in the egg. Add half the milk and, using a wooden spoon, gradually work in the flour. Beat the mixture until it is smooth, then add the remaining milk and 6–7 tbsp water. Beat until well mixed and the surface is covered with tiny bubbles.
4 Put 2 tbsp fat from the beef into a baking pan and place in the oven at 425°F for a few minutes until the fat is very hot.
5 Pour in the batter and return to the oven to cook until risen and golden brown, 40–45 minutes; do not open the oven door for 30 minutes.
6 After 30 minutes, transfer the cooked meat to a warmed serving plate and let it rest about 20 minutes, covered, before carving.
7 To make the gravy, the meat juices alone may be used. For a thicker gravy, skim some of the fat from the surface and place the pan over medium heat. Sprinkle the flour into the pan and stir it into the pan juices, scraping up the brown sediment. Cook over high heat, stirring constantly, until the flour has browned slightly. (When the meat is carved, any juices from the meat can be added to the gravy.) Add up to 1¼ cups beef stock to the pan and stir well. Bring it to a boil, simmer 2–3 minutes, and season to taste. Pour into a sauceboat.
8 Serve the carved beef with Yorkshire pudding, cut into portions. Accompany with the gravy and mustard or horseradish sauce, and seasonal vegetables.

NOTE: Allow about 8 oz per person for a boned and rolled roast; 10–12 oz for meat on the bone. For information on suitable cuts for roasting and advice on carving see page 165.

Variation
For individual Yorkshire puddings or popovers, use the batter to fill 12 muffin pans. Bake 15–20 minutes.

❖ Beef Tenderloin with ❖ Mushrooms and Sweet Peppers

SERVES 8

PREPARATION TIME
25 minutes
COOKING TIME
55 minutes, plus standing
FREEZING
Not suitable

- 3-lb beef tenderloin roast
- 4 oz flat mushrooms
- 9½-oz jar red and yellow peppers in oil
- salt and pepper
- 12 oz pancetta, sliced
- 2 tbsp olive oil
- 2 tsp flour
- ⅔ cup Italian red wine
- 1¼ cups beef stock
- 2 tbsp Marsala wine c red currant jelly
- 2 tsp dried mixed herl
- herb sprigs, for garni.

450 CALS/SERVING

1 Cut a slit along the side of the tenderloin roast, then open out to make a pocket.

2 Chop the mushrooms. Drain and slice peppers. Mix these with the mushrooms; use half to stuff the beef.

3 Grind black pepper over th meat, then wrap the pancetta around the tenderloin to enclose completely. Tie with string.

4 Heat the oil in a large non-stick frying pan, add the meat, and brown on all sides. Lift out and transfer to a roasting pan; reserve the pan juices. Roast the tenderloin in a preheated 375°F oven 45 minutes. Cover with foil and let rest in a warm place 15 minutes. Reheat reserved juices in frying pan. Add the flour and cook, stirring, 2 minutes. Stir in the wine and stock.

5 Add the Marsala, herbs, and seasoning. Cook, stirring, until thickened. Add remaining mushrooms and peppers; cook through. Remove string and carve the meat. Arrange on a warmed serving plate. Remove the mushrooms and peppers from the sauce with a slotted spoon and use to garnish the meat. Spoon on a little sauce; garnish with herbs. Serve remaining sauce separately.

1 Brush the beef with brandy and season with pepper. Melt the butter in a frying pan, add beef, and fry 2 minutes, turning to seal all over. Transfer to a roasting pan and roast in a preheated 400°F oven 15 minutes. Cool.

2 Meanwhile mince the onions and mushrooms. Add the onions to the pan and fry 10 minutes. Add the mushrooms and fry until most of the moisture has evaporated, 4–5 minutes longer. Season and let cool.

❖ *Boeuf en Croûte* ❖

3 Roll out the pastry to a large rectangle. Mix the pâté with ¼ cup of the mushroom mixture; spread it on top of the beef. Place meat, pâté-side down, in the center of the pastry and top with the remaining mushroom mixture.

4 Trim off the corners of the pastry. Brush the edges of the pastry with beaten egg and wrap the pastry around the beef to enclose. Press the edges to seal and place, seam-side down, on a baking sheet.

5 Re-roll pastry trimmings, cut leaves, and use to decorate. Brush with beaten egg. Bake at 400°F until the pastry is golden brown, about 20 minutes. Transfer to a warmed serving dish.

6 To make the sauce, mince onion and mushrooms. Melt the butter in a pan and fry onion 5 minutes, then add mushrooms and cook 3 minutes. Stir in the flour and cook 1 minute. Gradually stir in the stock and wine. Simmer 10 minutes. Season to taste; strain and serve with the Boeuf en Croûte.

SERVES 8

PREPARATION TIME
30 minutes
COOKING TIME
40 minutes
FREEZING
Not suitable

- 3½-lb beef tenderloin roast
- 4 tsp brandy
- salt and pepper
- 4 tbsp butter
- 2 onions, peeled
- 12 oz mushrooms
- 1 lb puff pastry
- 6 oz smooth pâté (chicken, duck, or goose liver)
- 2 eggs, lightly beaten

SAUCE:
- 1 small onion
- 4 oz mushrooms
- 4 tbsp butter
- 2 tbsp flour
- 2½ cups beef stock
- 1¼ cups red wine

800 CALS/SERVING

❖ Stir-Fried Beef ❖ with Mixed Vegetables

SERVES 4

PREPARATION TIME
25 minutes, plus
marinating
COOKING TIME
4–5 minutes
FREEZING
Not suitable
COLOR INDEX
Page 30

- 1¼ lb boneless sirloin or flank steak
- ¼ cup soy sauce
- 6 tbsp oil
- 1 large garlic clove, minced
- ½ oz fresh gingerroot
- 3–4 medium fresh green chili peppers
- salt and pepper
- 4 oz baby corn
- 6 oz snow peas
- 4 oz small cup mushrooms
- 1 bunch scallions
- 6 oz broccoli
- 6–8 tbsp vegetable stock

460 CALS/SERVING

1 Cut the steak into thin strips, about 2-inches long and ¼-inch thick, discarding any fat.

2 In a bowl, whisk the soy sauce with 2 tbsp oil and the garlic. Peel and mince the ginger; stir into the bowl.

3 Wearing rubber gloves to avoid skin irritation, split open the chilies and rinse away the seeds. Mince the flesh and add half to the bowl. Tightly cover the remainder and refrigerate.

4 Add the beef to the bowl with plenty of pepper; the soy sauce should add sufficient salt. Cover and refrigerate several hours, preferably overnight.

5 Slice the corn lengthwise into fine strips. Trim the snow peas; thinly slice the mushrooms. Cut each scallion into three.

6 Divide the broccoli into small florets; trim the stems and slice lengthwise into thin pieces. Blanch the baby corn and broccoli separately in boiling salted water about 1 minute each; drain thoroughly.

7 Heat 2 tbsp oil in each of two large frying pans. Add the beef and marinade to one and the vegetables to the other. Stir-fry both over high heat 2–3 minutes only.

8 Combine the contents of both pans, add the stock, and bubble up. Adjust seasoning, adding extra chilies to taste. Serve immediately, with noodles.

NOTE: This stir-fry can be made as spicy as you like by simply adding more chilies. Use sparingly to start with as some chilies can be very hot. It's a good idea to use two frying pans to allow room for the ingredients to fry quickly and not stew. If you use a large wok, stir-fry the beef first.

❖ Chili Beef with Noodles ❖

SERVES 4

PREPARATION TIME
10 minutes
COOKING TIME
10 minutes
FREEZING
Not suitable
COLOR INDEX
Page 31

- 1 lb boneless sirloin steak
- 8 oz red bell pepper
- 8 oz broccoli
- 1 onion, peeled
- 2 tbsp oil
- ½ tsp chili powder or few drops of hot pepper sauce
- 2 tsp dried oregano
- 2 tbsp sherry or
- medium white wine
- 1¼ cups beef stock
- 1 tbsp soy sauce
- 2 oz fresh or dried tagliarini (thin pasta noodles)
- pepper

270 CALS/SERVING

1 Trim the steak of any excess fat. Cut into bite-sized pieces. Halve, core, and seed the pepper and cut into similar-sized pieces. Divide the broccoli into small florets; thinly slice the stems. Chop the onion.

2 Heat the oil in a large sauté pan and brown the beef well on all sides about 2–3 minute. Remove with a slotted spoon. Add the vegetables, chili powder, and oregano. Sauté, stirring, 1–2 minutes.

3 Mix in the sherry, stock, and soy sauce, then add the tagliarini. Cover and simmer until the noodles and broccoli are tender, about 5 minutes. Return the beef to the pan. Bring to a boil and simmer 1 minute to heat through. Adjust seasoning, adding pepper as necessary.

❖ Hamburgers ❖

SERVES 4

PREPARATION TIME
15 minutes
COOKING TIME
8 minutes
FREEZING
Suitable (stage 2)

- 1 lb ground round
- ⅔ cup rolled oats
- 1 tsp dried mixed herbs
- 3 tbsp tomato chutney or relish
- salt and pepper
- 1 egg, beaten
- flour, for dusting
- vegetable oil, for brushing
  FOR SERVING:
- warm buns
- salad
- onion rings

380 CALS/SERVING

1 In a medium bowl, mix together the beef, oats, herbs, chutney, and seasoning, adding sufficient beaten egg to bind the mixture.
2 With lightly floured hands, shape into 4 or 8 patties.
3 Brush each one lightly with oil, and grill or broil until golden and cooked through, about 4 minutes on each side, depending on the thickness of the burgers.
4 Serve in warm buns on a salad base, topped with onion rings.

❖ Beef and Potato Moussaka ❖

3 Add the tomatoes, tomato paste, eggplant, and seasoning; mix well. Spread evenly in a 2-quart shallow flameproof casserole. Arrange the slices of potato neatly over the top to cover the beef mixture completely.

4 For the topping, beat together the egg yolks, yogurt, and shredded cheese. Pour over the potatoes to cover completely. Bake uncovered in a preheated 375°F oven about 1 hour. Brown under a hot broiler if necessary.

NOTE: This is a delicious, virtually oil-free moussaka that uses blanched eggplant, rather than the more usual fried ones. Serve it with a crisp green salad.

Variation
Replace the yogurt topping with 1¼ cups cheese sauce (page 92).

SERVES 4	
PREPARATION TIME 20 minutes	• 12 oz eggplant
COOKING TIME 1–1¼ hours	• salt and pepper
FREEZING Not suitable	• 1¾ lb potatoes

- 12 oz eggplant
- salt and pepper
- 1¾ lb potatoes
- 1 lb ground round
- 2 onions, peeled and chopped
- ½ tsp dried thyme
- 3 tbsp chopped parsley
- ¼ tsp ground cinnamon
- 16-oz can crushed tomatoes
- 1 tbsp tomato paste
- 2 egg yolks
- 1½ cups plain yogurt
- ½ cup shredded sharp Cheddar cheese

480 CALS/SERVING

1 Cut the eggplant into large chunks; blanch in boiling salted water 2 minutes; drain well. Peel and thickly slice the potatoes and blanch in boiling salted water 5–6 minutes; drain well.

2 In a medium sauté pan (preferably nonstick), fry the beef with the onions, thyme, parsley, and cinnamon until the meat begins to brown; stir frequently to prevent sticking.

❖ Chile Tacos ❖

SERVES 4	
PREPARATION TIME 10 minutes	
COOKING TIME 30 minutes	
FREEZING Not suitable	
COLOR INDEX Page 31	

- 1 onion, peeled
- 1 green bell pepper
- 1 lb ground round
- 1 garlic clove, minced
- 16-oz can crushed tomatoes
- 16-oz can red kidney beans, drained and rinsed
- 1 tbsp tomato paste
- ½ tsp chili powder
- 1 tbsp ground cumin
- salt and pepper
- 8 taco shells
- 1 cup shredded Cheddar cheese or Monterey Jack
- sour cream, for serving

470 CALS/SERVING

1 Chop the onion; halve, seed, and chop the green pepper. Place the beef, onion, garlic, and green pepper in a large nonstick saucepan and heat gently, stirring, until the beef begins to brown and the vegetables soften.
2 Add the tomatoes, kidney beans, tomato paste, spices, and seasoning, with 1¼ cups water and stir well. Simmer until well reduced, 20–25 minutes.
3 Just before serving, heat the taco shells in a preheated 300°F oven 2–3 minutes, until crisp. Spoon a little of the chile con carne into each taco shell.
4 Serve topped with shredded cheese and accompanied by sour cream. Serve with a crisp leafy salad.

NOTE: The chile also makes a good filling for flour tortillas or a tasty sauce for pasta.

❖ Pork with Prunes ❖

SERVES 4

PREPARATION TIME
10 minutes, plus
marinating
COOKING TIME
40 minutes
FREEZING
Not suitable

- 12 large prunes, pitted
- 1¼ cups Vouvray or similar fruity, dry white wine
- 8 thin pork chops or steaks, about 3 lb total weight
- seasoned flour, for coating
- 2 tbsp butter
- 1¼ cups light stock
- 2 tsp red currant jelly
- salt and pepper
- thyme sprigs, for garnish

600 CALS/SERVING

1 Place the prunes and wine in a bowl, cover, and let marinate overnight.

2 Dip the pork chops in seasoned flour to coat. Melt the butter in a flameproof casserole and brown the chops in two batches. Return all chops to the pan. Pour in the stock, wine, and prunes. Bring to a boil, cover, and simmer gently until the pork is tender, about 30 minutes, turning the meat once.

3 Transfer the pork and prunes to a warmed platter, cover, and keep warm.

4 Whisk the red currant jelly into the cooking liquid. Bring to a boil and boil until the sauce has reduced slightly, 4–5 minutes. Taste and adjust the seasoning, then pour over the meat. Garnish with thyme and serve immediately.

❖ Pork and Pasta Sauté ❖

SERVES 4

PREPARATION TIME
15 minutes, plus
marinating
COOKING TIME
15–20 minutes
FREEZING
Not suitable
COLOR INDEX
Page 35

- 1 lb pork tenderloin
- 4 bacon slices
- 2 red onions, peeled
- 1 tbsp wholegrain mustard
- ½ cup dry hard cider
- 1 garlic clove, minced
- 3–4 tbsp oil
- salt and pepper
- 1 green bell pepper
- 6 oz green beans, halved
- 3 oz dried pasta shells or bows
- 1 tbsp soy sauce
- ¼ cup light stock

445 CALS/SERVING

1 Trim the pork and cut into strips, about 2 × ¼ inch, discarding any excess fat. Chop the bacon. Finely slice the onions.

2 Put the pork, bacon, and onions in a bowl. Add the mustard, cider, garlic, 1 tbsp oil, and seasoning. Stir well. Cover and let marinate in the refrigerator at least 1 hour, preferably overnight.

3 Halve, core, and seed the pepper, then cut into strips. Blanch the green beans and pepper together in boiling salted water 2 minutes; drain, rinse under running cold water, and let cool.

4 Cook the pasta in boiling salted water until just cooked, 7–10 minutes. Drain and toss in a little oil to prevent the pasta sticking.

5 Remove the pork, bacon, and onions from the marinade, reserving the marinade. Heat 2 tbsp oil in a large sauté pan or frying pan. Add the meat and onions and sauté over high heat until lightly browned, 3–4 minutes.

6 Stir in the beans and green pepper with the marinade, soy sauce, and stock. Season to taste with pepper. Bring to a boil, stirring, then simmer gently about 4 minutes. Add the pasta and cook 1 minute, until piping hot. Serve immediately.

❖ Stir-Fried Pork ❖ with Baby Corn

3 Add the vegetables and continue stirring over high heat 2–3 minutes, until piping hot.

4 Mix in the remaining ingredients and bring to a boil, stirring well. Adjust the seasoning and serve, garnished with chives and parsley. Accompany with noodles tossed in oil and fresh herbs.

NOTE: Bottled chili and tomato sauce is available from specialty stores and larger supermarkets.

SERVES 4	

PREPARATION TIME
10 minutes
COOKING TIME
10 minutes
FREEZING
Not suitable

- *1 lb pork tenderloin*
- *6 oz carrots, peeled*
- *6 oz baby corn*
- *6 oz sugar-snap peas*
- *salt and pepper*
- *3 tbsp sunflower oil*
- *¼ cup stir-fry chili and tomato sauce*
- *1 tsp sugar*
- *2 tbsp wine vinegar*
- *¼ cup light soy sauce*

FOR GARNISH:
- *chives*
- *parsley sprigs*

`380 CALS/SERVING`

1 Trim the pork tenderloin and cut across into ¼-inch thick slices. Cut the carrots into sticks. Blanch the vegetables in boiling salted water 2 minutes; drain and refresh under cold water, then drain thoroughly.

2 Heat the oil in a large wok or frying pan (preferably non-stick). Add the pork and stir-fry over high heat until well browned and almost tender, 2–3 minutes.

❖ Pork Tenderloin ❖ in Wine and Coriander

SERVES 4	

PREPARATION TIME
15 minutes
COOKING TIME
20 minutes
FREEZING
Not suitable
COLOR INDEX
Page 35

- *1½ lb pork tenderloin*
- *1 small green bell pepper*
- *1 onion, peeled*
- *1 tbsp butter or margarine*
- *1 tbsp oil*
- *1½ tbsp flour*
- *1 tbsp coriander seeds, ground*
- *⅔ cup light stock*
- *⅔ cup dry white wine*
- *salt and pepper*
- *coriander sprigs (cilantro), for garnish*

`365 CALS/SERVING`

1 Trim the pork and cut into ½-inch slices. Place the pork slices between two sheets of wax paper and flatten with a meat pounder or rolling pin until thin. Slice the pepper into rings, discarding the core and seeds. Chop the onion.
2 Heat the butter and oil in a large saucepan, add the pork, and brown on both sides. Add the pepper and onion and cook gently until softened, 8–10 minutes.
3 Stir in the flour and ground coriander and cook 1 minute. Gradually add the stock and wine; cook, stirring, until the sauce is thickened and smooth. Season with salt and pepper. Simmer gently until the pork is tender and cooked through, about 5 minutes. Serve garnished with fresh coriander.

POULTRY & GAME

Poultry is the general name given to all domesticated birds bred for the table: chickens, ducks, geese, turkeys, and guinea fowl. Strictly speaking, game is any wild bird or beast that is hunted for food, but the term is now used rather loosely to include some farm-raised animals, such as rabbit and venison and birds such as quail, squab (young pigeon), and pheasant.

Choosing Poultry and Game

A grain diet and the freedom to roam in the open air produces the best-flavored poultry. At last consumers are realizing this and some farmers are being encouraged to move away from intensive mass-production methods to free-range birds.

These birds are fed a special diet free of antibiotics, hormones, and growth-enhancers. Each bird has double the area allotted to a mass-produced chicken (which is normally 1 square foot) plus access to the outdoors. All this doesn't come cheap, of course, and free-range birds are much more expensive than mass-produced chickens.

When choosing poultry in the market, look for a moist, unbroken skin with no dark patches, and a nice plump breast. In young birds the breast will be pliable. When choosing duck look for a plump bird with a good light-colored skin. Poultry that's past its best rapidly develops an unpleasant smell. It should not be eaten if it smells anything other than fresh. If buying from a supermarket, check the use-before date.

When choosing game look for soft, plump breast meat and unscarred feet. Badly calloused feet indicate an old bird. A flexible breastbone and short spurs are also signs of youth. Young pheasants and partridges (chukar) have a large pointed tail feather; in older birds it is rounded.

Handling and Storing Poultry

It is vital that poultry is handled, stored, and cooked correctly, because most, if not all, raw poultry contains low levels of salmonella and campylobacter, the bacteria responsible for food poisoning. Provided that poultry is correctly stored these bacteria will remain at low levels. As long as it is then cooked thoroughly they will be killed by the heat and rendered harmless. Always use the following guidelines:

❖ If buying frozen poultry, check that it's frozen solid. If buying fresh, ensure that it's well chilled and within the use-before date.

❖ Transfer poultry to the refrigerator or freezer as soon as possible after purchase. In warm weather it's advisable to carry it home in an insulated cool bag.

❖ Remove the giblets from fresh poultry, put the bird on a plate to catch any drips, then cover, and store in the refrigerator up to 2 days.

❖ Frozen poultry will keep up to 3 months. Frozen chicken should be thawed at cool room temperature, not in the refrigerator. Pierce the wrappings and put the chicken on a plate to catch any drips. Remove the giblets as soon as they are loose.

❖ Always check that poultry is completely thawed before cooking: Make sure that there are no ice crystals in the body cavity and that the legs are quite flexible. Once thawed, cover and refrigerate, but cook as soon as possible. For turkey thawing times, refer to the chart on page 220. Never re-freeze raw poultry.

❖ To avoid cross-contamination, always wash your hands before and after preparing poultry. NEVER use the same utensils for preparing raw and cooked poultry without first washing them thoroughly in hot soapy water. It's advisable to keep a separate chopping board for preparing raw poultry.

❖ Stuff the neck end only. Do not stuff the body cavity or the heat may not penetrate fully to kill the salmonella bacteria.

❖ Always cook poultry thoroughly until the juices run clear. Cool leftovers quickly, refrigerate, and use within 2 days.

❖ Chicken ❖

For taste, versatility, and nutritional value, chicken is hard to beat. It's full of protein and B vitamins and, once the skin is trimmed away, it has very little fat. It is, therefore, not surprising that this white meat is so popular and available in so many different shapes and sizes, both fresh and frozen.

❖ Broiler-fryers, or frying chickens, are all-purpose birds, suitable for both broiling and frying as well as roasting, baking, poaching, and grilling. These birds are around 2½ months old and generally weigh 3–4 lb.

❖ Roasters, or roasting chickens, are a little older (3–8 months) and thus have more flavor as well as more fat, which makes them ideal for dry heat cooking. Usual weight is about 5 lb.

❖ Squab chickens, or "poussins," are 4–6 weeks old. They weigh about 1–1½ lb. One will serve 1–2 people. If serving 2 the bird is usually halved along the breastbone.

❖ Rock Cornish game hens are 4–6 weeks old and weigh 1–2 lb. There is relatively little meat on these small birds, so each will serve just one person.

❖ Chicken with ❖ Nuts and Mushrooms

SERVES 4

PREPARATION TIME
15 minutes, plus
marinating
COOKING TIME
5–7 minutes
FREEZING
Not suitable
COLOR INDEX
Page 39

- 1 lb skinless, boneless chicken breast halves
- 2-inch piece fresh gingerroot
- 3 tbsp soy sauce
- ¼ cup dry sherry wine
- 1 tsp five-spice powder
- 4 oz mushrooms
- ¼ English cucumber
- 3 tbsp oil
- ¾ cup walnut pieces
- pepper

250 CALS/SERVING

1 Cut the chicken into thin strips and place in a bowl. Peel and thinly slice the ginger; add to the bowl with the soy sauce, sherry, and five-spice powder. Stir well, cover, and let marinate at least 1 hour.

2 Remove the chicken from the marinade with a slotted spoon, reserving the marinade. Halve the mushrooms; cut the cucumber into chunks.

3 Heat the oil in a wok or large frying pan. Add the chicken and cook 3–4 minutes, stirring constantly.

4 Add the mushrooms, cucumber, and walnuts and stir-fry until the chicken is cooked and the vegetables are tender but still crisp 1–2 minutes.

5 Stir in the reserved marinade and cook 1 minute. Season to taste with pepper. Serve immediately, with rice or noodles.

❖ Chicken with ❖ Tarragon and Juniper

SERVES 4

PREPARATION TIME
20 minutes
COOKING TIME
20–25 minutes
FREEZING
Not suitable

- 4 skinless, boneless chicken breast halves, about 5 oz each
- salt and pepper
- flour, for coating
- 2 tbsp butter or margarine
- ⅓ cup dry white wine
- ¼ cup chicken stock
- 6 juniper berries, lightly crushed
- ⅔ cup light whipping cream
- 1 tbsp chopped tarragon

335 CALS/SERVING

1 Dip the chicken breasts in seasoned flour to coat evenly, shaking off any excess.

2 Heat the butter in a sauté pan and brown the chicken brea on both sides. Add the wine, stock, and juniper berries. Cook covered, over low heat 10–12 minutes.

3 Add the cream, seasoning, and tarragon. Cook gently with boiling, until the chicken is cooked through, 5–10 minutes longer.

❖ Chicken Chow Mein ❖

SERVES 4

PREPARATION TIME
15 minutes
COOKING TIME
7–8 minutes
FREEZING
Not suitable

- 6 oz egg noodles
- salt and pepper
- 6 oz onions, peeled
- 8 oz skinless, boneless chicken breast halves
- 8 oz Napa cabbage
- 2 tbsp oil
- 2 tbsp sesame oil
- ½ tsp chili powder
- 6 oz bean sprouts
- 8 oz cooked peeled shrimp
- 1 garlic clove, mince
- 2 tbsp soy sauce
- 2 tbsp dry sherry wi

470 CALS/SERVIN

1 Cook the noodles in boiling salted water according to packag directions until just tender. Drain well and rinse under cold running water to stop them cooking further.

2 Meanwhile, thinly slice the onions and chicken; shred the cabbage into fine pieces.

3 Heat the oil and sesame oil in a large wok or frying pan. Add the onions and chicken with the chili powder and stir-fry over high heat until almost tender, 3–4 minutes.

4 Mix in the bean sprouts, cabbage, shrimp, garlic, and pepper to taste. Stir over high heat about 2 minutes.

5 Add the noodles, soy sauce, and sherry. Cook, stirring, until thoroughly hot. Adjust the seasoning and serve immediately.

Variations

Replace the chicken and shrimp with 1 lb boneless tender steak, pork, or lamb.

❖ Chicken and ❖ Avocado Stroganoff

SERVES 4
PREPARATION TIME
15 minutes
COOKING TIME
40 minutes
FREEZING
Not suitable

- 4 chicken legs, about 1¼ lb total weight
- 2 tbsp oil
- 5 oz small button mushrooms
- ⅔ cup chicken stock
- 2 tsp wholegrain mustard
- salt and pepper
- 1 avocado (ripe but firm)
- ⅔ cup thick plain yogurt
- parsley sprigs, for garnish

`400 CALS/SERVING`

1 Separate the chicken legs into thighs and drumsticks.
2 Heat the oil in a large sauté pan and fry the chicken, turning, until deep golden on both sides. Lift out with a slotted spoon and drain on paper towels.
3 Lower the heat, add the mushrooms to the pan, and cook, stirring, 2–3 minutes. Add the stock, mustard, and seasoning.
4 Replace the chicken in the pan, bring to a boil, then cover, and simmer until the chicken is cooked, about 30 minutes.
5 Peel the avocado, halve, pit, and cut into chunks. Stir into the chicken juices with the yogurt. Increase the heat and bubble 2–3 minutes to reduce. Adjust the seasoning.
6 Serve immediately, garnished with parsley and accompanied by rice and green beans.

❖ Honey-Barbecued Drumsticks ❖

SERVES 8
PREPARATION TIME
10 minutes, plus marinating
COOKING TIME
15–20 minutes
FREEZING
Suitable
COLOR INDEX
Page 39

- ¼ cup thin honey
- grated rind and juice of 2 lemons
- grated rind and juice of 2 oranges
- 6 tbsp soy sauce
- ½ tsp ground coriander
- pepper
- 16 chicken drumsticks, skinned

`225 CALS/SERVING`

1 Mix together the honey, lemon rind and juice, orange rind and juice, soy sauce, coriander, and pepper.
2 Score the drumsticks with a sharp knife, lay in a shallow dish, and pour on the honey marinade. Cover and let marinate in the refrigerator 1–2 hours, turning the chicken occasionally.
3 Cook the drumsticks on a preheated barbecue or under the broiler until tender, 15–20 minutes, turning frequently and basting with the marinade. Serve hot.

❖ Lemon Chicken Kebabs ❖

SERVES 4
PREPARATION TIME
20 minutes
COOKING TIME
15 minutes
FREEZING
Not suitable
COLOR INDEX
Page 40

- 4 boneless chicken thighs, about 1 lb total weight
- 4 tbsp butter, melted
- 3 tbsp lemon juice
- 1 tbsp light brown sugar
- 2 garlic cloves, minced
- salt and pepper
- 1 small onion, peeled
- 4 oz zucchini
- 4 oz cherry tomatoes

`280 CALS/SERVING`

1 Cut the chicken into ¾-inch cubes. Thread onto 4 bamboo skewers and place in a foil-lined broiler pan.

2 Whisk together the butter, lemon juice, sugar, and garlic; season with a little salt and plenty of black pepper. Brush over the chicken.

3 Quarter the onion and separate the layers. Thickly slice the zucchini. Thread the tomatoes, onion, and zucchini onto 4 bamboo skewers and brush with the lemon butter.

4 Cook the chicken kebabs under the broiler (or grill them) about 7–8 minutes each side, adding the vegetable kebabs for the last 5–6 minutes of the cooking time, basting and turning occasionally. Serve with rice.

❖ Grilled Chicken ❖ with Spiced Butter

SERVES 4

PREPARATION TIME
10 minutes
COOKING TIME
20 minutes
FREEZING
Not suitable
COLOR INDEX
Page 40

- 1 small green chili pepper
- about ¼ cup chopped coriander (cilantro) or parsley
- 6 tbsp butter, softened
- salt and pepper
- 4 boneless chicken breast halves, about 5 oz each
- 2 tbsp lemon juice
- coriander sprigs (cilantro), for garnish

360 CALS/SERVING

1 Wearing rubber gloves to avoid skin irritation, halve, seed, and mince the chili. In a small bowl, beat the chili and coriander into the softened butter. Season with salt and pepper.

2 Make three or four slashes on each side of the chicken to a depth of about ¼ inch.

3 Place, skin-side down, on a rack. Spread with half the butter and sprinkle with half the lemon juice.

4 Broil or grill, 4–5 inches from the heat, 7 minutes. Turn, spread with the remaining butter, and sprinkle with lemon juice. Grill until tender, about 7 minutes longer. Serve with seasonal vegetables, spooning any remaining spiced butter over them. Garnish with coriander.

NOTE: Use chili with care. It's better to sprinkle more over the chicken when you're serving it than to make the initial flavor too strong. For a milder flavor replace the chili with 1–2 minced garlic cloves.

❖ Cider Roast Poussins ❖

SERVES 4

PREPARATION TIME
15 minutes
COOKING TIME
55 minutes
FREEZING
Not suitable
COLOR INDEX
Page 40

- 2 squab chickens (poussins), about 1 lb each
- ½ cup cream cheese with garlic and herbs
- 2 tbsp chopped mixed herbs (parsley, chives, thyme, etc.)
- 1¼ cups medium-dry hard cider
- 1¼ cups chicken stock
- 2 crisp apples
- 2 tbsp butter or margarine
- salt and pepper

300 CALS/SERVING

1 Place the poussins breast-side down on a board and halve lengthwise by cutting either side of the backbone, then turning the bird and cutting along the breastbone.

2 Mix together the cream cheese and herbs. Ease up the breast skin of the poussins and fill the "pocket" with the cheese mixture. Carefully secure with wooden toothpicks.

3 Place the poussins, in a small roasting pan. Pour in the cider and stock.

4 Quarter, core, and thickly slice the apples into the pan, tucking some under the birds.

5 Roast in a preheated 400°F oven until the poussins are tender, about 50 minutes. Remove the toothpicks; cover with foil and keep warm in a serving dish.

6 Pour the cooking juices into a saucepan, boil to reduce by half, then whisk in the butter; season. Serve the poussins and apple slices with the sauce.

❖ Deviled Poussins ❖

SERVES 6

PREPARATION TIME
15 minutes, plus
marinating
COOKING TIME
35 minutes
FREEZING
Suitable (stage 3)
COLOR INDEX
Page 40

- 1 tbsp mustard powder
- 1 tbsp paprika
- 4 tsp turmeric
- 4 tsp ground cumin
- ¼ cup tomato ketchup
- 1 tbsp lemon juice
- 4 tbsp butter, melted
- 3 squab chickens (poussins), about 1½ lb each
- 1 tbsp poppy seeds
- watercress sprigs and cherry tomatoes, for garnish

290 CALS/SERVING

1 Place the mustard powder, paprika, turmeric, and cumin in a small bowl. Add the tomato ketchup and lemon juice. Beat well to form a thick, smooth paste. Slowly pour in the melted butter, stirring all the time.

2 Place the poussins on a board, breast-side down. With a small sharp knife, cut right along the backbone of each bird through skin and flesh. With shears, cut through the backbone to open the birds up. Turn the birds over and continue cutting along the breastbone which will split the birds into 2 equal halves.

3 Lay the birds, skin-side uppermost, on a large edged baking sheet. Spread the spice paste evenly over the surface of the birds and sprinkle with the poppy seeds. Cover loosely and leave in a cool place at least 1–2 hours.

4 Roast the poussins in a preheated 425°F oven until the skin is well browned and crisp, about 15 minutes. Reduce the temperature to 350°F and roast until the poussins are tender, about 20 minutes longer. Serve immediately, on a bed of watercress sprigs, garnished with cherry tomatoes.

Variations

HERBY ORANGE POUSSINS: Replace the spice paste with a marinade of ⅔ cup dry white wine, 3 tbsp olive oil, juice of 2 oranges, 1 tsp each chopped rosemary, thyme, and marjoram, and 1 minced garlic clove.

CHINESE POUSSINS: Use a marinade of ½ cup soy sauce, 2 tbsp dry sherry wine, 2 sliced scallions, 2 tbsp light brown sugar and ½ tsp ground ginger.

❖ Poussins ❖ with Pepper Stuffing

SERVES 8

PREPARATION TIME
30 minutes
COOKING TIME
45–50 minutes
FREEZING
Not suitable
COLOR INDEX
Page 40

- 3 red bell peppers, about 6 oz each
- 3 yellow bell peppers, about 6 oz each
- 1 bunch scallions
- 3 celery stalks
- 3 oz sun-dried tomatoes in oil
- 2⅓ cups fresh whole wheat bread crumbs
- salt and black pepper
- 4 boned squab chickens (poussins), about 9 oz each
- 1¼ cups dry white wine
- 1¼ cups chicken stock
- 1 garlic clove, minced
- 2 tbsp fromage blanc or sour cream
- 2 tbsp chopped parsley
- parsley sprigs, for garnish

350 CALS/SERVING

1 Cut the peppers in half and place skin-side up on a large baking sheet. Place under a hot broiler until the skin is charred, about 15 minutes. Cover with a damp towel and cool, then peel off the skin under cold running water. Discard seeds and stem, then cut the flesh into long thin strips.

2 Chop the scallions, celery, and sun-dried tomatoes, reserving the oil. Place the peppers, scallions, celery, and tomatoes in a nonstick frying pan and sauté until tender, about 10 minutes, adding a little reserved oil if necessary. Stir in the bread crumbs and seasoning.

3 Place the boned poussins breast-side down on a flat surface. Scrape a little of the meat away from the sides toward the middle and trim away any excess skin.

4 Put a quarter of the stuffing inside each bird. Bring the sides together to enclose the stuffing. Secure with toothpicks, or sew with fine string. Turn the poussins over and plump back into shape.

5 Put the birds in a roasting pan just large enough to hold them without squashing them together. Add the wine, stock, and garlic. Bring to a boil on top of the stove, then transfer to a preheated 400°F oven and cook until the juices run clear when you insert a fine skewer, 45–50 minutes.

6 Transfer the poussins to an ovenproof serving dish; cover and keep warm. Boil the cooking juices until reduced by one-third; adjust seasoning. Whisk in the fromage blanc and chopped parsley; do not boil. Halve the poussins lengthwise and serve immediately with the sauce.

❖ Crêpes ❖

MAKES 8

PREPARATION TIME
10 minutes, plus
standing
COOKING TIME
15–20 minutes
FREEZING
Suitable
COLOR INDEX
Page 44

- ¾ *cup flour*
- *pinch of salt*
- *1 egg*
- *about 1¼ cups milk*
- *1 tbsp oil*
- *oil for frying*

105 CALS/CRÊPE

1 Sift the flour and salt into a bowl and make a well in the center. Break the egg into the well and add a little of the milk. Mix the liquid ingredients together, then gradually beat in the flour until smooth.

2 Beat in the oil and the remaining milk to obtain the consistency of thin cream. (Alternatively, the batter can be mixed in a blender.) Cover the batter and let stand in the refrigerator about 20 minutes.

3 Heat a crêpe pan; when hot, brush with the minimum of oil. Add a little extra milk to the batter if it is thick. Pour a small amount of batter into the pan and swirl around until it is evenly and thinly spread over the bottom of the pan.

4 Cook over medium-high heat until the edges are curling away from the pan and the underside is golden, about 1 minute. Flip the crêpe over using a metal spatula and cook the second side.

5 Turn the crêpe onto a sheet of wax paper (or parchment paper if the crêpes are to be frozen). Loosely fold a clean towel over the top. Repeat until all the batter has been used, lightly oiling the pan between crêpes.

Variations

WHOLE WHEAT CRÊPES: Use a mixture of half all-purpose, half whole wheat flour.

BUCKWHEAT CRÊPES: Use a mixture of half all-purpose, half buckwheat flour. Don't sift the buckwheat flour.

SPICED CHICK PEA CRÊPES: Use 1 cup chick pea (gram) flour. Toast 2 tsp cumin seeds under the broiler, then grind to a powder. Add to the flour with ¼ tsp turmeric. Replace ⅔ cup of the milk with water. Make slightly thicker crêpes. Use more oil if necessary.

Fillings

Almost any mixture of cooked vegetables, fish, or chicken, and herbs or nuts – moistened with a little white sauce, cream, or cream cheese – can be used as a crêpe filling.

❖ Chicken and ❖ Mushroom Crêpes

SERVES 6

PREPARATION TIME
40 minutes
COOKING TIME
25 minutes
FREEZING
Not suitable

- *12 oz cooked chicken meat*
- *8 oz button mushrooms*
- *4 tbsp butter or margarine*
- *3 tbsp flour*
- *1¼ cups chicken stock*
- *salt and pepper*
- *12 Buckwheat Crêpes (see above)*
- *1 cup shredded Gruyère cheese*

460 CALS/SERVING

1 Roughly shred the chicken; slice the mushrooms. Melt the butter in a saucepan. Add the mushrooms and cook 2–3 minutes. Stir in the flour and cook, stirring, 1 minute, then stir in the stock. Bring to a boil, stirring, then simmer 2–3 minutes. Stir in the chicken and seasoning to taste.
2 Spoon some of the chicken and mushroom mixture onto a quarter of each crêpe. Fold in half, and then in half again to form neat pockets. Arrange in a lightly greased baking dish.
3 Sprinkle liberally with the shredded cheese and bake in a preheated 375°F oven until golden and bubbly, about 25 minutes

❖ Ratatouille Crêpes ❖

SERVES 4

PREPARATION TIME
minutes
COOKING TIME
0 minutes
FREEZING
Not suitable

- ½ quantity Ratatouille (page 269)
- 8 Buckwheat Crêpes (see left)
- about ½ cup freshly grated Parmesan or Cheddar cheese
- chervil or parsley sprigs, for garnish

375 CALS/SERVING

Divide the ratatouille among the crêpes. Roll up to enclose the filling, then arrange in a single layer, seam-side down, in a lightly greased gratin dish. Sprinkle with the cheese.

Cover with foil and bake in a preheated 400°F oven until the crêpes are heated through, about 20 minutes. Serve immediately, garnished with herbs, accompanied by a salad.

❖ Mediterranean Vegetables with Eggs

SERVES 4

PREPARATION TIME
20 minutes
COOKING TIME
0 minutes
FREEZING
Not suitable
COLOR INDEX
Page 45

- 1 onion, peeled
- 12 oz zucchini
- 1 medium green bell pepper
- 2 tbsp olive oil
- 1 garlic clove, minced
- salt and pepper
- 2 tsp chopped rosemary or ½ tsp dried rosemary
- 16-oz can crushed tomatoes
- 4 eggs
- ½ cup shredded sharp Cheddar or Gruyère cheese

280 CALS/SERVING

1 Slice the onion and zucchini; roughly chop the pepper, discarding the core and seeds. Heat the oil in a large flameproof sauté pan. Add the zucchini, bell pepper, and onion and cook until beginning to soften and brown, stirring occasionally.

2 Stir in the garlic, seasoning, rosemary, and tomatoes. Simmer, uncovered, until the vegetables are tender and the liquid is well reduced.

3 Make four slight hollows in the vegetable mixture and carefully break an egg into each. Season the eggs with salt and plenty of pepper and top with the shredded cheese.

4 Cook under a preheated broiler about 10 minutes, depending on how well cooked you like your eggs.

NOTE: Protect the sauté pan handle with foil if necessary. Alternatively, use individual flameproof dishes for this recipe if you have them.

❖ Smoked Haddock ❖ and Egg Crêpes

SERVES 3–4

PREPARATION TIME
30 minutes
COOKING TIME
20 minutes
FREEZING
Not suitable

- 12 oz smoked haddock fillet (finnan haddie)
- 2 eggs
- 3 tbsp butter or margarine
- 3 tbsp flour
- 1 cup milk
- ⅔ cup sour cream
- 1 tbsp snipped chives
- pepper
- 6 Crêpes (see left)
- 1⅓ cups fresh brown bread crumbs

720–540 CALS/SERVING

1 Poach the fish in enough water to cover until tender, 5–7 minutes. Drain, skin, and flake into large pieces, removing any bones. Hardboil the eggs 7 minutes, then shell and chop roughly.

2 Melt 2 tbsp butter in a saucepan, add the flour, and cook, stirring, 1 minute. Remove from the heat and gradually stir in the milk and sour cream. Bring to a boil, stirring constantly, then lower the heat and cook gently, stirring, 2–3 minutes.

3 Add the flaked fish and roughly chopped eggs to the sauce. Stir in the chives and season with plenty of black pepper; the fish adds sufficient salt. Divide the mixture among the prepared crêpes and roll up.

4 Place in a shallow baking dish and sprinkle with the bread crumbs. Melt the remaining butter and drizzle over the top. Bake in a preheated 375°F oven until bubbling and thoroughly heated through, about 20 minutes.

❖ Spanish Tortilla ❖

SERVES 6

PREPARATION TIME
15 minutes
COOKING TIME
40 minutes
FREEZING
Not suitable
COLOR INDEX
Page 45

- 12 oz onions, peeled
- about ½ cup olive oil
- 1½ lb boiling potatoes, peeled
- 6 eggs
- salt and pepper

355 CALS/SERVING

1 Thinly slice the onions. Heat the oil in a large non-stick frying pan, about 9–10 inches in diameter. Add the onions and cook gently until quite soft, about 10 minutes.

2 Meanwhile thinly slice the potatoes, using a food processor if possible. Add to the pan and cook over medium heat, stirring frequently, until the potatoes are golden and almost tender, 10–15 minutes.

3 Lift the potatoes and onions into a colander, draining and reserving the oil. In a large bowl, whisk the eggs with plenty of seasoning. Stir in the potatoes and onions.

4 Heat the reserved oil in the clean frying pan, adding a little more if necessary to give a good film. Add the potato, onion, and egg mixture, pressing it down gently.

5 Cook over medium heat until well browned underneath and the top is nearly set, 6–8 minutes. Place under a hot broiler about 3 minutes to brown the top. Serve either warm or cold, cut into wedges and accompanied by a tomato, olive, and onion salad and crusty bread.

NOTE: When cooking the tortilla, you need to use plenty of oil otherwise it will refuse to come out of the pan. Remember to protect the pan handle with foil if necessary, when broiling.

❖ Baked Eggs ❖ with Chorizo

SERVES 4

PREPARATION TIME
20 minutes
COOKING TIME
15–20 minutes
FREEZING
Not suitable
COLOR INDEX
Page 45

- 1 large onion, peeled
- 2 tbsp olive oil
- 1 garlic clove, minced
- ½ tsp paprika
- 16-oz can crushed tomatoes
- salt and pepper
- 8 oz thin asparagus spears
- ⅓ cup fresh or frozen green peas
- 7-oz can pimientos, drained
- 3 oz prosciutto or other raw ham
- 4 oz ready-to-eat chorizo sausage
- 4 eggs

370 CALS/SERVING

1 Chop the onion. Heat the oil in a small saucepan, add the onion and garlic, and cook over medium heat until beginning to brown. Stir in the paprika, then cook 1 minute. Mix in the crushed tomatoes and seasoning. Simmer about 5 minutes.

2 Meanwhile, trim the asparagus and cut into 2-inch lengths. Cook the asparagus and peas separately in boiling salted water until tender; drain. Shred the pimientos into fine strips. Cut the ham and chorizo sausage into small pieces.

3 Divide the tomato sauce among four 1½- to 2-cup shallow ovenproof dishes. Make a well in the center of the sauce and break an egg into each one.

4 Arrange the asparagus, peas, pimiento, ham, and chorizo sausage around the egg. Season with pepper. Bake in a preheated 425°F oven 15–20 minutes. Serve immediately.

NOTE: Spicy chorizo is the most typical Mexican and Spanish sausage. It is sold both raw for use in cooked dishes and cured, ready to slice and serve.

❖ Cheese Soufflé ❖

3 Stir the cheese into the sauce until evenly blended. Using an electric mixer, beat the egg whites until they stand in soft peaks.

4 Mix one large spoonful of egg white into the sauce to lighten it. Gently pour the sauce over the remaining egg whites and carefully fold the ingredients together, using a metal spoon; do not overmix.

5 Pour the soufflé mixture gently into the prepared dish; it should come about three-quarters of the way up the side of the dish.

6 Sprinkle with the reserved cheese and run a knife around the edge of the mixture. Stand the dish on a baking sheet and bake in a preheated 350°F oven until golden brown on the top, well risen, and just firm to the touch, about 30 minutes. Serve immediately. There should be a hint of softness in the center of the soufflé.

SERVES 4

PREPARATION TIME
20 minutes, plus standing
COOKING TIME
30 minutes
FREEZING
Not suitable

- 1 tbsp freshly grated Parmesan cheese
- 1 cup milk
- few onion and carrot slices
- 1 bay leaf
- 6 black peppercorns
- 2 tbsp butter or margarine
- 2 tbsp flour
- 2 tsp Dijon mustard

- salt and pepper
- cayenne pepper
- 4 eggs, separated, plus 1 egg white
- ¾ cup shredded sharp Cheddar cheese

295 CALS/SERVING

NOTE: Use a straight-sided soufflé dish to get the best rise. Running a knife around the edge of the mixture before it goes into the oven helps to achieve the classic "hat" effect. If necessary, the soufflé can be prepared ahead to the end of stage 2 and kept several hours before completing.

Variations

Don't use too great a weight of flavoring ingredient or the soufflé will be heavy. Replace the Cheddar cheese with one of the following:

BLUE CHEESE: Use a semi-hard blue cheese, such as Stilton or Danish Blue.

MUSHROOM: Add 4 oz mushrooms, chopped and sautéed in butter.

SMOKED HADDOCK: Add 3 oz finely flaked cooked smoked haddock (finnan haddie).

1 Grease a 1½-quart soufflé dish with butter. Sprinkle the Parmesan into the dish and tilt the dish, tapping the sides gently until they are evenly coated with cheese. Put the milk in a saucepan with the onion and carrot slices, bay leaf, and peppercorns. Bring slowly to a boil, remove from the heat, cover, and let infuse 30 minutes; strain.

2 Melt the butter in a saucepan and stir in the flour and mustard. Season with salt, pepper, and cayenne, and cook 1 minute, stirring. Remove from the heat and gradually stir in the milk. Bring to a boil slowly and cook, stirring, until the sauce thickens. Cool a little, then beat in the egg yolks, one at a time. Sprinkle the Cheddar cheese over the sauce, reserving 1 tbsp for the topping.

VEGETABLES

Never has the choice of vegetables been so good. Modern methods of production, transportation, and refrigeration ensure that a constant supply reaches the markets no matter what the season. The influence of other cultures and cuisines brings us more unusual vegetables such as fresh bamboo shoots and water chestnuts and genetic engineering brings us more and more hybrids and baby vegetables.

Traditionally vegetables are categorized into family groups. First are the *brassicas*, the cabbage family, which include Brussels sprouts, kohlrabi, cauliflower, broccoli, and curly kale, as well as the many varieties of cabbage. *Roots and tubers* are the vegetables that grow underground, such as carrot, potato, turnip, beet, parsnip, Jerusalem artichoke, and salsify. *Pods and seeds* takes in the many varieties of bean, along with green peas, snow peas, and corn. *Vegetable fruits* include the tomato, okra, eggplant, and cucumber. Some would also put the avocado in this category, but strictly it is a fruit rather than a vegetable. *Leafy vegetables* include the many varieties of salad leaves, which are described in more detail in the next chapter.

Other categories are *stalks and shoots* – celery, asparagus, fennel, and chard; *squashes* – both summer and winter; and, of course, the much loved family of *onions* comprising garlic, leek, and shallot, as well as red, white, Bermuda, and scallion. Finally come *mushrooms* in all their many varieties and *thistles* – notably the globe artichoke – the thistle with the delicately flavored heart.

With all this variety and choice it is no surprise that the vegetable has been lifted from its previously underrated position, to something other than a mere accompaniment. Nutritionally vegetables are, of course, excellent. They are low in fat and cholesterol and high in vitamins, minerals, and fiber. However, to retain the maximum nutrients they should be eaten as fresh as possible; long-stored vegetables have a much lower vitamin content than those that have been freshly picked.

When choosing vegetables look for a good bright color, and crisp, firm leaves. Avoid those that show signs of discoloration or bruising, or that look shriveled. Always look for firm root vegetables; those that are wrinkled and flabby have lost flavor and goodness. Don't buy potatoes with a green tinge, as these are unfit for eating. At home, always store potatoes in the dark: The exposure to light will turn them green. Resist buying the largest vegetables, particularly when choosing roots, since as they swell and enlarge they become tough and woody. Generally the younger and smaller the vegetable the sweeter and more tender it will be, although you may find that some of the baby vegetables lack flavor because they are so immature.

Store all vegetables in a cool, dark, well-ventilated place, preferably in a rack or in the bottom of the refrigerator. It is important that they are kept in the dark because light destroys vitamins B and C. Paper bags are preferable to plastic for wrapping; pierce holes in plastic bags and loosen or remove plastic wrap to increase ventilation. Root vegetables should stay fresh 5–6 days, and green vegetables 3–4 days. Most vegetables freeze well if blanched beforehand. They are best used within 6 months, and cooked from frozen.

❖ Organic Fruit and Vegetables ❖

The demand for organic produce – obtained by farming methods that do not utilize artificial fertilizers or insecticides – is increasing. There is a growing awareness of the possible health risks of these chemicals and consumers are responding accordingly. Many supermarket chains now stock a reasonably good range of organic produce, but it tends to be rather expensive. This is because organic farming is labor intensive, yields are relatively low, and there is a high demand for a restricted supply.

❖ Preparing Vegetables ❖

If vegetables are incorrectly prepared they may not cook through in the stated time or they may spoil the appearance of the finished dish, so do pay attention to instructions given in recipes.

Cleaning

Always shake or brush off loose earth before washing. With the exception of mushrooms, all vegetables must be thoroughly washed before cooking. To ensure that leeks are thoroughly cleaned, slit the green part in half lengthwise and wash under cold running water to remove any accumulated grit inside. Brush or wipe mushrooms, rather than wash them, or they will soak up water and become spongy.

Vegetables with inedible skins, such as onion, thick-skinned roots and tubers, and winter squash, must be peeled. If you're particularly worried about residual contamination from insecticides, peel vegetables with edible skins too – washing alone is not enough to remove all traces.

Peeling and Cutting

A vegetable peeler or small paring knife is best for peeling. A really sharp knife and a good, heavy chopping board are essential for slicing and chopping. Some recipes call for a specific method of preparation, such as a julienne or chiffonade. To cut into juilienne the aim is to cut the vegetable into neat, equal-sized pieces the shape of a matchstick. Simply cut into thin slices (which are the width of a matchstick), trim into 2-inch lengths, then stack the slices and cut lengthwise again into strips. To make a chiffonade (usually of lettuce, arugula, or basil) stack several

❖ Citrus Leeks ❖
with Sugar-Snap Peas

SERVES 6

PREPARATION TIME
10 minutes
COOKING TIME
5–6 minutes
FREEZING
Not suitable

- 1½ lb trimmed leeks
- 1 lb sugar-snap peas or snow peas
- 1½ –2 tbsp olive oil
- salt and pepper
DRESSING:
- 3 tbsp olive oil
- 1 tbsp balsamic vinegar
- ½ tsp light brown sugar
- 2–3 tsp lemon juice
- ½ tsp Dijon mustard

- finely grated rind and juice of ½ orange

150 CALS/SERVING

1 Cut the leeks into ½-inch slices. Trim the sugar-snap peas.

2 Heat the oil in a large sauté pan, add the leeks, and sauté gently until just tender, 5–6 minutes.

3 Meanwhile cook the sugar-snap peas in boiling salted water 5 minutes. Drain, then mix with the leeks. Whisk together all the ingredients for the dressing and season with salt and pepper to taste. Pour over the hot vegetables and toss to mix. Serve immediately.

❖ Squash with ❖
Tomato and Onion

SERVES 4–6

PREPARATION TIME
20 minutes
COOKING TIME
30 minutes
FREEZING
Not suitable

- 1 large summer squash
- 2 onions, peeled
- 6 large tomatoes
- 2 tbsp butter or margarine
- 1 garlic clove, minced
- 2 tbsp tomato paste

- 2 tbsp chopped mixed herbs or 2 tsp dried her
- salt and pepper
- parsley sprigs, for garnish

100–65 CALS/SERVI

1 Peel the squash, cut in half lengthwise, and scoop out the seeds. Cut the flesh into 1-inch cubes. Chop the onions; skin a chop the tomatoes.
2 Melt the butter in a large saucepan and gently fry the onions and garlic until soft, about 5 minutes. Add the squash and cook 5 minutes longer.
3 Stir in the tomatoes, tomato paste, and herbs. Cover and simmer until the vegetables are tender, about 20 minutes. Seaso to taste. Serve at once, garnished with parsley.

❖ Baked Mushrooms ❖
with Parsley

SERVES 4–6

PREPARATION TIME
10 minutes
COOKING TIME
30 minutes
FREEZING
Not suitable
COLOR INDEX
Page 51

- 1¼ lb large flat mushrooms
- 1 garlic clove, minced
- 2 tbsp chopped parsley
- salt and pepper

- olive oil, for basting
- parsley sprig, for garnish

55–35 CALS/SERVIN

1 Thickly slice the mushrooms and arrange in a greased baking dish. Sprinkle with the garlic, parsley, and seasoning to taste. Drizzle over enough oil to moisten the mushrooms.
2 Bake in a preheated 400°F oven about 30 minutes. Serve hot, garnished with parsley.

❖ Mushrooms Sautéed ❖ with Thyme and Garlic

SERVES 4–6

PREPARATION TIME
10 minutes
COOKING TIME
10 minutes
FREEZING
Not suitable

- *2 lb mixed mushrooms, such as open cup, oyster, and button*
- *3 tbsp olive oil*
- *1 large garlic clove, minced*
- *few thyme sprigs or ¼ tsp dried thyme*
- *juice of ½ small lemon*

- *salt and pepper*
- *¼ cup crème fraîche or heavy whipping cream*
- *½ tsp Dijon mustard*
- *lemon rind shreds, for garnish*

145–95 CALS/SERVING

1 To clean the mushrooms, wipe them with a clean cloth or brush or pick off any lumps of dirt; do not wash them or they will become waterlogged. Slice any large mushrooms, but try to leave some whole.

2 Heat the oil in a large, heavy-based frying pan, preferably nonstick. Add the mushrooms and sauté over high heat until slightly softened, shaking the pan occasionally.

3 Add the garlic, thyme, lemon juice, and plenty of seasoning. Reduce the heat and simmer gently until the mushrooms are tender. Blend the crème fraîche with the mustard and add to the pan. Let bubble 1–2 minutes to reduce. Serve hot, garnished with lemon rind shreds.

❖ Spinach and ❖ Mushroom Bhaji

SERVES 8

PREPARATION TIME
15 minutes
COOKING TIME
45 minutes
FREEZING
Suitable

- *2 garlic cloves*
- *1-inch piece fresh gingerroot*
- *1 tbsp black mustard seeds*
- *2 tsp coriander seeds*
- *1 tsp cumin seeds*
- *3 tbsp oil or ghee*
- *2 large onions, peeled and thinly sliced*
- *2 tsp turmeric*
- *1–2 tsp chili powder, to taste*
- *1 lb button mushrooms, thickly sliced*

- *16-oz can crushed tomatoes*
- *2 lb spinach leaves*
- *salt and pepper*
- *about ¼ cup toasted shredded coconut, for garnish*

120 CALS/SERVING

1 Roughly chop the garlic and ginger. Put the mustard, coriander, and cumin seeds in a large heavy-based pan and fry over medium heat 2–3 minutes, stirring all the time. Remove the spices from the pan and crush with the garlic and ginger using a mortar and pestle.

2 Heat the oil in the pan, add the onions, and cook gently, stirring frequently, until softened and golden, about 10 minutes. Add the spice paste, turmeric, and chili powder and cook gently, stirring all the time, about 5 minutes.

3 Add the mushrooms and stir well, then add the tomatoes and bring to a boil, stirring. Simmer 10 minutes, stirring occasionally.

4 Roughly shred the spinach and add to the pan. Stir well, then season with salt and pepper to taste. Lower the heat, cover, and simmer 15 minutes, stirring frequently to blend in the spinach as it cooks down. Check the seasoning and sprinkle with the coconut to serve.

NOTE: Frozen spinach can be used for this recipe. You will need 1 lb frozen leaf spinach, thawed and well drained.

VEGETARIAN DISHES

An ever-increasing number of people are choosing to eat more and more meatless meals based on ingredients like pasta, rice, grains, and vegetables. Many others – sometimes known as the "demi-veggies" – choose to exclude red meat from their diet completely but still eat the occasional meal containing fish, shellfish, or chicken. As for vegetarians, there are as many types of vegetarian diet as there are reasons for being one. Vegans are very strict vegetarians, who won't eat any animal product whatsoever and that includes gelatin and in some cases honey. Less strict vegetarians eat cheese, butter, and milk. Some also eat eggs.

The reasons for becoming vegetarian are numerous. Some look to it as a healthier way of eating; current research seems to suggest that many so-called "diseases of Western civilization" such as heart disease, strokes, obesity, and high blood pressure are related to a diet that's high in animal fats. Others are influenced by their religion or choose to avoid meat because they're concerned about animal welfare. Many vegetarians are worried about the environment and believe that a vegetarian diet is a more economical method of food production in terms of the world's limited resources.

❖ Balancing a Vegetarian Diet ❖

Many people make the mistake of assuming that a vegetarian diet is automatically healthier than a carnivore's. This isn't always the case. It is not enough simply to stop eating meat; the nutrients that would have been obtained from meat must be derived from other sources. It's quite common for vegetarians to rely too heavily on dairy products – like cheese – which are high in saturated fats and calories.

As with any diet, variety is important. If a wide range of foods is eaten, a vegetarian diet is no more likely to be lacking nutritionally than any other diet. There are lots of good vegetable sources of protein such as beans, grains, nuts, tofu, Quorn, and TVP as well as dairy products. Animal proteins contain almost all of the essential amino acids and are regarded as "complete protein" foods. With the exception of soybean products and quinoa, vegetable proteins are lacking or low in one or more of the essential amino acids. However, by eating certain foods together at the same meal any deficiency is overcome. This isn't as complicated as it sounds and tends to happen automatically when menu planning. For example, cereals should be eaten with dairy products, legumes, or nuts: granola with yogurt or milk; chile with rice or tortillas; nut roast made with bread crumbs. Legumes and nuts should also be eaten with dairy products: dhal with raita; nut burgers with a cream-based sauce; bean stew with cheese topping, for example.

Vegetarians and vegans should be careful to regulate their intake of vitamins B12 and D, although contrary to popular belief a deficiency of either is unlikely. Both are found in dairy products and fortified products such as breakfast cereals. Anemia or a lack of dietary iron is often discussed in relation to a vegetarian diet because meat and liver are commonly believed to be the best sources of iron. In fact, iron is found in a wide range of foods including leafy green vegetables, cereals, legumes, nuts, eggs, and dried fruits – especially apricots. The absorption of iron is greatly increased if vitamin C rich foods are eaten at the same meal. It is decreased by the presence of tannin, which is found in large amounts in tea – so don't drink tea at meal times!

❖ The Vegetarian Pantry ❖

Vegetarian alternatives to ingredients of animal origin are becoming increasingly available. You can now buy a wide range of cheeses produced using vegetarian rennet, for example. Other useful products include agar-agar which is an alternative for gelatin. Certain foods are particularly significant in a vegetarian diet; these are described below.

Legumes

The term legume covers all the various beans, peas, and lentils that have been preserved by drying. Legumes are an important source of protein, carbohydrate, and fiber in a vegetarian diet.

Legumes should be stored in airtight containers in a cool, dark place. They keep well, but after about 6 months their skins toughen and they take increasingly longer to cook, so buy them from a supplier with a fast turnover.

Before cooking, with the exception of lentils and split peas, all legumes should be soaked overnight in a large bowl of cold water. In the morning, drain them, bring to a boil in fresh water, and boil rapidly 10 minutes to destroy any toxins present. Although fast-boiling is not strictly necessary for all types of legume it does them no harm and saves the problem of remembering which ones require it. After fast-boiling, lower the heat, cover, and simmer until tender. The flavor can be subtly enhanced by adding a couple of bay leaves or garlic cloves, or an onion studded with a

PASTA

It's difficult to remember what we did for fast, satisfying meals before pasta became readily available. Because it keeps well and is quick to cook, cheap, and tasty, pasta has become one of our most popular foods. Nutritionally speaking pasta is high in fiber and low in fat and calories – it's the sauce that makes pasta dishes fattening. If you're watching your weight use low-calorie ingredients like vegetables, skim milk and low- or medium-fat cheese to replace full-fat equivalents, and keep the use of ingredients like olive oil, butter, olives, and salami to a minimum.

❖ Fresh and Dried Pasta ❖

Fresh pasta is now widely available in a good range of shapes and flavors, in supermarkets as well as Italian grocers. It cooks in a matter of minutes and is considered superior to dried pasta. Of course, you can make your own at home following our recipe overleaf – homemade pasta is incomparable. The best flour to use is a very fine-textured soft wheat flour known as "type 00." This yields a dough that is easier to stretch by hand. Durum or hard wheat semolina flour is only really suitable if you are using a pasta machine that flattens, rather than stretches the dough. Both types of flour are available from Italian grocers.

If you make pasta frequently, it is probably a good idea to invest in a pasta machine to do the rolling and cutting for you. One of these machines will take all the hard work out of rolling and get the dough really thin. It will also ensure that the dough is cut into neat, uniform shapes, so that it cooks evenly.

Dried pastas are available in a bewildering range of sizes, shapes, and flavors. The best are made from 100% durum wheat (pasta di semola di grano duro); some include eggs (all'uovo).

Shapes, Sizes, and Flavors

The choice of shape and size is a matter of personal taste but it's worth bearing in mind that some varieties – such as conchiglie (shells) – are particularly suited to holding lots of sauce, while other chunkier shapes – such as penne – are good with robust vegetable-based sauces. Fine spaghetti and noodles are excellent with delicate fish sauces, while tiny ditalini are perfect for soups and young children's meals. There are the classic recipes, such as macaroni with cheese, spaghetti bolognese, and spaghetti alla carbonara, but do experiment with your own combinations.

Colored and flavored pastas (fresh and dried) can add a new twist to a familiar meal. These are colored with puréed vegetables; although the colours are fun the flavors are rarely pronounced. If you're looking for extra flavor choose those flavored with garlic and herbs. Whole wheat pasta is made with whole wheat flour and has a rather heavy chewy texture. If you're trying to increase your intake of dietary fiber you may prefer to eat plain pasta with a high fiber vegetable-based sauce.

Quantities

It is difficult to give specific quantity guidelines for pasta since it really depends on how rich the sauce is, and even on the size and shape of the pasta – some are easier and quicker to eat than others! Of course appetites, particularly for pasta, vary enormously, too. As a very rough guide allow about 3–4 oz uncooked weight, per person.

❖ Cooking Pasta ❖

All pasta, fresh and dried, should be cooked until al dente – firm to the bite, definitely not soft, and without a hard, uncooked center. The most important thing to remember is that pasta requires lots of fast-boiling salted water; a small pan containing insufficient water will produce unevenly cooked stodgy pasta. Some cooks add a little olive oil to the water in the belief that it will prevent sticking, but this is not necessary. Fresh pasta will cook in a few minutes, while dried pasta usually takes 8–12 minutes. Whether you're cooking fresh or dried pasta the time will depend on the size and shape; obviously thin shapes like capellini (angel's hair) will cook more quickly than chunky or filled shapes. Manufacturers' recommended cooking times vary, too. The only accurate way to determine when pasta is cooked is by tasting.

❖ Serving Suggestions ❖

Toss cooked pasta with the chosen sauce or butter as soon as it is cooked, or it will stick together as it cools. Always have warm plates or bowls ready as it quickly loses heat. If cooking pasta to serve cold, drain and rinse with cold water to prevent further cooking and rinse away surface starch. Toss with dressing while still slightly warm for optimum flavor. If you store the salad in the refrigerator, bring it to room temperature before serving.

Parmesan cheese is a must for serving with most hot pasta – although some seafood pasta dishes are better without it. Do buy a piece of Parmesan; the taste is far superior to the "soapy" ready-grated alternatives sold in tubs and packages. A well wrapped piece of Parmesan will keep in the refrigerator several weeks. Rather than grating it on the fine side of the grater, try using a cheese slice or swivel-bladed peeler to shave off large flakes of cheese. But: dieters be warned. Just one tablespoon of grated Parmesan adds an extra 70 calories!

Should you find yourself with leftovers, the only satisfactory method of reheating pasta is in the microwave. Both dressed and plain pasta can be reheated in this way without loss of texture or flavor. To reheat plain pasta, toss with a little olive oil, cover, and cook on HIGH about 2 minutes. Alternatively, toss plain leftover pasta with a well-flavored dressing and salad ingredients and serve as a salad.

❖ Pesto ❖

SERVES 4-6

PREPARATION TIME
5-10 minutes
FREEZING
Not suitable

75 CALS/1 TBSP

- 1 cup basil leaves (without stems)
- 2 garlic cloves, skinned
- 2 tbsp pine nuts
- salt and pepper
- ½ cup olive oil
- ½ cup freshly grated Parmesan cheese

1 Put the basil, garlic, pine nuts, salt, pepper, and olive oil in a mortar and pound with a pestle, or place in a blender or food processor and blend at high speed until very creamy.
2 Transfer the mixture to a bowl, fold in the cheese, and mix thoroughly. Store up to 2 weeks in a screw-topped jar in the refrigerator.

❖ Spaghetti alla Carbonara ❖

SERVES 4

PREPARATION TIME
5 minutes
COOKING TIME
About 10 minutes
FREEZING
Not suitable

720 CALS/SERVING

- 1 onion, peeled
- 6 pancetta or unsmoked bacon slices
- 2 tbsp olive oil
- 1 garlic clove, minced
- 14 oz dried spaghetti or other long thin pasta
- salt and pepper
- 3 eggs
- ¼ cup freshly grated Parmesan cheese
- 2 tbsp light whipping cream
- 2 tbsp chopped parsley

1 Mince the onion. Remove any rind from the pancetta, then cut into thin strips. Heat the oil in a pan, add the onion, and fry gently until soft but not colored, about 5 minutes. Add the garlic and cook 1 minute longer.

2 Cook the spaghetti in a large pan of boiling salted water until *al dente* (tender but still firm to the bite), 8–10 minutes. Meanwhile, add the bacon to the onion and fry 2 minutes over high heat.

3 In a bowl, lightly beat the eggs with the Parmesan, cream, chopped parsley, and salt and pepper to taste.

4 Drain the spaghetti and return to the pan with the bacon and onion mixture. Stir well over a medium heat 1 minute.

5 Remove from the heat and add the egg mixture, mixing well; the heat from the spaghetti will lightly cook the egg. Turn into a warmed serving dish and serve immediately.

❖ Pasta with Bacon Sauce ❖

SERVES 4

PREPARATION TIME
10 minutes
COOKING TIME
15 minutes
FREEZING
Not suitable
COLOR INDEX
Page 61

720 CALS/SERVING

- 12 oz dried pasta, such as vermicelli, spaghetti, or penne
- salt and pepper
- 4 oz black olives (preferably Kalamata), pitted
- 8 oz smoked bacon
- ¼ cup olive oil
- 2 garlic cloves, minced
- two 16-oz cans crushed tomatoes
- ¼ cup chopped herbs, such as basil, marjoram, or parsley
- chopped herbs, for garnish

1 Cook the pasta in a large pan of boiling salted water until *al dente* (tender but still firm to the bite), about 10 minutes.
2 Meanwhile, roughly chop the olives and bacon. Heat 2 tbsp oil in a frying pan and fry the garlic and bacon until golden. Stir in the tomatoes, olives, and herbs and heat through 2–3 minutes until piping hot. Adjust the seasoning.
3 Drain the pasta and toss with the remaining oil. Add the bacon sauce and toss well. Leave, covered, for 1 minute, then toss again and serve immediately, garnished with chopped herbs.

❖ Seafood Spaghetti ❖

3 Drain the spaghetti, toss with the seafood sauce, and season to taste. Serve immediately, garnished with plenty of chopped parsley.

SERVES 4-6

PREPARATION TIME
15 minutes
COOKING TIME
About 25 minutes
FREEZING
Not suitable

- 2 lb mussels
- 2 leeks
- 1 onion, peeled
- 2 tbsp olive oil
- 1 garlic clove, minced
- large pinch of saffron strands
- 12 oz dried spaghetti
- salt and pepper
- ⅛ cup dry white wine
- ⅔ cup heavy whipping cream

- 3 tbsp chopped parsley
- 8 oz large cooked peeled shrimp
- 6 oz sea scallops (optional)
- chopped parsley, for garnish

745–495 CALS/SERVING

1 Scrub the mussels (see page 134). Thinly slice the leeks; mince the onion. Heat the oil in a large saucepan, add the leeks, onion, garlic, and saffron, and sauté 3–4 minutes, stirring all the time. Cover the pan, lower the heat, and cook until the vegetables are really soft, about 10 minutes.

2 Cook the spaghetti in a large pan of boiling salted water until *al dente* (tender but still firm to the bite), 8–10 minutes. Meanwhile, add the wine, cream, and parsley to the leek mixture. Bring to a boil and boil a few minutes to reduce slightly. Add the seafood, re-cover, and cook, shaking the pan frequently, until the mussels have opened, 2–3 minutes; discard any that stay closed.

❖ Spaghetti with Garlic ❖

SERVES 4-6

PREPARATION TIME
5 minutes
COOKING TIME
8–10 minutes
FREEZING
Not suitable

- about 1 lb dried spaghetti
- salt and pepper
- ⅓ cup virgin olive oil
- 2 garlic cloves, minced
- hot chili pepper, seeded and chopped

- 2 tbsp chopped parsley, coriander (cilantro), or basil (optional)
- freshly grated Parmesan cheese, for serving (optional)

560–370 CALS/SERVING

1 Cook the spaghetti in a large pan of boiling salted water or until *al dente* (tender but still firm to the bite), 8–10 minutes.
2 Meanwhile, heat the oil in a heavy-based saucepan, add the garlic and chili and fry 2–3 minutes, stirring occasionally. Don't let the garlic and chili become too brown or the oil will taste bitter. Remove from the heat and set aside until the pasta is cooked.
3 Drain the pasta thoroughly. Reheat the oil over very high heat for 1 minute, then pour over the pasta with the herbs, if using. Season with salt and pepper and serve immediately, with Parmesan if desired.

NOTE: Increase or decrease the quantity of garlic and chili used in this recipe according to taste. It's an intensely flavored dish, best served with a crisp mixed leaf and watercress salad dressed lightly with a sharp vinaigrette.

RICE, GRAINS, & NOODLES

Rice is one of our staple foods. It contains protein and B vitamins, but no fat, and it is cheap and quick to cook. There are many types of rice, each with its own characteristics, and for many dishes it is important to choose the correct variety.

❖ Types of Rice ❖

❖ Brown rice is the whole grain with only the tough outer husk removed. Like other unrefined grains it is higher in fiber, B vitamins, and protein than its refined counterpart. Because the bran is retained, the rice has a chewy texture and nutty flavor, and it takes longer to cook than white varieties.

❖ Long-grain white rice is brown rice that has been further milled to remove the bran and germ. When cooked the grains should be separate, quite dry, and fluffy. Varieties include Patna and Carolina.

❖ Basmati rice is a wonderfully aromatic long-grain rice that was originally harvested mainly in the foothills of the Himalayas. It is the perfect accompaniment to curries and other spicy dishes, and is used to make a pilaf. Brown basmati rice is also available.

❖ Thai rice is a newcomer to our supermarkets. The large plump grains are extremely fragrant with a slightly sweet flavor. Try it flavored with chopped hot chilies and fresh coriander (cilantro), as an accompaniment to spicy foods.

❖ Arborio rice is a special short-grain variety from Italy that is essential for an authentic risotto. It has the unique ability to absorb a lot of liquid during cooking without turning mushy.

❖ Glutinous rice is another Asian variety which is also known as sticky rice. It has oval cream-colored grains that cook into a sticky mass. It is a vital ingredient in Japanese sushi.

❖ Short-grain rice is indispensable for a rice pudding. The small grains absorb lots of liquid during cooking, softening in the process to produce the characteristic creamy result.

Cooking Rice

Contrary to popular belief, cooking rice isn't difficult. Some of the "specialty rices" are cooked in specific ways: The liquid is usually added gradually to arborio for a risotto; rice pudding is usually baked slowly in a low oven; glutinous rice is steamed; but in general long-grain rice varieties can be treated in the same way.

Many cooks like to wash or rinse the rice before cooking to remove excess starch. With some varieties this is not necessary, but others – particularly basmati – tend to be very starchy and may contain small pieces of grit so washing is advisable. Simply put the rice in a strainer and wash under cold running water until the water runs clear, shaking the strainer and picking out any bits of grit.

To cook the rice you will need a large saucepan and plenty of fast-boiling salted water. Sprinkle the rice into the boiling water and keep the heat high until the water returns to a boil. Stir once with a fork to loosen any rice grains that have sunk to the bottom, lower the heat, and cook, uncovered, fairly vigorously. As long as you have sufficient water the rice will not stick.

There are so many varieties of long-grain rice on the market that it is impossible to give exact cooking times. Most varieties take a minimum of 10 minutes; to test, pick out a few grains and taste. As soon as the rice is cooked, drain in a strainer and rinse with boiling water to remove excess starch. Fluff up the grains with a fork and tip into a heated serving dish or warmed plates.

The alternative method relies on accurately estimating the volume of liquid to that of rice (usually double liquid to rice). It is a little trickier because the rice has a habit of sticking to the bottom of the pan, so you need to use a pan with a really solid base, and control the heat carefully. Always keep a careful watch on the time and resist lifting the lid during cooking because this lets precious steam escape. Rice can also be cooked by this method in the oven, usually at about 350°F, but it will take much longer. If converting a white rice recipe to use brown rice, don't forget to add extra liquid and increase the cooking time.

Rice may be cooked in advance, stored in the refrigerator, and reheated in the microwave or in the oven – in a well-buttered covered dish. Cooked rice can also be frozen, but takes ages to thaw, so freeze it in portion sizes to reduce defrosting time.

❖ Grains and Noodles ❖

The interest in natural foods and healthy eating means that a better range of grains can be found in supermarkets than ever before. Grains are high in vitamins. They are also extremely versatile and can be used for making all sorts of dishes or at the very least as a change from rice or potatoes as an accompaniment.

One of the most delicious and expensive grains is wild rice. It is not as the name suggests a rice but the seed of an aquatic grass. It is dark brown in color and has a strong, nutty flavor. Because of its cost, wild rice is usually mixed with other grains or rice. Look out for commercially prepared mixtures. Other useful grains include bulgur wheat, couscous, barley, and cornmeal.

Noodles can be derived from soybeans, such as cellophane noodles; rice flour, as in rice stick noodles; and of course from wheat flour. Some varieties need to be soaked before cooking. Like rice and grains, noodles are often served as an accompaniment.

❖ Thai Fried Rice ❖

SERVES 4

PREPARATION TIME
10 minutes
COOKING TIME
15 minutes
FREEZING
Not suitable

- 1⅓ cups basmati rice
- salt
- 1 hot red chili pepper
- 2 scallions
- 3 tbsp oil
- 2 tsp nam pla (fish sauce)
- 1 egg, beaten (optional)
- 1 tbsp soy sauce
- 1 tsp brown sugar

335 CALS/SERVING

1 Cook the rice in boiling salted water until almost tender, about 10 minutes. Drain, then rinse with boiling water. Spread out on a tray and let cool while cooking the vegetables.
2 Seed and chop the chili; chop the scallions. Heat the oil in a wok, then add the fish sauce, chili, and scallions and stir-fry 1–2 minutes to flavor the oil.
3 Add the egg, if using, and stir-fry until the egg scrambles, stirring all the time so that the egg sets in small pieces rather than one large lump.
4 Stir the rice with a fork to separate the grains, then tip into the hot oil. Stir-fry with the eggs until thoroughly heated through. Mix the soy sauce with the sugar, then stir into the rice mixture. Serve immediately.

❖ Basmati Pilaf ❖

SERVES 4

PREPARATION TIME
10 minutes, plus soaking
COOKING TIME
25 minutes
FREEZING
Not suitable
COLOR INDEX
Page 65

- 1⅓ cups basmati rice
- 4 cardamom pods, split
- 4 black peppercorns
- 3 whole cloves
- 1-inch cinnamon stick
- 1½ tsp cumin seeds
- 2 tbsp oil
- 1 small onion, peeled and minced
- 1 tsp turmeric
- 2 curry leaves or bay leaves, torn into pieces
- salt and pepper
- ⅓ cup pistachio nuts, roughly chopped
- 3 tbsp raisins (optional)

365 CALS/SERVING

1 Rinse the rice in several changes of cold water to remove excess starch. Place in a bowl, cover with cold water, and let soak 30 minutes. Drain off the water, transfer the rice to a strainer and rinse under cold running water until the water runs clear.
2 Put the cardamom pods, peppercorns, cloves, cinnamon stick and cumin seeds in a large, heavy flameproof casserole and fry over medium heat, stirring all the time until the seeds pop and release their flavor, 2–3 minutes. Add the oil and stir until hot, then add the onion and turmeric and cook gently, stirring frequently, until the onion is softened, about 10 minutes.
3 Add the rice and stir until coated in the spiced onion mixture, then slowly pour in 5 cups boiling water. (Take care as the water may sizzle and splash.) Add the curry or bay leaves and seasoning, bring to a boil, and stir well. Lower the heat, cover, and cook very gently about 10 minutes, without lifting the lid. Remove from the heat and let stand 10 minutes to let the flavors develop.
4 Uncover the rice, add half the pistachio nuts and the raisins if using, and gently fork through to fluff up the grains. Taste and adjust the seasoning. Spoon the pilaf onto a warmed serving platter and sprinkle with the remaining pistachio nuts to serve.

❖ Asparagus Risotto ❖

SERVES 4

PREPARATION TIME
30 minutes
COOKING TIME
30–35 minutes
FREEZING
Not suitable

- 1 quart vegetable stock
- ⅔ cup dry white wine
- 1 lb thin green asparagus
- 1 onion, peeled
- 6 tbsp butter
- 1½ cups arborio rice
- pinch of saffron strands
- salt and pepper

FOR SERVING:
- ½ cup freshly grated Parmesan cheese

455 CALS/SERVING

Bring the stock and wine to boil in a large saucepan and keep at barely simmering point. Meanwhile, cut off the tips of the asparagus and set side. Peel the asparagus stalks and cut into 2-inch engths.

2 Mince the onion. Melt 2 tbsp butter in a large heavy-based saucepan. Add the onion and fry gently until soft, about 5 minutes. Add the asparagus stems and the arborio rice to the pan and stir over low heat until the rice is well coated with the butter, about 5 minutes.

Add a ladleful of stock to he pan and cook gently, tirring occasionally, until the tock is absorbed. Stir in more tock as soon as each ladleful s absorbed.

4 When the rice becomes creamy, sprinkle in the saffron with salt and pepper to taste. Continue adding stock and stirring until the risotto is thick and creamy, tender but not sticky. This process should take 20–25 minutes; it must not be hurried. You may not need to add all of the stock.

5 Meanwhile, steam the asparagus tips until just tender. Just before serving the risotto, add the asparagus tips with the remaining butter. Check the seasoning and serve sprinkled with the Parmesan cheese.

❖ Mushroom Risotto ❖

SERVES 4
PREPARATION TIME
15 minutes
COOKING TIME
20–25 minutes
FREEZING
Not suitable

- 1 onion, peeled
- 1 lemon
- 6 oz flat mushrooms
- 8 oz broccoli florets
- 6 oz thin green beans
- salt and pepper
- 1 quart vegetable stock
- 2 tbsp olive oil
- 1½ cups arborio rice
- *pinch of saffron strands (optional)*
- ¼ cup dry white wine

- freshly grated Parmesan cheese, for serving

420 CALS/SERVING

1 Mince the onion. Finely pare the rind from the lemon in one piece, then squeeze the juice from the lemon. Slice the mushrooms.
2 Break the broccoli into small florets; halve the green beans. Blanch the beans and broccoli together in boiling salted water about 4 minutes. Drain and refresh under cold running water.
3 Bring the stock to a boil in a large saucepan and keep at barely simmering point.
4 Heat the oil in a large heavy-based saucepan, add the onion, and cook until beginning to soften, 2–3 minutes. Stir in the rice and saffron, if using, season well, and add the wine, pared lemon rind, 2 tbsp lemon juice, and a ladleful of stock. Cook gently, stirring occasionally, until the stock is absorbed. Continue adding the stock, a ladleful at a time as each addition is absorbed.
5 When most of the stock has been added and the rice is creamy (after about 15 minutes), stir in the mushrooms, broccoli, green beans, and a little more stock. Cover and simmer until the rice is just tender and most of the liquid absorbed, about 5 minutes longer. Remove the lemon rind and check the seasoning. Serve the risotto with freshly grated Parmesan.

PIES, QUICHES, & PIZZAS

The art of successful pastry-making lies in light careful handling and accurate measuring. Except when making choux pastry, the golden rule is to keep everything cool – the kitchen, work surface, utensils, ingredients, and yourself!

There are three main types of pastry: short (for piecrust), puff, and choux or cream puff. The classic French *pâte sucrée* is similar to short pastry although it is richer and *pâte sucrée* is mixed differently. (Recipes for sweet pastries are on page 354.)

For most pastries, all-purpose flour is the best, as it gives a light, crisp result. Self-rising flour produces a soft spongy pastry, while using all whole wheat flour tends to give a heavy pastry. For whole wheat pastry it is best to use half whole wheat and half all-purpose flour. Cake flour is not suitable for pastry making.

A little lemon juice is usually added to puff pastry to soften the gluten and make the dough more elastic. This enables it to be rolled out and folded many times during its preparation.

Traditionally short, or basic pie, pastry is made with a mixture of shortening and either butter or margarine, or all shortening, butter, or margarine is used instead. For a rich flavor, butter is undoubtedly the best, although for savory pastries shortening gives good results. Generally hard margarine should be used in preference to soft margarine.

Be careful when adding the water to the dough: Too much will make the cooked pastry tough while too little will make a dry dough that's hard to handle and is crumbly when cooked.

❖ Mixing Pastry ❖

Most pastries involve cutting the fat into the flour. To do this, cut the fat into small cubes, then tip them into the flour and salt. Mix them around briefly to evenly coat the exposed surfaces with flour, then using a pastry blender, cut the fat and flour together until the fat breaks down into small pieces. Try to do this as quickly and lightly as possible. You can also rub in the fat with your fingertips, but don't use the palms of your hands or you will end up with a sticky mess. Another alternative is to use 2 table knives scissor-fashion.

Sprinkle the water evenly over the mixture and stir it in with a round-bladed knife. You may need to add a little more or a little less than stated in the recipe since the absorbency of different flours varies, so don't add the liquid all at once. Collect the dough into a ball and knead lightly for a few seconds. If it feels very sticky, simply sprinkle with a little extra flour.

❖ Using a Food Processor ❖

Short pastry can be made very quickly and successfully in a food processor. It's important to pulse the machine or turn it on in short bursts only so that the dough doesn't get overworked. Don't try to make too much pastry at one time, or you will overload the machine.

❖ Commercial Pastries ❖

If you don't have the time or inclination to make your own pastry, choose from the good range of commercial pastries now available – both frozen and from the chilled cabinet. Piecrust mixes, sticks of piecrust, and refrigerated piecrust dough are widely available. For real time-saving look for frozen ready-to-use pie shells and patty shells (puff pastry).

❖ Rolling Out Pastry ❖

Dust the work surface and the rolling pin – never the pastry – with as little flour as possible. Roll the dough lightly and evenly in one direction only. Always roll away from you, using light, firm strokes, and rotate the pastry frequently re-dusting the work surface as necessary to keep an even shape and thickness. Roll it out until it is quite thin – very thick pastry is unpleasant to eat – but avoid over-rolling or stretching the pastry as you roll or it will shrink badly during cooking.

❖ Making a Two-Crust Pie ❖

If you are making two-crust pie, divide the pastry dough into two portions – one a little larger than the other. Use the larger portion for the bottom crust. Roll out this dough to a round about 2 inches larger all around than the pie plate. Lift the dough and drape it into the plate, gently easing it in to cover the bottom and side. Trim the edge so there is about 1 inch hanging over the rim of the plate. Put the filling into the bottom crust. Moisten the edge. Roll out the second portion of dough into a round. Cut slashes or a design in the center and lay the round over the filling. Press the edges of top and bottom crust together, folding up the overhang. Finish the edge plainly or in a more decorative way as desired (see page 329).

❖ Sausage Rolls ❖

MAKES 28

PREPARATION TIME
25 minutes
COOKING TIME
30 minutes
FREEZING
Suitable
COLOR INDEX
Page 67

- 1 quantity Puff Pastry (page 330)
- 1 lb pork sausage meat
- flour, for dusting
- a little milk
- beaten egg, to glaze

`230 CALS/ROLL`

1 On a lightly floured surface roll out half the pastry to a 16-×8-inch oblong. Cut lengthwise into 2 strips. Divide the sausage meat into 4 pieces, dust with flour, and form into rolls the length of the pastry. Lay a sausage-meat roll on each pastry strip.

2 Repeat with remaining pastry and sausage-meat rolls. Brush the pastry edges with a little milk, fold one side of the pastry over the sausage meat, and press the two long edges firmly together to seal.

3 Brush the pastry with egg, then cut each roll into 2-inch lengths. Place on a baking sheet and bake in a preheated 425°F oven 15 minutes. Reduce the temperature to 350°F and bake 15 minutes longer. Serve hot or cold.

❖ Gougère ❖

SERVES 4

PREPARATION TIME
25 minutes
COOKING TIME
45–50 minutes
FREEZING
Not suitable
COLOR INDEX
Page 68

CHOUX PASTRY:
- ¾ cup flour
- large pinch of salt
- large pinch of cayenne
- 6 tbsp butter
- 3 eggs, lightly beaten
- ¾ cup shredded sharp Cheddar cheese
- 2 tbsp chopped parsley

FILLING:
- 2 tbsp butter
- 1 onion, peeled and chopped
- 1 garlic clove, minced
- 4 oz mushrooms, sliced

- 1¼ cups thick Béchamel Sauce (page 92)
- 12 oz cooked boneless chicken, chopped
- 2 tbsp chopped parsley
- salt and pepper
- 1–2 tbsp fresh bread crumbs
- 2 tbsp freshly grated Parmesan cheese

`780 CALS/SERVING`

1 To make the filling, melt the butter in a saucepan and fry the onion and garlic until softened. Add the mushrooms and cook until softened, 2–3 minutes. Stir in the Béchamel sauce. Let cool.

2 To make the choux pastry, sift the flour, salt, and cayenne onto a piece of paper. Melt the butter with ⅞ cup water in a saucepan, then quickly bring to a boil. Off the heat, immediately tip in all the flour and beat vigorously with a wooden spoon.

3 Return to the heat and continue beating until the mixture is smooth and leaves the sides of the pan clean to form a ball; do not over-beat. Let cool 1–2 minutes.

4 Gradually beat in the eggs, adding just enough to give a consistency that will drop off the spoon. The pastry should be smooth and shiny. Fold in the cheese and parsley.

5 Spoon the pastry around the edge of a greased gratin dish. Bake in a preheated 400°F oven until well risen and golden brown, about 25 minutes. Meanwhile add the chicken to the cold sauce with the parsley and seasoning.

6 Pile the filling in the center of the choux ring. Sprinkle with the bread crumbs and Parmesan and bake 15 minutes longer until the filling is hot. Serve immediately.

Variation

VEGETABLE GOUGÈRE: Replace the filling with stir-fried mixed vegetables. Sprinkle with toasted cashew nuts to serve.

PIZZAS

Rapid rise dry yeast has revolutionized pizza-making. It is mixed straight into the flour without any proving and the dough only needs to be left to rise once. Packaged bread or pizza mix also makes a good, speedy pizza base; as a guide one 10-oz package is roughly equivalent to a pizza dough made with 1⅔ cups flour. When making up the mix, substitute a little olive oil for some of the liquid to improve the flavor. Included below is a recipe for a quick biscuit-like alternative base that doesn't need rising.

❖ Pizza Toppings ❖

Before the toppings are added, the dough is usually covered with a layer of tomato. This may be homemade tomato sauce, canned crushed tomatoes, canned or bottled purée, or even sliced tomatoes. The golden rule here is to make sure that the tomato mixture isn't too wet or it will make the base soggy. If using homemade tomato sauce ensure it is well reduced and thick; drain excess juice from canned tomatoes. Tomato paste has an intense, almost bitter, flavor and is best avoided. If you don't like tomatoes in any form, brush the dough with a well-flavored olive oil instead.

The sky's the limit when it comes to toppings! All manner of ingredients can be arranged on the tomato base. Uncooked meat and most vegetables need to be cooked first, as they will not cook through sufficiently on the pizza. In addition to the main ingredients, don't forget flavorings such as garlic, herbs, chili flakes, olives, and capers. Try the following suggestions:

VEGETABLE: Almost any vegetable is good on a pizza. Try steamed fresh spinach (or well-drained frozen leaf spinach); grilled, peeled, and sliced bell peppers; sliced canned artichoke hearts; or mushrooms, eggplant, zucchini, or baby onions, cut into chunks or sliced and sautéed in olive oil.

SPICY SAUSAGE: Scatter sliced peperoni, chorizo, chopped salami, or other spicy sausage over the pizza(s) before cooking.

CHEESE: Most firm cheeses with good melting properties are suitable for topping pizzas. Mozzarella is traditional, but try Bel Paese, fontina, Taleggio, Swiss, or Parmesan.

❖ Quick Pizza Dough ❖

MAKES 1 LARGE PIZZA BASE	• 1½ cups flour	• 6–8 tbsp milk
PREPARATION TIME 15 minutes	• ¼ tsp salt	
FREEZING Suitable	• 1 tsp baking powder	
	• 3 tbsp butter or margarine	
	• 1 tbsp olive oil	
	• 1 egg	310 CALS/SERVING

1 In a bowl, stir together the flour, salt, and baking powder. Cut in the butter until the mixture resembles crumbs.
2 Whisk together the olive oil, egg, and milk in a bowl. Make a well in the center of the dry ingredients and add the liquid.
3 Stir the mixture quickly by hand until it forms a soft dough. (Cover if not using immediately – while making up the topping.)
4 Turn the dough onto a well-floured surface and knead about 30 seconds; do not overwork. Place a lightly oiled flat cookie sheet in a preheated 425°F oven to heat.

5 Roll out the dough to a round roughly 10-inches in diameter. Place on the heated baking sheet and press up the edges. Complete and bake with your choice of toppings.

❖ Basic Pizza Dough ❖

MAKES 1 LARGE PIZZA BASE	• 1¼ cups flour	• 1 tbsp olive oil
PREPARATION TIME 1 hour	• ¼ tsp salt	
FREEZING Suitable	• 1 tsp rapid rise dry yeast	
		185 CALS/SERVING

1 In a warm bowl, mix the flour, salt, and yeast. Make a well in the center and add ⅔ cup warm water and the olive oil.

2 Stir the mixture by hand or with a wooden spoon until it forms a wet dough. Beat 2–3 minutes longer.

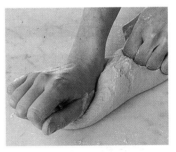

3 Turn the dough onto a well-floured surface and knead until smooth and elastic, about 5 minutes. Place in a bowl, cover, and let rise in a warm place until doubled in size, about 45 minutes.

4 Turn the dough onto a floured surface and knead again for 2–3 minutes. Place a lightly oiled cookie sheet in a preheated 425°F oven to heat.

5 Roll out the dough to a round roughly 10-inches in diameter. Place on the heated baking sheet and press up the edges. The pizza dough is now ready to complete and bake with your choice of toppings.

NOTE: Each of these pizza dough recipes makes a large enough base to serve 4, if the topping is generous.

DESSERTS

Few of us can resist something sweet at the end of a meal. No matter how full we might feel, somehow there always seems to be room for a refreshing fruit sorbet, a feather-light mousse or meringue, or a creamy, fragrant custard. Texture and weight are all-important, so always choose a dessert that balances the rest of the meal. Complement a rich, cream-based main course with a crisp and tangy fruit tart; follow a substantial stew or potpie with an airy soufflé; supplement a light fish dish with a satisfying baked pudding.

At one time season dictated choice, but now ingredients like soft fruits are available virtually all year round (at premium prices), so it is possible to serve strawberries and cream midwinter if you wish. But imported soft fruits tend to lack the flavor of home-produced summer berries, so they are generally best avoided. Instead you can opt for traditional autumn and winter fare like fruit crisps or bread and butter pudding; these old-fashioned favorites are enjoying a revival. But bear in mind that winter puddings don't have to be hearty: there are many lighter alternatives, using seasonal fruits and other readily available ingredients.

Counting Calories

It's the traditional hot puddings that have given desserts a bad name as far as weight watching is concerned. Of course, not all desserts are so fattening, and there are various guidelines you can follow to cut down on calories still further.

In summer, make fruit salads with fresh soft fruits and fragrant exotic fruits; in winter, poach apples and plums and serve as warm compotes. Don't steep the fruit in sugary syrup: instead, use natural fruit juices – preferably homemade, though there are now plenty of commercially prepared varieties to choose from; and try adding extra interest with a vanilla bean, a little minced fresh ginger, or some lemon, lime, or orange rind. Let the fruit macerate in the juice at least an hour before serving, to let the full flavors develop.

As a change from fruit salad, try pears poached in red wine, served warm in winter and chilled in summer. Sweeter but still fruity alternatives include sorbets, mousses, and pies (pastry on top only). Serve these with low-fat cream or plain yogurt.

❖ Adding the Finishing Touches ❖

Attractive presentation can turn a simple dessert into something quite irresistible. A generous dusting of confectioners' sugar transforms pies and pastries, while chocolate curls (shaved with a potato peeler) add texture to mousses and creams. Fresh fruits can be relied on to give a touch of color and interest; strawberries always look good, but for something a little more extravagant try Cape gooseberries (with the papery calyxes peeled back to reveal the gleaming orange berries inside) or tiny, sparkling bundles of seedless grapes, dipped in egg white and sugar.

Don't forget dried fruits either: Dip whole fruits in both dark and white chocolate, to create a spectacular effect. Chopped or sliced nuts are another way to add texture and color: Toast them first under the broiler or in the oven to enhance the flavor.

❖ Some Key Ingredients ❖

Sugar, cream, eggs, fruit, and of course chocolate all play leading roles in the creation of delectable desserts. The one thing all desserts have in common is a varying degree of sweetness.

❖ VANILLA SUGAR: One of those ingredients that's well worth keeping in the cabinet, vanilla sugar can be used to flavor not only custards and ice creams but also meringue and pastry. It adds a subtle sophistication to whatever it touches. Don't buy the overpriced commercially prepared type. Make your own at home by burying a whole vanilla bean in a jar of sugar; leave it about two weeks before using. Whenever vanilla itself is called for, always use a bean or pure vanilla extract in preference to synthetic vanilla flavoring.

❖ CREAM: When choosing cream, look for real fresh cream and not sugar-loaded synthetic substitutes. Don't be misled by some of these products. Although they do contain fewer calories than cream, many are still high in saturated fat, and they don't taste nearly as good as the real thing. So unless you are following a strict calorie-controlled diet it's probably better to use real cream but eat a smaller portion.

❖ CHOCOLATE: Many of the most tempting desserts are based on chocolate. Don't spoil them by using cheap brands with a low chocolate liquor content or, worse still, chocolate-flavored imitations of the real thing. Instead, buy intensely flavored, almost bitter brands with less sugar and more chocolate liquor. Read the labels: Look for at least 50 percent chocolate liquor. Good specialty stores offer expensive imported French and Belgian brands, and it is worth buying these for special chocolate desserts. Otherwise, bittersweet chocolate, with at least 35 percent chocolate liquor, is a good choice.

❖ EGGS: Many classic desserts – including mousses, soufflés, ice creams, and sorbets – are prepared with raw eggs. Others, such as egg custards, are based on lightly cooked eggs. There is a very slight risk of salmonella if raw or undercooked eggs are eaten, which most people choose to ignore. However if you are in the at-risk group (see page 435) you should avoid these desserts just to be on the safe side.

❖ Peach and ❖ Nectarine Croustade

PREPARATION TIME
35 minutes
COOKING TIME
About 30 minutes
FREEZING
Not suitable

- *1 stick (½ cup) butter*
- *5 tbsp sugar*
- *1 egg, beaten*
- *6 tbsp self-rising flour*
- *finely grated rind of 1 orange*
- *6 large sheets of filo pastry*
- *1 ripe peach*
- *2 ripe nectarines*
- *confectioners' sugar, for dusting*

- *¼ cup clear honey*
- *2 tbsp lemon juice*
- *2 tbsp pistachio nuts*
- *a little Armagnac (optional)*

215 CALS/SERVING

1 Cream together half of the butter with the sugar until very light and pale. Gradually beat in the egg. Lightly fold in the flour and orange rind.
2 Melt the remaining butter. Cut nine 10-inch rounds from the filo pastry sheets; keep covered with a damp dish towel. Place one filo round on a large baking sheet and brush lightly with melted butter. Add another two rounds, brushing each with butter. Spread the creamed mixture on the pastry, leaving a 1-inch clear edge.
3 Halve, pit, and thickly slice the fruits. Scatter over the mixture and around the pastry edges. Cover the fruit with three more pastry rounds, brushing with melted butter between each layer.
4 Scrunch up the remaining three rounds and place on top of the pie. Drizzle the remaining butter over the top and dust with confectioners' sugar. Bake in a preheated 400°F oven until the filling is cooked and the pastry is golden brown and crisp, about 30 minutes, covering with foil if necessary to prevent overbrowning.
5 Heat together the honey, lemon juice, and nuts. Spoon over the hot croustade and drizzle with Armagnac, if wished. Serve warm or cold, with cream.

❖ Individual Fruit Tarts ❖

PREPARATION TIME
20 minutes, plus pastry and crème pâtissière
COOKING TIME
20–25 minutes
FREEZING
Not suitable
COLOR INDEX
Page 73

- *double quantity Pâte Sucrée (page 354)*
- *1¼ cups Crème Pâtissière (see page 359)*

APRICOT GLAZE:
- *⅔ cups apricot preserves*
- *1 tbsp Kirsch*

FILLING:
- *selection of seasonal fruits, such as raspberries, strawberries, blueberr figs, grapes, kiwi fruit*

385 CALS/TART

1 Roll out the pastry on a lightly floured surface and cut out ten 5-inch rounds with a plain cutter. Use to line individual 4-inch loose-based fluted tartlet molds. Prick the bases with a fork, then chill 30 minutes.

2 Bake "blind" (see page 328 in a preheated 375°F oven until golden and crisp, about 20 minutes. Let the tartlet shells cool a little in the molds, then carefully remove to a wire rack to cool.

3 To make the apricot glaze, put the preserves and Kirsch in a saucepan with 1 tbsp water and heat gently until melted. Simmer 1 minute, then strain. Brush the inside of each pastry shell evenly with glaze.

4 Spread a generous layer of crème pâtissière in each pastr shell. Arrange the sliced or whole fruit on top.

5 Reheat the remaining apricot glaze, then carefully brush over the fruits to glaze evenly. Serve as soon as possible.

❖ Cream Puffs ❖

3 Beat in the eggs, a little at a time, adding only just enough to give a piping consistency. It is important to beat the mixture vigorously at this stage to incorporate as much air as possible.

4 Put the choux pastry in a pastry bag fitted with a ½-inch plain nozzle. Pipe about 20 small puffs on 2 dampened baking sheets. Alternatively simply spoon the mixture into small mounds.

5 Bake in a preheated 425°F oven until well risen and golden brown, 20–25 minutes. Reduce the oven temperature to 350°F. Make a hole in the side of each puff, then return to the oven for 5 minutes to dry out completely. Let cool on a wire rack.

6 For the chocolate sauce, melt the chocolate, butter, 2 tbsp water, the corn syrup, and vanilla extract in a small saucepan over very low heat. Stir until smooth and well blended.

SERVES 4

PREPARATION TIME
30 minutes
COOKING TIME
20–25 minutes
FREEZING
Suitable (unfilled puffs and sauce separately)

CHOUX PASTRY:
• ½ cup flour
• 4 tbsp butter or margarine
• 2 eggs, lightly beaten
CHOCOLATE SAUCE:
• 4 oz bittersweet chocolate
• 1 tbsp butter or margarine
• 2 tbsp light corn syrup

• 2–3 drops of vanilla extract
TO FINISH:
• ⅔ cup heavy whipping cream or Crème Pâtissière (below)
• confectioners' sugar, for dusting

575 CALS/SERVING

7 Whip the cream until it just holds its shape. Spoon into a pastry bag fitted with a medium nozzle and use to fill the puffs through the hole in the sides. Alternatively simply split the puffs and spoon in the cream. Dust with confectioners' sugar and serve with the chocolate sauce spooned over.

1 To make the choux pastry, sift the flour onto a plate or piece of paper. Put the butter and ⅔ cup water in a saucepan. Heat gently until the butter has melted, then bring to a boil. Remove pan from heat and immediately tip in the flour. Beat thoroughly with a wooden spoon.

2 Continue beating over a low heat until the mixture is smooth and forms a ball in the center of the pan (take care not to overbeat or the mixture will become fatty). Remove from the heat and let cool 1–2 minutes.

CRÈME PÂTISSIÈRE (PASTRY CREAM): Heat 1¼ cups milk with a split vanilla bean almost to a boil; set aside to infuse. Whisk 3 egg yolks and 5 tbsp sugar together in a bowl until pale and thick. Whisk in 2 tbsp each flour and cornstarch. Strain in milk, whisking constantly. Return to pan, bring to a boil, and cook, whisking, until thickened, 2–3 minutes. Pour into a bowl and cool, with a circle of damp wax paper on top to prevent a skin forming. When cool, fold in 1 stiffly beaten egg white.

MERINGUE

The light, crisp texture of meringue is the perfect foil to creamy fillings and soft fruit. Meringue is made with beaten egg whites into which sugar is incorporated.

To make a meringue "suisse," the egg whites must be beaten until they are very stiff and will hold an unwavering peak. The sugar can then be beaten in a little at a time; or part beaten, part folded into the whites.

To make meringue "cuite," the unbeaten egg whites and sugar are put in a bowl, then beaten over a pan of gently simmering water until stiff and thick. As soon as the mixture becomes thick, the bowl should be removed from the heat. This meringue has a smooth texture and wonderful gloss. It also holds its shape well.

❖ Meringue Shells with Grand ❖ Marnier and Chocolate Sauce

SERVES 8

PREPARATION TIME
35 minutes, plus
cooling
COOKING TIME
About 2 hours
FREEZING
Suitable (unfilled
shells and sauce
separately)

MERINGUE:
• 4 egg whites
• 1 cup + 2 tbsp superfine sugar
FILLING AND SAUCE:
• ¾ cup golden raisins, roughly chopped
• 3 tbsp Grand Marnier or Cointreau
• 1¼ cup heavy whipping cream
• 7 oz bittersweet chocolate
• confectioners' sugar, for dusting

485 CALS/SERVING

1 Put the raisins and Grand Marnier in a small bowl, and let soak at least 4 hours. To make the meringue, line 2 baking sheets with parchment paper. Beat the egg whites in a bowl until stiff. Beat in 3 tbsp sugar, keeping the mixture stiff, then fold in the remaining sugar.

2 Spoon the meringue into a pastry bag fitted with a ½-inch plain nozzle and pipe ovals onto the prepared baking sheets, making about 32 meringue shells. Bake in a preheated 200°F oven until the meringues are well dried out, about 2 hours; switch the baking sheets around halfway through the cooking time. Cool on wire racks.

3 About 2 hours before serving, whip all but 3 tbsp of the cream in a bowl until it holds its shape, then fold in the raisins and Grand Marnier Put pairs of meringue shells together with the cream mixture and pile in a serving dish. Grate over a little chocolate and dust with confectioners' sugar. Cover and chill until required.

4 To make the sauce, break the remaining chocolate into a saucepan and add the cream and ⅔ cup water. Warm gently until chocolate melts, stirring occasionally. Simmer gently, stirring frequently, until slightly thickened, about 3 minutes. Serve with the meringues shells.

❖ Brown Sugar and ❖ Hazelnut Meringue Shells

MAKES 18
PREPARATION TIME
30 minutes, plus
cooling
COOKING TIME
2–3 hours
FREEZING
Suitable (unfilled)
COLOR INDEX
Page 74

MERINGUE:
• 3 tbsp hazelnuts
• 3 egg whites
• ¾ cup packed light brown sugar

FILLING:
• 1½ cups ice cream or whipping cream, whipped

110 CALS/MERINGUE

1 Line 2 large baking sheets with parchment paper. Toast the hazelnuts under the broiler until golden brown. Tip onto a clean dish towel and rub off the loose skins. Chop roughly.
2 Beat the egg whites in a bowl until stiff. Beat in the sugar, 1 tbsp at a time. Spoon the meringue mixture into a pastry bag fitted with a large star nozzle and pipe about 36 small swirls on the prepared baking sheets. Sprinkle with the nuts.
3 Bake in a preheated 225°F oven until dry, 2–3 hours; switch the positions of the sheets halfway through cooking. Let cool.
4 Put pairs of meringue shells together with ice cream or whipped cream to serve.

❖ Meringue Basket ❖

SERVES 6-8	MERINGUE:	• 1 lb prepared fresh
PREPARATION TIME	• 4 egg whites	fruit in season, such as
35 minutes, plus	• 2 cups confectioners'	strawberries, rasp-
cooling	sugar, sifted	berries, and blueberries
COOKING TIME	FILLING:	
4–5 hours	• 1¼ cups heavy cream	
FREEZING	• 2 tbsp Kirsch	
Suitable (unfilled)		375–280 CALS/SERVING

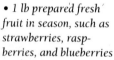

1 Line 3 baking sheets with parchment paper and draw a 7½-inch circle on each. Turn the paper over so that the pencilled circle does not come into contact with the meringue.

2 To make the meringue, place 3 egg whites and 1½ cups of the sugar in a large bowl set over a pan of simmering water. Beat until the mixture stands in stiff peaks; do not let the bowl get too hot or the meringue will crust around the edges.

3 Using a pastry bag fitted with a large star nozzle, pipe rings of meringue inside two of the circles. From the center, pipe a continuous coil of meringue on the third circle, for the base. Bake in a preheated 200°F oven until dry, 2½–3 hours; switch the positions to ensure even cooking.

4 Use the remaining egg white and sugar to make meringue as before. Remove the cooked meringue rings from the paper and layer on the base, piping a ring of fresh meringue between each. Return to the oven to dry 1½–2 hours longer.

5 Let cool, then peel off the base paper. Place on a flat serving plate. To make the filling, lightly whip the cream and fold in the Kirsch. Spoon half into the meringue basket and cover with fruit. Top with the remaining cream and fruit. Serve as soon as possible.

Variation

INDIVIDUAL MERINGUE BASKETS: Prepare the baking sheets as above, but draw eight 4-inch circles on the paper. Make the meringue as above, using 3 egg whites and 1½ cups confectioners' sugar. Pipe a continuous coil of meringue on each circle to make the bases, then pipe a ring on top of each circle. Bake as in step 3 above for 2½ hours to dry out.

❖ Snow Eggs ❖

SERVES 6	• 2 tsp coffee beans	• blackberries, for
PREPARATION TIME	• 3 eggs, separated	decoration (optional)
25 minutes, plus	• ½ cup superfine sugar	
chilling	• 2 cups milk	
COOKING TIME	• 2 oz milk chocolate	
30 minutes	• 2 tbsp Scotch whisky	
FREEZING		
Not suitable		
COLOR INDEX		
Page 74		200 CALS/SERVING

1 Toast the coffee beans under the broiler for a few minutes.
2 To make the meringue, beat the egg whites until stiff but not dry. Add half the sugar and continue beating until the mixture is firm and shiny.
3 Put the milk in a large, deep, frying pan. Bring to a boil, then reduce the heat to a gentle simmer. Drop five or six spoonfuls of the meringue mixture into the milk and poach about 5 minutes, turning once. Remove with a slotted spoon and drain on paper towels. Repeat until all the mixture is used: There should be about 18 meringues.
4 Whisk the egg yolks and remaining sugar into the poaching milk, then add the coffee beans. Stir over very low heat until slightly thickened, 10–12 minutes, making sure it does not boil. Strain the coffee custard into a serving dish and arrange the meringues on top.
5 Melt the chocolate with 1 tbsp water in a heatproof bowl over a pan of hot water until smooth, then stir in the Scotch. Drizzle over the meringues. Chill 15–20 minutes before serving, decorated with blackberries if desired.

CAKES &
COOKIES

There's something wonderfully uplifting about baking a cake, particularly a spectacular layer cake, or a batch of cookies. However health-conscious we may be, few can resist the aroma of a freshly baked cake or tray of cookies. And no matter how hard you try to keep your baked goods, they'll just disappear, and quickly. The following notes should help you to achieve perfect results with your home baking.

❖ Essential Ingredients ❖

The following ingredients are commonly used in baking recipes, in addition to a wide variety of flavorings, including spices, extracts, nuts, dried fruit, and chocolate. Remember to check the use-before dates on these items before use.

❖ FAT: Butter gives a rich flavor and color, which many prefer, but the flavor of margarine has improved enormously in recent years. Shortening, is ideal for all-in-one methods. If you are using butter (or one of the hard margarines) bring it to room temperature first. Alternatively microwave on LOW about 1 minute, but watch carefully – if it melts you'll have to start again.

Avoid using low-fat spreads: Many contain high proportions of water and, although they look like margarine, they do not behave identically during cooking. Oil can be used in suitably proportioned recipes only.

❖ SUGAR AND SWEETENERS: Sugar is needed for texture and volume as well as flavor. Granulated sugar is generally the best choice since it has small regular granules that dissolve easily. Superfine sugar, with its finer granules, is the one to use for the more delicate sponge cakes. Confectioners' sugar can also be used, but it is unsuitable for butter cakes and others made with an initial creaming stage. Other sugars lend a particular effect: raw brown makes a delicious crunchy topping, while dark brown sugar imparts a rich color and distinctive flavor. Corn syrup, honey, and molasses are generally added for flavour only and are used in addition to sugar. Sugar substitutes and artificial sweeteners cannot be substituted for sugar in cakes.

❖ EGGS: Avoid using eggs straight from the refrigerator – a cake batter is much more likely to curdle if it's made with cold eggs. Eggs act as a leavening agent in many cakes so it's important to select the right size – use extra large eggs in these recipes unless otherwise stated. Using the wrong size could result in failure.

❖ FLOUR: Self-rising flour is used in some cake recipes as it conveniently includes a leavening agent. All-purpose flour can be converted to self-rising, by blending it with baking powder. Cake flour is widely available; its lower gluten content and high starch make it eminently suitable for cake-making. The results are very tender and crumbly. Ideally you should use the type of flour specified in a recipe, but if you have no cake flour you can substitute all-purpose by replacing 2 tbsp of the flour quantity with cornstarch.

Whole wheat flour is nutritionally preferred to white flour but produces cakes with a darker color and denser texture. If you wish to use whole wheat flour, a mixture of white and whole wheat with a little extra baking powder works best. If you sift it don't forget to tip in the bran from the sifter or valuable fiber and nutrients will be wasted.

❖ Cake-Making Methods ❖

The following standard mixing methods employ different techniques that largely determine the texture of the cake. Some recipes use more than one method – for example, creamed cakes sometimes have beaten egg whites folded in.

❖ CREAMING: This is the traditional method used to make a butter cake. Softened fat makes creaming considerably easier, as does an electric mixer. As soon as the fat and sugar are creamed to a pale-colored mixture, fluffy and light in texture, you can start adding the beaten egg. Don't be tempted to add it all at once or the mixture will curdle, producing a dense cake. If the mixture looks as if it is about to curdle, add a spoonful of the sifted flour. Finally fold in all of the flour with a large metal spoon.

❖ ALL-IN-ONE: For speedy last-minute cakes, this is the ideal method. Simply throw all the ingredients together in a bowl and beat thoroughly. If using a food processor, don't over-process or you will beat out all the air. Softened butter or margarine or shortening are the best fats to use. It's prudent to add a little extra leavening agent to compensate for the lack of creaming.

❖ WHISKING: This is the method used to produce the classic fat-less sponge. Because the cake relies on the volume of air trapped in the egg mixture to make it rise, the eggs must be beaten really thoroughly. This is virtually impossible unless you use an electric mixer or a good rotary egg beater plus strong arms and a lot of patience! Setting the bowl over a pan of simmering water helps to increase volume and stabilize the foamy mass. (This isn't necessary if you use a heavy-duty mixer.) Keep the base of the bowl clear of the water or you will end up with scrambled eggs! The whisked mixture is ready for the flour when you can lift the beaters and write the numeral 8 on the surface with the trail of mixture.

A Genoese sponge is a whisked sponge that's enriched with melted butter. It is probably the most difficult of all cakes to perfect, but well worth the effort since it is rich yet light, and keeps much better than a fatless sponge. The tricky part is getting the butter to the correct consistency – it should be melted but cooled until almost cold. Add the butter gradually by pouring a small amount around the edge of the bowl. Fold this in and then add a little more, but take your time.

❖ MELTING: Cakes made by this method usually contain a high proportion of syrup, honey, or molasses and it is vital that they are measured accurately; if you add too much the cake will be dense and it will probably sink in the middle. If the measurements are given in tablespoons, use a warmed measuring spoon, preferably metal.

This measured syrup is then heated gently with fat and sugar until melted; cool slightly before mixing with the dried ingredients. The mixture should have the consistency of a thick batter; it should find its own level when poured into the pan. For best results wrap these cakes in wax paper, then overwrap with foil and store 1–2 days before cutting.

❖ CUTTING IN: As the name suggests these cakes are made in the same way as basic piecrust, by cutting the fat into the flour. Once you have cut in the fat, add the liquid carefully – too much will result in a heavy doughy cake, while too little will make it dry. Remember that flour absorbencies vary; use the recipe as a fairly accurate guide but don't be afraid to add a little more or a little less. In general, for large cakes the mixture should be soft enough to drop from a spoon. Because cut in cakes are comparatively low in fat they stale quickly and are best eaten on the day of making.

Cake Pans

Using the correct size pan can make all the difference between success and failure. It goes without saying that if you put a cake batter in a pan that's too big you will end up with a pancake and if the pan is too small the batter will spill out over the top. Because pans come in a confusing array of sizes – particularly loaf pans – a volume measurement is sometimes given as well. To check the capacity of a pan, simply fill with water from a measure, noting how much it will hold.

Grease pans and line the bottoms with lightly greased wax paper, or parchment paper (this does not require greasing). We advise doing this even when using nonstick cake pans, to ease unmolding. For rich mixtures and fruit cakes, line the sides of the pan, too. For large rich fruit cakes, stand the pan on a double thickness of brown paper and tie a band of brown paper around the outside of the pan to prevent the outside overcooking.

What Went Wrong?

Unfortunately it's not always easy to determine why a cake hasn't come out looking like the picture. It is important to measure everything accurately – using standard cups and spoons – and to use the right size pan. Once the cake is in the oven resist the temptation to open the door until at least three-quarters of the cooking time has elapsed – a sudden gush of cold air will make it sink in the middle. If your cake appears to be browning too quickly cover it with wax paper toward the end of cooking. Here are some other common problems and possible causes:

CLOSE, DENSE TEXTURE
❖ Too much liquid.
❖ Too little leavening agent, or leavening agent past its use-before date.
❖ Insufficient creaming of the fat and sugar.
❖ Creamed mixture curdled.
❖ Flour folded in too vigorously.

PEAKED AND CRACKED TOP
❖ Oven too hot, or the cake was too near the top of the oven.
❖ Not enough liquid.
❖ Pan too small.

SUNKEN FRUIT
❖ Fruit too sticky or too wet.
❖ Batter too soft to support the weight of the fruit.

SUNK IN THE MIDDLE
❖ Wrong size pan.
❖ Inaccurately measured ingredients (gingerbread in particular).
❖ Oven too hot or too cool, or cooking time too short.
❖ Oven door opened too soon.

Storing Cakes

Make sure that the cake is completely cold before you put it into a cake tin or plastic airtight container. If you don't have a large enough container, wrap in a double layer of wax paper and overwrap with foil. Avoid putting rich fruit cakes in direct contact with foil; the fruit may react with it. Most cakes freeze well; they are best frozen undecorated. If you want to freeze a decorated cake, open freeze, then pack in a rigid container.

❖ Cookies and Biscuits ❖

Cookies are quick and easy to make, taste much better than many commercial varieties, and they're cheaper too! Exaggerate the fact that they are homemade by using interesting or quirky cutters; you'll find a wide range in most cookshops. Don't be alarmed if the cookies seem soft when you have baked them; some, particularly those containing syrup or honey, crisp as they cool. Homemade cookies freeze well and thaw in a matter of minutes, so it's a good idea to make double quantities and freeze some.

Homemade biscuits are delicious served warm from the oven. To ensure a good rise, avoid heavy handling, or rolling the dough too thinly: it should be at least ¾-inch thick. Remember too that the leavening agent begins to work as soon as it is mixed with liquid, so put the biscuits into a hot oven as quickly as possible.

❖ Peanut and Raisin Cookies ❖

MAKES 30	• 1 stick (½ cup) butter	• ½ cup crunchy peanut
PREPARATION TIME	or margarine, softened	butter
15 minutes	• ¾ cup sugar	• 1 cup raisins
COOKING TIME	• 1 egg	
15 minutes	• 1 cup flour	
FREEZING	• ½ tsp baking powder	
Suitable	• pinch of salt	

110 CALS/COOKIE

1 Put all the ingredients except the raisins in a bowl and beat together until well blended. Stir in the raisins.
2 Spoon large teaspoonfuls of the dough onto lightly greased cookie sheets, leaving room for spreading.
3 Bake in a preheated 375°F oven until golden brown around the edges, about 15 minutes. Let cool slightly before lifting onto a wire rack to cool completely.

Variations

CHOCOLATE CHIP-NUT COOKIES: Omit the peanut butter and raisins and add 1 tsp vanilla extract. Stir in ¾ cup chocolate chips and ¾ cup roughly chopped walnuts.

COCONUT AND CHERRY COOKIES: Omit the peanut butter and raisins, reduce the sugar to ½ cup and stir in ½ cup dried shredded coconut and ⅔ cup rinsed, dried, and roughly chopped candied cherries.

OAT AND CINNAMON COOKIES: Omit the peanut butter and raisins and add 1 tsp vanilla extract. Stir in 1 tsp ground cinnamon and 1 cup rolled oats.

❖ Inverness Gingersnaps ❖

MAKES 36	• 1⅔ cups flour	• ½ cup molasses
PREPARATION TIME	• 2 tsp ground ginger	• 4 tbsp butter
20 minutes	• 1 tsp apple pie spice	
COOKING TIME	• 1 cup rolled oats, finely	
20–25 minutes	ground in a food	
FREEZING	processor	
Suitable	• ½ cup sugar	
COLOR INDEX	• ½ tsp baking soda	
Page 78		

75 CALS/COOKIE

1 Put the flour, ginger, spice, ground oats, sugar, and baking soda in a bowl and mix together.
2 Heat the molasses and butter in a pan until melted. Pour onto the dry ingredients and mix to a smooth dough. Knead well.
3 Roll out to about a ¼-inch thickness. Prick with a fork and cut out 2½-inch rounds with a plain cutter. Place on greased cookie sheets. Bake in a preheated 325°F oven until firm to the touch, 20–25 minutes. Transfer to wire racks to cool.

❖ Caraway Cookies ❖

MAKES 24	• 1⅔ cups flour	• caraway seeds, for
PREPARATION TIME	• 6 tbsp butter, diced	sprinkling
20 minutes	• ½ cup sugar	
COOKING TIME	• 1 egg, beaten	
10 minutes	• 1 egg white, beaten, to	
FREEZING	glaze	
Suitable		
COLOR INDEX		
Page 78		

70 CALS/COOKIE

1 Sift the flour into a bowl and cut in the butter until the mixture resembles crumbs. Stir in the sugar. Add the egg and mix to a stiff paste.
2 Roll out on a lightly floured surface, until ¼-inch thick. Prick with a fork and cut into rounds with a 2-inch plain cutter. Brush with egg white and sprinkle on a few caraway seeds.
3 Place on greased cookie sheets. Bake in a preheated 350°F oven until lightly browned, about 10 minutes. Cool on wire racks.

❖ Shrewsbury Biscuits ❖

MAKES 24	• 1 stick (½ cup) butter	• finely grated rind of
PREPARATION TIME	or hard margarine	1 lemon or orange
20 minutes	• ¾ cup sugar	• ⅓ cup chopped dried
COOKING TIME	• 2 egg yolks	fruit (optional)
15 minutes	• 1⅔ cups flour	
FREEZING		
Suitable		
COLOR INDEX		
Page 78		

100 CALS/COOKIE

1 Cream the butter and sugar together in a bowl until pale and fluffy. Add the egg yolks and beat well. Stir in the flour, grated lemon rind, and dried fruit if using. Mix to a fairly firm dough with a round-bladed knife.
2 Turn onto a lightly floured surface and knead lightly. Roll out to a ¼-inch thickness and cut out rounds with a 2½-inch fluted cutter. Place on lightly greased cookie sheets.
3 Bake in a preheated 350°F oven until golden, about 15 minutes.

❖ Coconut Macaroons ❖

MAKES 24	
PREPARATION TIME	• 2 egg whites
20 minutes	• 1 cup confectioners'
COOKING TIME	sugar, sifted
25 minutes	• 1⅓ cups ground
FREEZING	almonds
Suitable	• few drops of almond
	extract

• 1 cup dried shredded coconut

`70 CALS/COOKIE`

1 Line 2 cookie sheets with parchment paper. Beat the egg whites in a bowl until stiff but not dry. Lightly fold in the sugar.

2 Gently stir in the ground almonds, almond extract and all but 2 tbsp of the coconut until the mixture forms a sticky dough.

3 Spoon walnut-sized pieces of dough onto the lined cookie sheets. Press a few strands of coconut on the top of each one.

4 Bake in a preheated 300°F oven until the outer crust is golden and the inside soft, about 25 minutes. Cool on a wire rack.

❖ Easter Cookies ❖

MAKES 30	
PREPARATION TIME	• 1 stick (½ cup) butter
20 minutes	• ½ cup sugar
COOKING TIME	• 1 egg, separated
15 minutes	• 1½ cups flour
FREEZING	• pinch of salt
Suitable	• ½ tsp apple pie spice
COLOR INDEX	• ½ tsp ground cinnamon
Page 78	• ⅓ cup currants
	• 1 tbsp chopped mixed
	candied peel

• 1–2 tbsp brandy or milk
• sugar, for sprinkling

`65 CALS/COOKIE`

1 Cream the butter and sugar together in a bowl until pale and fluffy, then beat in the egg yolk. Sift the flour, salt, and spices together over the mixture. Stir well, then add the fruit and mixed peel, with enough brandy or milk to give a fairly soft dough.
2 Knead lightly on a lightly floured surface and roll out to a ¼-inch thickness. Cut into 2-inch rounds using a fluted cutter. Place on lightly greased cookie sheets.
3 Bake in a preheated 400°F oven 10 minutes, then brush with the lightly beaten egg white and sprinkle with a little sugar. Return to the oven and bake until golden brown, about 5 minutes longer. Transfer to wire racks to cool.

❖ Shortbread ❖

MAKES 8	
PREPARATION TIME	• 1 cup flour
20 minutes	• 3 tbsp ground rice
COOKING TIME	• ⅓ cup sugar
About 40 minutes	• 1 stick (½ cup) butter,
FREEZING	at room temperature
Suitable	• sugar, for dredging
COLOR INDEX	
Page 79	

`200 CALS/PIECE`

1 Sift the flour and ground rice into a bowl and add the sugar. Work in the butter with your fingertips – keep it in one piece and gradually work in the dry ingredients. Knead well.
2 Pack into a floured shortbread mold, then unmold on to a baking sheet. Alternatively, pack into a 7-inch layer cake pan, prick well with a fork, and pinch up the edges decoratively with finger and thumb.
3 Bake in a preheated 325°F oven until firm and pale golden, about 40 minutes. Mark into 8 triangles while still hot. Cool slightly before transferring to a wire rack.
4 When cool, dredge with sugar. Serve cut in wedges.

NOTE: Traditional Scottish shortbread molds are made with a thistle design in the center. These can be bought at specialty food stores, but are not essential; an ordinary cake pan will do the job just as well. Be sure to use a good-quality butter. The flavor of shortbread relies heavily on the butter in the mixture, and margarine is no substitute.

❖ Florentines ❖

MAKES 20–24

PREPARATION TIME
30 minutes, plus
cooling
COOKING TIME
10 minutes
FREEZING
Suitable (stage 3)

- *7 tbsp butter or margarine*
- *⅔ cup sugar*
- *1⅓ cups sliced almonds, roughly chopped*
- *3 tbsp golden raisins*
- *5 candied cherries, chopped*
- *3 tbsp chopped mixed candied peel*
- *1 tbsp light whipping cream*
- *8 oz semisweet or white chocolate, in pieces*

`165–140 CALS/COOKIE`

1 Line 3 baking sheets with parchment paper. Melt the butter in a saucepan over low heat. Add the sugar and heat gently until dissolved, then boil 1 minute. Remove from the heat and add the remaining ingredients, except the chocolate, stirring well to mix.

2 Drop the mixture in small, well-rounded heaps on the prepared baking sheets, leaving enough room between each for the mixture to spread. Bake in a preheated 350°F oven until golden brown, about 10 minutes.

3 Remove from the oven and press around the edges of the cookies with the blade of a knife to neaten the shape. Leave on the baking sheets for 5 minutes until beginning to firm, then lift on to a wire rack. Cool 20 minutes.

4 Melt the chocolate in a heatproof bowl over a pan of simmering water. Stir until smooth, then let cool until beginning to set, 10–15 minutes. Spread over the back of the cookies and mark wavy lines with a fork. Leave to set.

❖ Gingerbread Men ❖

MAKES 10–12

PREPARATION TIME
20 minutes
COOKING TIME
12–15 minutes
FREEZING
Suitable
COLOR INDEX
Page 79

- *2½ cups flour*
- *1 tsp baking soda*
- *2 tsp ground ginger*
- *1 stick (½ cup) butter or hard margarine*
- *¾ cup light brown sugar*
- *¼ cup light molasses syrup*
- *1 egg, beaten*
- *currants, to decorate*

`300–250 CALS/COOKIE`

1 Sift the flour, baking soda, and ginger into a bowl. Cut in the butter until mixture resembles fine crumbs. Stir in the sugar. Beat the molasses with the egg, then stir in.

2 Mix to form a dough and knead until smooth. Divide in half and roll out each piece on a lightly floured surface to a ¼-inch thickness.

3 Using suitable cutters, cut out gingerbread figures and place them on lightly greased baking sheets. Decorate with currants to represent eyes and buttons. Bake in a preheated 375°F oven until golden, 12–15 minutes. Cool slightly, then transfer to a wire rack to cool completely.

❖ Brandy Snaps ❖

4 Bake in a preheated 375°F oven until the brandy snaps have spread considerably and are golden brown, 8–10 minutes. The texture will be open and lacy. Remove from oven and let firm up slightly, about 15 seconds only. Loosen with a metal spatula and roll them around the spoon handles.

5 Place on a wire rack and leave until set, then twist gently to remove and let cool completely and crisp up. Just before serving, fill with whipped cream, if desired, using a pastry bag fitted with ½-inch fluted tube.

NOTE: If the cookies set too hard to roll while on the baking sheet, return to the oven for a few moments to soften.

Variations

LACY TUILES: Instead of using wooden spoon handles, curve the brandy snap rounds over a lightly oiled large rolling pin. These cookies take their name from the French *tuile*, meaning roof tile, which they resemble.

LACY PETALS: Let the cookies cool on the baking sheets until beginning to set, then carefully lift off and pinch 2 edges together to form a point. The cookies will then resemble petals.

MAKES 12–16	• 6 tbsp butter or hard margarine	TO SERVE:
PREPARATION TIME 25 minutes	• ½ cup sugar	• ⅔ cup heavy whipping cream, whipped (optional)
COOKING TIME 8–10 minutes	• 3 tbsp dark corn syrup	
FREEZING Suitable (unfilled)	• 9 tbsp flour	
	• 1 tsp ground ginger	
	• 2 tbsp brandy	
	• 1 tbsp lemon juice	

165–125 CALS/COOKIE

1 Lightly oil the handles of several wooden spoons and line 2–3 baking sheets with parchment paper.

2 Place the butter, sugar, and corn syrup in a heavy-based pan and warm gently until evenly blended. Let cool 2–3 minutes. Stir in the flour and ginger sifted together, the brandy, and lemon juice.

3 Taking 1 tbsp of batter at a time, spoon onto the lined baking sheets, leaving plenty of room for spreading. There is no need to flatten the batter: It will spread itself.

❖ Pistachio Rings ❖

MAKES 20	• 1½ sticks (¾ cup) butter, softened	• ⅓ cup skinned and chopped pistachio nuts
PREPARATION TIME 30 minutes	• ⅓ cup sugar	
COOKING TIME 8–10 minutes	• 1⅔ cups flour, sifted	
FREEZING Suitable (undecorated)	• 1 tbsp milk	
COLOR INDEX Page 79	SUGAR ICING:	
	• 1 cup confectioners' sugar, sifted	
	• 1–2 tbsp fresh lime juice	

150 CALS/COOKIE

1 Cream the butter and sugar together until light and creamy. Add the flour and milk and mix to form a fairly soft dough. Put the mixture into a pastry bag fitted with a ½-inch star tube.

2 Pipe the cookie dough into 2¼-inch diameter rings, spaced well apart, on greased baking sheets. Bake in a preheated 350°F oven until lightly golden and cooked through, 8–10 minutes.

3 Transfer the cookies to wire racks to cool slightly. Meanwhile, blend the confectioners' sugar with enough lime juice to make a thin icing. Brush the icing over the rings while still warm, to glaze.

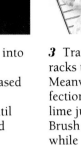

4 Sprinkle at once with chopped nuts. Leave to set before serving.

4 Spread the chocolate and nut spread evenly over the base in the pan. Cover with the cake batter. Bake in a preheated 350°F oven until golden, 45–50 minutes, covering loosely with foil if necessary.

5 Leave in the pan about 10 minutes before unmolding onto a wire rack to cool. Cut into bars and store in an airtight container up to 2 days.

❖ Fruit and Nut Bars ❖

❖ Chocolate-Pecan Bars ❖

MAKES 25	BASE:	• ¾ cup milk chocolate
PREPARATION TIME	• ¾ cup flour	chips
15 minutes	• ¼ cup confectioners'	• ¾ cup pecan halves
COOKING TIME	sugar	TO ASSEMBLE:
About 1 hour	• 5 tbsp butter, in pieces	• 6 tbsp chocolate and nut
FREEZING	• 1 egg yolk	spread
Suitable	CAKE:	
COLOR INDEX	• ¾ cup self-rising flour	
Page 80	• 1 tsp baking powder	
	• ⅔ cup sugar	
	• 3–4 drops of vanilla	
	extract	
	• 2 eggs	
	• 10 tbsp butter, softened	**200 CALS/BAR**

1 Grease and bottom-line a 1½-inch deep baking pan measuring 10¼ × 6½ inches.

2 To make the base, put the flour, confectioners' sugar, and butter in a food processor and work the mixture until crumblike in texture. Add the egg yolk and blend until the mixture begins to come together, 10–15 seconds. Turn into the pan and press into a thin layer. Bake in a preheated 400°F oven until golden, about 15 minutes.

3 Meanwhile, prepare the cake batter. Put the flour, baking powder, sugar, vanilla, eggs, and butter in the food processor and blend until smooth, about 15 seconds. Turn into a bowl and fold in the chocolate chips and pecans.

MAKES 12	• 1 lb apples	• ⅔ cup self-rising whole
PREPARATION TIME	• ⅓ cup unsweetened	wheat flour
20 minutes	fruit juice	• ¼ cup dried shredded
COOKING TIME	• 8 oz mixed dried fruit,	coconut
About 40 minutes	such as no-soak dried	• ⅓ cup pumpkin seeds
FREEZING	apricots, dates, golden	• 2 tbsp oil
Not suitable	raisins, chopped if	• 2 tbsp pear and apple
	necessary	spread, or apricot
	• 1 cup chopped mixed	preserves
	nuts	
	• 1 cup rolled oats	**235 CALS/BAR**

1 Grease and bottom-line an 8-inch square pan. Peel, core, and chop the apples and place in a heavy-based saucepan with the fruit juice. Cover and cook gently until the apples are very soft, 10–15 minutes, shaking the pan occasionally (don't remove the lid). Beat thoroughly to make a smooth purée.

2 Add all the remaining ingredients except the spread or preserves, and beat well. Spoon the mixture into the prepared pan. Bake in a preheated 350°F oven until firm to the touch, about 40 minutes.

3 Let cool in the pan 5 minutes, then unmold onto a wire rack. Brush with the spread or preserve while still warm and mark into 12 bars. Let cool, then cut into bars.

❖ Vanilla Streusel Bars ❖

MAKES 25

PREPARATION TIME
15 minutes
COOKING TIME
50–55 minutes
FREEZING
Suitable

STREUSEL TOPPING:
• 6 tbsp butter, softened
• ½ cup sugar
• ¾ cup flour

CAKE BATTER:
• 1½ sticks (¾ cup) butter
• 1 cup sugar
• 1¼ cups self-rising flour

• finely grated rind of 1 lemon
• 3 eggs
• 1½ tsp vanilla extract

160 CALS/BAR

1 Grease and bottom-line a 1½-inch deep baking pan, measuring 10¼ × 6½ inches.
2 To make the streusel topping, put the butter and sugar in a food processor and blend until smooth. Add the flour and blend to a very rough crumb mixture, 8–10 seconds; remove and set aside.
3 To make the cake batter, place the butter, sugar, self-rising flour, grated lemon rind, eggs, and vanilla extract in the food processor and blend until smooth, about 15 seconds. Pour into the prepared pan.
4 Sprinkle the streusel topping over the surface of the batter to cover and press down lightly.
5 Bake in a preheated 350°F oven for 50–55 minutes, covering loosely with foil if necessary. Let cool in the pan 5 minutes before turning out onto a wire rack to cool completely. Cut into bars. Store in an airtight container up to 3 days.

Cherry and Coconut Streusel Bars
Make the batter as above, adding ½ cup dried shredded coconut at the end of stage 2. Fold in 1⅓ cups rinsed, dried, and quartered candied cherries at the end of stage 3. Cook as above.

❖ Lemon and Almond Bars ❖

MAKES 25

PREPARATION TIME
15 minutes
COOKING TIME
About 1 hour
FREEZING
Suitable
COLOR INDEX
Page 80

BASE:
• ¾ cup flour
• ¼ cup confectioners' sugar
• 5 tbsp butter, in pieces
• 1 egg yolk

CAKE BATTER:
• ¾ cup self-rising flour
• 1 tsp baking powder
• ½ tsp ground nutmeg
• ⅔ cup sugar
• ¼ tsp almond extract
• 2 eggs
• 10 tbsp butter, softened
• 1½ cups sliced almonds

TO ASSEMBLE:
• ⅓ cup lemon curd or fruit butter
• confectioners'g sugar, for dusting

170 CALS/BAR

1 Grease and bottom-line a 1½-inch deep baking pan, measuring 10¼ × 6½ inches.
2 To make the base, put the flour, confectioners' sugar, and butter in a food processor and blend until crumblike in texture. Add the egg yolk and blend until the mixture begins to come together, 10–15 seconds. Turn into the prepared pan and press into a thin layer. Bake in a preheated 400°F oven until golden, about 15 minutes.
3 Meanwhile, prepare the cake batter. Put the flour, baking powder, nutmeg, sugar, almond extract, eggs, and butter in the food processor and blend until smooth, about 15 seconds. Turn into a bowl and fold in two-thirds of the sliced almonds; set aside.
4 Spread the lemon curd evenly over the base in the pan. Cover with the cake batter and sprinkle with the remaining almonds. Bake in a preheated 350°F oven until golden, 45–50 minutes, covering loosely with foil if necessary.
5 Let cool in the pan for about 10 minutes before turning out onto a wire rack to cool completely. Cut into bars and store in an airtight container up to 2 days. Dust with confectioners' sugar to serve.

Date and Banana Bars
Omit the lemon curd, almond extract, and almonds. Instead, place 1 cup chopped dates in a small saucepan with the grated rind and juice of 1 lemon and 2 tbsp water. Simmer very gently until tender, about 4 minutes; there should be very little liquid left. Let cool slightly. Blend 1 roughly chopped banana with the batter in step 3. Fold in the date mixture. Finish as above, omitting the confectioners' sugar.

❖ Chocolate Brownies ❖

MAKES 24
PREPARATION TIME
20 minutes
COOKING TIME
40–45 minutes
FREEZING
Suitable

- 1¼ lb semisweet chocolate
- 2 sticks (1 cup) butter
- 3 eggs
- 2 tbsp freshly made strong coffee
- 1 cup + 2 tbsp sugar
- ½ cup self-rising flour
- ¼ tsp salt
- 1½ cups walnut halves, chopped
- 1 tsp vanilla extract

300 CALS/CAKE

1 Grease and line a baking pan measuring 8½ × 11½ inches across the top and 7½ × 10½ inches across the base. (Or use a similar-sized pan.)

2 Using a sharp knife, roughly chop 8 oz of the chocolate and set aside. Melt the remaining chocolate with the butter in a heatproof bowl over a pan of simmering water. Let cool slightly.

3 Mix the eggs, coffee, and sugar together in a large bowl until smooth, then gradually beat in the melted chocolate mixture. Fold in the flour, salt, walnuts, vanilla extract, and chopped chocolate.

4 Pour into the prepared pan and bake in a preheated 375°F oven until just firm to the touch in the center, 40–45 minutes. Let cool in the pan, then turn out. Trim off the edges and cut into squares.

NOTE: Do not overcook or the fudgy texture will be ruined.

❖ Madeleines ❖

MAKES 24
PREPARATION TIME
20 minutes
COOKING TIME
12 minutes
FREEZING
Suitable
COLOR INDEX
Page 79

- 3 eggs
- ¾ cup sugar
- 1 cup cake flour
- ½ tsp baking powder
- pinch of salt
- finely grated rind of 1 lemon
- 10 tbsp butter, melted and cooled
- confectioners' sugar, for dusting

120 CALS/CAKE

1 Grease two trays of Madeleine molds with shortening, then dust with flour, shaking out any excess.
2 Beat the eggs and sugar together in a bowl until pale and creamy. Sift in the flour with the baking powder and salt. Add the lemon rind and beat well. Pour in the melted butter and fold in until blended.
3 Half-fill the Madeleine molds with the batter and let stand 10 minutes. Bake in a preheated 425°F oven until well risen and golden, about 12 minutes. Ease out of the pans and cool on a wire rack. Serve dusted with confectioners' sugar.

NOTE: If you have only 1 Madeleine tray, bake in 2 batches.

❖ Queen Cakes ❖

MAKES 16
PREPARATION TIME
15 minutes
COOKING TIME
15–20 minutes
FREEZING
Suitable
COLOR INDEX
Page 79

- 1 stick (½ cup) butter
- ⅔ cup sugar
- 2 eggs, beaten
- ¾ cup self-rising flour
- ⅓ cup golden raisins

110 CALS/CAKE

1 Put 16 paper cupcake cases into a tray of muffin pans.
2 Cream the butter and sugar together until pale and fluffy. Gradually beat in the eggs, a little at a time, beating well after each addition. Fold in the flour, then the fruit.
3 Half-fill the paper cases. Bake in a preheated 375°F oven until golden, 15–20 minutes. Transfer to a wire rack to cool.

Variations
Replace the raisins with: ⅓ cup chopped dates; ⅓ cup chopped candied cherries; or ¼ cup chocolate chips.
FAIRY CAKES: Omit the raisins. Frost the cakes with Glacé Icing (page 410).

❖ Marbled Chocolate Loaf ❖

14 SLICES

PREPARATION TIME
20 minutes
COOKING TIME
1¼–1½ hours
FREEZING
Suitable
COLOR INDEX
Page 81

- 2 sticks (1 cup) butter or margarine
- 1 cup + 2 tbsp sugar
- 3 eggs, beaten
- ¾ cup self-rising white flour
- finely grated rind of 1 large orange
- 2 tbsp orange juice
- few drops of orange flower water (optional)
- 3 oz semisweet chocolate
- 1 tbsp unsweetened cocoa powder
- ¾ cup self-rising whole wheat flour
- 1 tbsp milk

290 CALS/SLICE

1 Grease a 5-cup capacity loaf pan and line the bottom and sides with wax paper.

2 Cream the fat and sugar together in a bowl until pale and fluffy, then gradually beat in the eggs, beating well after each addition.

3 Transfer half of the mixture to another bowl and beat in the white flour, orange rind, juice, and orange flower water, if using.

4 Break the chocolate into pieces, put into a small bowl, and set over a pan of simmering water. Stir until the chocolate melts. Stir into the remaining cake mixture with the cocoa powder, whole wheat flour, and milk.

5 Put alternate spoonfuls of the two batters in the prepared pan. Use a knife to swirl through the batters to make a marbled effect, then level the surface. Bake in a preheated 350°F oven until well risen and firm to the touch, 1¼–1½ hours. Unmold onto a wire rack to cool.

❖ Layered Butter Cake ❖

8 SLICES

PREPARATION TIME
20 minutes
COOKING TIME
20 minutes
FREEZING
Suitable (unfilled)

- 1½ sticks (¾ cup) butter or margarine, softened
- 1 cup sugar
- 3 eggs, beaten
- 1¼ cups self-rising cake flour

TO FINISH:
- ¼ cup fruit preserves
- sugar, for dredging

370 CALS/SERVING

1 Grease and bottom-line two 7-inch layer cake pans. Beat the butter and sugar together until pale and fluffy.

2 Add the eggs, a little at a time, beating well after each addition.

3 Fold in half the flour using a metal spoon, then fold in the rest.

4 Divide evenly between the pans and level the surface. Bake in a preheated 375°F oven until well risen, firm to touch, and beginning to shrink from sides of pans, about 20 minutes.

5 Unmold onto a wire rack and let cool. When the cakes are cool, put them together with the preserves and sprinkle the top with sugar.

Variations

CHOCOLATE: Replace 3 tbsp flour with unsweetened cocoa powder. Layer the cakes with Chocolate Butter Frosting (page 410).

COFFEE: Add 2 tsp instant coffee powder, dissolved in a little warm water, to the creamed butter and sugar mixture with the eggs, or use 2 tsp coffee extract. Layer the cakes with Coffee Butter Frosting (page 410).

ORANGE OR LEMON: Add the finely grated rind of an orange or lemon to the batter. Layer the cakes with Orange or Lemon Butter Frosting (page 410).

ONE-BOWL CAKE: Add 1 tsp baking powder to the basic recipe. Simply put all the ingredients in a large bowl or food processor and beat until smooth and glossy.

❖ Orange and Poppy Seed Cake ❖

12 SLICES

PREPARATION TIME
10 minutes
COOKING TIME
50–55 minutes
FREEZING
Suitable (without icing)
COLOR INDEX
Page 81

- 2 sticks (1 cup) butter or margarine
- 1 cup sugar
- 3 eggs
- 1½ cups self-rising whole wheat flour
- 1 tsp baking powder
- pinch of salt
- finely grated rind and juice of 2 oranges
- ⅓ cup poppy seeds

TOPPING:
- ¾ cup confectioners' sugar
- 2–3 tsp orange juice
- shredded orange rind, to decorate

335 CALS/SLICE

1 Grease and line a 1½-quart capacity loaf pan. Put all the cake ingredients except the poppy seeds in a food processor and process until smooth and well mixed. Fold in the poppy seeds.
2 Spoon the batter into the prepared pan and level the surface. Bake in a preheated 350°F oven until well risen and firm to the touch, 50–55 minutes. Unmold onto a wire rack to cool.
3 For the topping, mix the confectioners' sugar with enough orange juice to form a smooth coating consistency. Spread over the top of the cake and decorate with orange rind shreds.

❖ Pound Cake ❖

12 SLICES

PREPARATION TIME
20 minutes
COOKING TIME
About 1 hour
FREEZING
Suitable
COLOR INDEX
Page 81

- ¾ cup flour
- ¾ cup self-rising flour
- 1½ sticks (¾ cup) butter or hard margarine, softened
- 1 cup sugar
- 1 tsp vanilla extract
- 3 eggs, beaten
- 1–2 tbsp milk (optional)
- 2–3 thin slices citron peel

245 CALS/SLICE

1 Grease and line a deep 7-inch round cake pan. Sift the flours together.
2 Cream the butter and sugar together in a bowl until pale and fluffy, then beat in the vanilla extract. Add the eggs, a little at a time, beating well after each addition.
3 Fold in the sifted flours with a metal spoon, adding a little milk if necessary to give a soft consistency.
4 Spoon the batter into the pan and level the surface. Bake in a preheated 350°F oven for 20 minutes. Lay the citron peel on top of the cake and bake until firm, 40 minutes longer. Unmold onto a wire rack to cool.

❖ Honey Cake ❖

12–16 SLICES

PREPARATION TIME
20 minutes
COOKING TIME
1¼ hours
FREEZING
Suitable
COLOR INDEX
Page 81

- 1 cup thin honey
- 6 tbsp butter
- 1½ cups whole wheat flour
- pinch of salt
- 1 tsp apple pie spice
- 1 tsp baking soda
- ⅓ cup candied cherries, halved
- ⅓ cup chopped mixed candied peel
- 3 eggs
- 3 tbsp milk
- grated rind of 1 large lemon
- ¼ cup sliced almonds

TO FINISH:
- 3 tbsp thin honey

250–185 CALS/SLICE

1 Grease and line a deep 8-inch square cake pan. Put the honey in a saucepan, add the butter, and heat gently, stirring, until smooth.
2 Sift the flour, salt, spice, and baking soda into a large bowl, stirring in any bran left in the sifter. Add the cherries and peel.
3 Beat the eggs and milk together and stir into the honey mixture with the lemon rind. Pour gradually onto the dry ingredients, beating well after each addition, until well blended.
4 Turn the batter into the prepared pan and sprinkle with the sliced almonds. Bake in a preheated 325°F oven until the cake is firm to the touch and a skewer inserted in the center comes out clean, about 1¼ hours.
5 Keeping the cake in the pan, prick the top all over with a skewer and spoon over the honey. Leave in the pan 5 minutes longer, then unmold and place the cake the right way up on a wire rack. Let cool. Do not remove the wax lining paper until the cake is cold.

❖ Black Forest Cake ❖

SERVES 10

PREPARATION TIME
40 minutes, plus
caraque
COOKING TIME
40 minutes
FREEZING
Suitable
(undecorated)

- 6 tbsp butter
- 6 eggs
- 1 cup superfine sugar
- ¾ cup cake flour
- ⅔ cup unsweetened cocoa powder
- ½ tsp vanilla extract
- two 16-oz) cans pitted sweet cherries
- ¼ cup Kirsch
- 2½ cups heavy whipping cream
- 4 oz Chocolate Caraque (see right)
- 1 tsp arrowroot

600 CALS/SERVING

1 Line and grease a deep 9-inch round cake pan. Put the butter in a bowl over a pan of warm water; beat until very soft.

2 Beat the eggs and sugar together in a large bowl set over a pan of simmering water until pale and creamy, and thick enough to leave a trail on the surface when the beaters are lifted. Remove from the heat and beat until cool.

3 Sift the flour and cocoa together, then lightly fold into the egg mixture. Fold in the vanilla and softened butter. Turn into the prepared pan and tilt to spread evenly.

4 Bake in a preheated 350°F oven until well risen, firm to the touch, and beginning to shrink away from the sides of the pan, about 40 minutes. Unmold onto a wire rack covered with wax paper, and let cool. Cut the cake into three layers.

5 Place one layer on a flat plate. To make the filling, drain the cherries, reserving the syrup. Mix ⅓ cup of the cherry syrup and the Kirsch together. Spoon 3 tbsp over the cake layer. Whip the cream until it holds its shape, then spread a thin layer over the soaked cake. Reserve a third of the cherries for decoration; scatter half the remainder over the cream.

6 Repeat the layers of cake, syrup, cream, and cherries. Top with the third cake layer and spoon over the remaining Kirsch-flavored syrup.

7 Spread a thin layer of cream around the side of the cake. Press on the chocolate caraque, reserving some. Pipe whirls of cream around the edge of the cake and top each with a chocolate curl.

8 Fill the center with the reserved cherries. Blend the arrowroot with 3 tbsp cherry syrup. Place in a small pan, bring to a boil, and boil, stirring, for a few minutes until the mixture is clear. Brush the glaze over the cherries.

❖ Chocolate Mousse Cake ❖

SERVES 12–16

PREPARATION TIME
30 minutes, plus
cake
FREEZING
Not suitable
COLOR INDEX
Page 82

- 9-inch Genoese cake (page 395)
  FILLING:
- 6 oz bittersweet chocolate, in pieces
- 2 tbsp brandy
- 2 eggs, separated
- 1¼ cups heavy whipping cream
- 1 tsp unflavored gelat
  CHOCOLATE CARAQU
- 10 oz bittersweet or white chocolate
  TO DECORATE:
- ⅔ cup heavy whipping cream
- confectioners' sugar, for dusting

640–480 CALS/SERVIN

1 To make the filling, melt the chocolate in a heatproof bowl set over a pan of simmering water. Remove from the heat and stir in the brandy and egg yolks. Whip the cream until it stands in soft peaks, then fold in.

2 Sprinkle the gelatin over 1 tbsp water in a small bowl and let soak 2–3 minutes, the dissolve over a pan of simmering water. Cool, then stir into the chocolate mixture. Beat the egg whites until stiff, then fold in.

3 Cut the cake into two layers. Put one layer back in the cake pan. Pour the mousse filling on top. Put the second layer on top. Leave in a cool place to set.

4 To make the chocolate caraque, melt the chocolate as in step 1. Spread out thinly on a marble slab or clean work surface. Let set until no longer sticky to touch.

5 Holding a large knife with both hands, push the blade across the surface to shave off long chocolate curls. Adjust the angle of the blade to get the best curls. Alternatively, use a clean wallpaper scraper as shown.

6 When the mousse is set, whip the cream until it holds its shape. Release the side of the pan and carefully ease the cake out. Place on a serving plate. Cover with the cream. Coat completely with the chocolate curls and dust lightly with confectioners' sugar.

5 For the filling, softly whip the cream. Mash half of the strawberries with the confectioners' sugar; fold into the cream with the yogurt. Fold in the remaining sliced strawberries. Spread the cream over the cake. Starting from one of the narrow ends, carefully roll it up, using the paper to help.

6 Dust the roulade generously with confectioners' sugar. Decorate with strawberries. Serve with a fruit Coulis (page 95), if desired.

NOTE: Don't worry if the roulade cracks as you are rolling – this is usual and adds to the appearance!

❖ Chocolate Roulade ❖

SERVES 8–10

PREPARATION TIME
35 minutes
COOKING TIME
20–25 minutes
FREEZING
Suitable (unfilled and rolled with lining paper)
COLOR INDEX
Page 83

- 4 oz semisweet chocolate, in pieces
- 4 eggs, separated
- ⅔ cup superfine sugar
FILLING:
- ⅔ cup heavy whipping cream
- 8 oz strawberries or raspberries, sliced

- 1 tbsp confectioners' sugar
- ⅔ cup thick plain yogurt
TO DECORATE:
- confectioners' sugar, for dusting
- strawberries or raspberries

395–315 CALS/SERVING

1 Grease a 13-×9-inch jelly roll pan, line with parchment paper, and grease the paper. Melt the chocolate in a bowl set over a pan of simmering water.

2 Beat the egg yolks with the sugar until very thick and pale in color. Beat in the chocolate. Beat the egg whites until stiff, then fold into the chocolate mixture.

3 Pour into the prepared pan and spread out evenly. Bake in a preheated 350°F oven until well risen and firm to the touch, 20–25 minutes.

4 Unmold the cake onto a sheet of wax paper generously sprinkled with granulated sugar. Carefully peel off the lining paper. Cover the cake with a warm, damp dish towel and let cool.

❖ Sachertorte ❖

SERVES 8–10

PREPARATION TIME
30 minutes
COOKING TIME
40–45 minutes
FREEZING
Suitable (without frosting)
COLOR INDEX
Page 83

- 5 oz semisweet chocolate, in pieces
- 1 stick (½ cup) unsalted butter or margarine, softened
- ⅔ cup sugar
- 1⅓ cups ground almonds
- 4 eggs, separated

- 1⅓ cups fresh brown bread crumbs
- 2 tbsp apricot preserves, melted
FROSTING:
- 7 oz semisweet chocolate, in pieces
- 1 cup heavy whipping cream

690–550 CALS/SERVING

1 Grease a 9-inch springform cake pan, line with wax paper, and grease the paper.
2 Melt the chocolate in a bowl set over a pan of simmering water. Remove from the heat.
3 Cream the butter and sugar together until light and fluffy. Stir in the almonds, egg yolks, bread crumbs, and melted chocolate and beat until well combined.
4 Beat the egg whites until stiff and fold half into the chocolate mixture, then fold in the other half. Pour into the prepared pan and level the surface. Bake in a preheated 350°F oven until firm to the touch, 40–45 minutes.
5 Cover with a damp dish towel, leave 5 minutes to cool slightly, then unclip the sides of the pan, and invert onto a wire rack. Remove the base. Turn the cake the right way up, cover, and let cool. When cold, brush the top with the jam.
6 To make the frosting, put the chocolate and cream in a heatproof bowl over a pan of simmering water until the chocolate has melted and evenly blended with the cream. Cool a few minutes until the frosting just coats the back of a spoon.
7 Pour the frosting over the cake and gently shake the cake to spread it evenly; use a spatula, if necessary, to ensure that the sides are completely covered. Let set in a cool place, but do not refrigerate or the frosting will lose its shine.

❖ Celebration Cake ❖

SERVES 20

PREPARATION TIME
30 minutes, plus
standing
COOKING TIME
1–1¼ hours
FREEZING
Suitable (cake
only)

• 2 sticks (1 cup) butter
or margarine, softened
• 1 cup + 2 tbsp sugar
• 4 eggs, lightly beaten
• 1⅔ cups self-rising
cake flour
• grated rind and juice of
1 lemon
TO DECORATE:
• red, blue, or yellow
food coloring

• 1½ lb ready-made icing
fondant
• 1¼ cups heavy
whipping cream
• ½ cup black cherry
conserve or ¼ cup sliced
strawberries
• ribbon and fresh
flowers, to decorate

315 CALS/SERVING

1 Grease and bottom-line a 9-inch round cake pan.
2 Cream the butter and sugar together until pale and fluffy. Add the eggs a little at a time, beating well after each addition, and adding a little flour if the mixture begins to curdle.
3 Sift the flour over the mixture and fold in with the lemon rind and juice. Spoon into the prepared pan and level the surface.
4 Bake in a preheated 350°F oven until golden and firm to the touch, 1–1¼ hours. Cover the top with wax paper, if necessary, toward the end of the cooking time. Unmold onto a wire rack to cool.
5 Meanwhile tint the icing fondant a pale shade by kneading in a little coloring until evenly blended. Wrap tightly in plastic wrap.
6 Cut the cake into two equal layers. Whip the cream until it just holds its shape. Put the cake layers together with preserves or fruit and all but 3 tbsp cream. Place on a serving plate. Spread the reserved cream thinly around the sides and over the top of the cake.
7 Dust the work surface lightly with confectioners' sugar and roll out the icing fondant to a circle large enough to cover the cake completely. Lift the fondant over a rolling pin and carefully onto the cake; gently smooth the sides. Trim the excess fondant from the base of the cake.
8 Decorate with a ribbon and fresh flowers just before serving.

❖ Teddy Bear Cake ❖

SERVES 20

PREPARATION TIME
About 2 hours
COOKING TIME
1¼ hours
FREEZING
Suitable

• 3½ sticks (1¾ cups)
butter or margarine,
softened
• 2¼ cups sugar
• 6 eggs, lightly beaten
• 3 cups self-rising cake
flour
• ⅔ cup unsweetened
cocoa powder
• 2 tsp baking powder

TO DECORATE:
• 3½ lb ready-made icing
fondant
• blue, brown, yellow,
red, and green food
colorings
• 3 tbsp apricot
preserves, strained

555 CALS/SERVING

1 Grease and bottom-line a 1½-quart and a 3-cup pudding basin. Place 3 paper cupcake cases in muffin pans. Cream together the butter and sugar in a bowl. Gradually beat in the eggs, adding a little flour if the mixture begins to curdle. Sift the remaining flour with the cocoa and baking powder and fold in. Half fill the cupcake cases; divide remaining batter between the pudding basins. Bake in a preheated 325°F oven, allowing 15 minutes for the cupcakes, 45 minutes for the small basin, and 1–1¼ hours for the large basin. Test by inserting a skewer into the center: It should come out clean. Let cool in the basins and paper cases for 15 minutes, then unmold onto a wire rack to cool completely.

2 Trim off top edges from basin cakes to give rounded shapes. Cut one cupcake in half for ears. Make two sloping cuts on remaining cupcakes to shape feet.

3 Cut a slice from one side of the large cake to make a firm base when the cake is lifted on its side. Cut another slice from the opposite side to support the head. Cut a slice from one side of the small basin cake.

5 To make vest, thinly roll 2 oz of the reserved white fondant. Cut 2 front sections of vest, each 3½ inches from neck to waist and 4 inches from center front to sides. Cut away V neck and armholes and secure to cake. Re-roll trimmings and cut out back of vest, about 4-inches deep and 9-inches wide. Cut away armholes and shape around back of teddy, easing to fit.

9 To make the arms, halve the remaining brown fondant and roll out 2 sausage shapes, each 4-inches long and slightly thicker in the middle. Secure to sides of teddy, letting ends rest on the legs or down sides. Mark stitching lines with teaspoon.

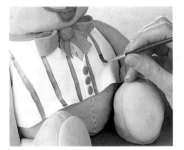

4 Color 8 oz of the fondant blue and roll out thinly on a surface dusted with cornstarch. Use to cover a 11-inch dampened board. Smooth out using hands dusted with cornstarch; trim off excess fondant around edge. Mix the preserves with 1 tbsp boiling water; spread over the round cakes.

5 Reserve 8 oz of the fondant; color remainder pale brown. Thinly roll a generous third of the brown fondant to an 11-inch round. Lift over the large cake. Using hands dusted with cornstarch, smooth fondant around sides to eliminate creases and folds. Tuck excess fondant under the base. Position cake on board.

10 Color another 4 oz white fondant yellow, adding a little brown color to tone down if preferred. Roll half into a ball, then flatten into a snout shape and secure to cake. Use remainder to shape feet, paw, and ear pads. Press into position.

11 Color a little of the remaining fondant red and use to shape small round buttons, a semi-circle for the mouth, and a neck tie; secure in place. Shape and position 2 small diskes of white fondant for eyes. Color remaining fondant dark brown and use to shape nose and mouth; secure to cake. To finish cake, use diluted colors to paint centers of eyes and candy stripes on vest. Let dry and harden in a cool place, preferably for 2 days.

6 Use another 8 oz brown fondant to cover the smaller round cake and sit it on top of the large cake. Using the tip of a teaspoon impress "stitching" lines around head, front, and sides of teddy.

7 To make each leg, roll out 3 oz brown fondant. Lay one cupcake in the center. Mold fondant around cake and shape excess into foot. Press into position on cake. Mark stitching lines. Use 2 oz brown fondant to cover ears and position. Mark stitching lines.

NOTE: As you work, keep any fondant not in use wrapped in plastic wrap, otherwise it will dry out and become difficult to use. The cake can be stored in a cool place 2–3 weeks. Alternatively, you could freeze it longer, but the fondant will develop a moist sheen. Apply any painted-on color once the cake has thawed.

❖ Dinosaur Cake ❖

SERVES 16

PREPARATION TIME
About 2 hours,
plus standing
COOKING TIME
1¼ hours
FREEZING
Suitable

580 CALS/SERVING

- 2 sticks (1 cup) butter or margarine, softened
- 1 cup + 2tbsp sugar
- 4 eggs, lightly beaten
- 2 cups self-rising cake flour
- 1 tsp baking powder
- grated rind of 1 orange
- 1 tbsp orange juice
- ½ quantity Butter Frosting (page 410)

TO DECORATE:
- 3½ lb ready-made icing fondant
- brown, green, yellow, red, and blue food colorings

1 Line and grease an 8-inch round cake pan. Cream together the butter and sugar. Gradually beat in the eggs, with a little flour if needed. Sift flour with baking powder; fold in with orange rind and juice. Turn into the pan. Bake in a preheated 325°F oven for 1–1¼ hours. Leave in pan 15 minutes, then cool on a wire rack. Halve cake vertically and put pieces together with one-third of the butter frosting. With cut sides down, trim cake edges to shape dinosaur's underside.

2 Roughly knead brown food coloring into 12 oz of the fondant until streaked with color. Roll out thinly on a surface dusted with cornstarch and use to cover a dampened 12-inch cake board. Smooth out fondant using hands dusted with cornstarch, then trim off excess around edge.

3 Reserve 2 oz of the fondant. Color the remainder green. Take 4 oz of the green fondant and roll out to a thick sausage, about 4½-inches long and thicker at one end. Cut a slice off the thick end. Press a "neck" 1½ inches from the rounded end, then bend fondant to create the head.

4 Using a sharp knife cut a ½-inch slice through rounded end to form the mouth, curving cut upward at ends to create "smiling" expression. Take a pea-sized piece of green fondant and cut in half. Press onto the top of the head to shape eye sockets. Press 2 small holes into fondant, just above mouth, to make nostrils. Thread a bamboo skewer through fondant as far as neck. Transfer to a sheet of parchment paper or foil and let harden 1–2 days.

5 Once head has hardened, push skewer into cake to secure head to body. Place on cake board and spread body with remaining butter frosting. Brush lower end of neck with water. Reserve 1¼ lb of the green fondant. Color another 3 oz a darker shade of green and reserve. Roll out remainder to an 11-inch round. Make a 3-inch cut from edge toward center. Lift fondant over cake so the slit falls around neck of dinosaur. Using hands dusted with cornstarch, smooth fondant eliminating as many creases and folds as possible. Smooth fondant around the neck until join barely shows. Trim off excess at base.

6 To shape tail take another 8 oz green fondant and roll out to a sausage, about 2-inches thick at one end and tapering to a point at other end. Dampen thick end and attach to cake, letting tail bend around front of board. Using fingers, smooth the fondant onto dinosaur body until join barely shows.

7 Color 1½ oz reserved white fondant with an equal quantity of yellow and brown color. Thinly roll and press onto front of dinosaur and around base of sides.

8 To shape each hind leg, roll 4 oz green fondant and mold into a pear shape. Bend the thin end of the pear shape around the back of a knife. Gently press against side of cake. Halve remaining green fondant and roll each piece to a 3½-inch sausage tapering slightly at one end. Bend fondant around back of knife, then press into position for front legs. Use a toothpick to make markings on feet and crease lines at leg joints.

9 Roll out the dark green fondant as thinly as possible. Cut 30–40 strips of fondant, varying in length from 5 inches to 1 inch and tapering to a point at each end. Lay over the back of dinosaur. Continue adding strips, decreasing in size as you work toward head and tail ends. (Use strips to cover any visible joins where neck and tail meet body.) Re-roll trimmings and use to shape spikes. Position along back, again decreasing in size toward head and tail ends.

10 Color a little fondant red and shape a small pointed tongue; press into mouth. Roll 2 small balls of white fondnat and press into eye sockets. Paint centers of eyes blue. Shape small claws from remaining white fondant and secure to feet. Finish cake by painting brown streaks between the dark green markings down the dinosaur's back. Remove the skewer before cutting the cake.

NOTE: Always keep any fondant not in use tightly wrapped in plastic wrap. This cake will keep 2–3 weeks in a cool place. It can be frozen for longer, but the fondant will develop a moist sheen. If freezing, painted-on color should be added once thawed.

❖ Simnel Cake ❖

SERVES 20

PREPARATION TIME
40 minutes
COOKING TIME
About 2½ hours
FREEZING
Suitable
(undecorated)
COLOR INDEX
Page 84

- 1½ sticks (¾ cup) butter or hard margarine, softened
- 1 cup sugar
- 3 eggs, lightly beaten
- 1⅓ cups cake flour
- pinch of salt
- ½ tsp ground cinnamon
- ½ tsp grated nutmeg
- ½ cup candied cherries, rinsed, dried, and cut into quarters
- ⅓ cup chopped mixed candied peel
- 1⅓ cups currants
- ⅔ cup golden raisins
- finely grated rind of 1 lemon

- 1–2 tbsp milk (if necessary)
- 1 lb Almond Paste (page 411)

TO DECORATE:
- 1 egg white, lightly beaten
- ribbon
- fresh or sugared flowers

345 CALS/SERVING

1 Line and grease a 7-inch round cake pan.
2 Cream the butter and sugar together until pale and fluffy. Gradually beat in the eggs.
3 Sift in the flour, salt, and spices and fold into the mixture with a metal spoon. Add all the fruit and the lemon rind, folding in to give a smooth, soft consistency. If a little too firm add 1–2 tbsp milk.
4 Divide the almond paste in half. Lightly dust a surface with confectioners' sugar and roll out one half to a 6½-inch round.
5 Spoon half of the cake batter into the prepared pan. Place the round of almond paste on top and cover with the remaining cake batter. Press down gently with the back of a spoon to level the surface.
6 Tie a double thickness of brown paper around the outside of the pan. Bake in a preheated 300°F oven about 2½ hours. When cooked the cake should be a rich brown color, and firm to the touch.
7 Cool in the pan about 1 hour, then unmold and let cool completely on a wire rack.
8 Divide the remaining almond paste in half. Roll out one half to a 7½-inch round and the rest into 11 small balls. Brush the top of the cake with egg white. Place the round of almond paste on top, crimp the edges, and, with a little of the egg white, fix the balls around the top edge of the cake.
9 Brush the almond paste with the remaining egg white and place under a hot broiler until the paste is well browned, 1–2 minutes. Tie ribbon around the cake and decorate with flowers.

Variation
Before broiling, apply a rope edging of almond paste around the top edge of the cake. When cool, cover the top of the cake with a layer of white Sugar Icing (page 410).

❖ Wedding Cake ❖

ABOUT 125 SLICES

PPREPARATION TIME
About 12–15 hours, plus standing

COOKING TIME
7–9 hours

FREEZING
Suitable (cakes only)

- *2 lb (5½ cups) plump raisins*
- *1½ cups candied cherries*
- *1¼ cups shelled almonds*
- *1 lb (2⅔ cups) currants*
- *1½ lb (4 cups) golden raisins*
- *1⅓ cups chopped candied peel*
- *3 cups ground almonds*
- *7 tbsp brandy*
- *6 oz semisweet chocolate, in pieces*
- *1½ lb (3 cups) butter or margarine*
- *4 cups packed dark brown sugar or Barbados sugar*
- *finely grated rind of 3 large lemons*
- *13 eggs*
- *5⅔ cups flour*
- *1½ tsp ground cinnamon*
- *1½ tsp grated nutmeg*
- *¼ cup molasses*

TO MATURE:
- *7 tbsp brandy*

TO COVER:
- *Apricot Glaze (page 411)*
- *about 4½ lb Almond Paste (page 411)*
- *about 4½ lb Icing Fondant (page 412)*

TO DECORATE:
- *about 1 lb Royal Icing (page 413)*

SUGAR-PASTE FLOWERS:
- *about 1 lb petal paste*
- *lemon-yellow dusting powder*
- *about 72 white stamens (double-headed)*

TO FINISH:
- *ribbon or board edging*
- *fresh flowers*

325 CALS/SLICE

1 Use 6-inch, 8-inch, and 11-inch round deep cake pans. Line the 3 cake pans with a double thickness of wax paper. Tie a double thickness band of brown paper around the outside of the pan. To mix the ingredients for all 3 cakes together, use a very large bowl. Alternatively you may find it easier to mix the cakes separately (see chart for quantities).

2 Prepare the fruit and nuts: chop the plump raisins; rinse, d and halve the cherries; blanch and shred the almonds. In a lar bowl, mix these together with the currants, golden raisins, pe ground almonds, and brandy.

3 Melt the chocolate in a heatproof bowl over a pan of simmering water; let cool.

4 In a separate bowl, cream the fat, sugar, and lemon rind un pale and fluffy. Add the eggs one at a time, beating well.

5 Sift the flour with the spices. Fold half carefully into the creamed mixture. Add the other half to the fruit; mix well and add to the creamed mixture with the chocolate and molasses. S

6 Divide the batter among the 3 pans, taking care to make the largest cake slightly deeper than the others.

7 Bake the two small cakes together first; cover the large cake p and put in a cool, dry place until ready to cook. Bake in a preheated 300°F oven for the first hour, then reduce to 275°F. Bake the small cake 1–1½ hours longer, the medium cake 1½–2 hours longer, and the large cake 3½–5 hours longer. (If the cake are baked together they will take considerably longer.) After 2 hours' baking, cover with wax paper. Cool in the pans, then transfer to wire racks.

8 Pierce the cakes at regular intervals with a fine skewer, spoo a little brandy over each, and let soak several hours. Wrap in wax paper, then overwrap with foil and leave to mature in a co dry place set aside 1–3 months, impregnating with a little bran at regular intervals.

9 Cover the cakes with almond paste; refer to page 411.

10 Cover the cakes with icing fondant; refer to page 412.

❖ Wedding Cake Quantities ❖

INGREDIENTS	6-INCH ROUND ❖	8-INCH ROUND ❖	11-INCH ROUND ❖
plump raisins	*1 cup*	*1⅔ cups*	*3 cups*
candied cherries	*¼ cup*	*½ cup*	*1 cup*
whole almonds	*3 tbsp*	*⅓ cup*	*¾ cup*
currants	*⅓ cup*	*⅔ cup*	*1⅔ cups*
golden raisins	*⅔ cup*	*1 cup*	*2 cups*
chopped candied peel	*¼ cup*	*½ cup*	*1 cup*
ground almonds	*½ cup*	*¾ cup*	*1⅔ cups*
brandy	*1 tbsp*	*2 tbsp*	*¼ cup*
semisweet chocolate	*1 oz*	*2 oz*	*3 oz*
margarine/butter	*6 tbsp*	*14 tbsp*	*1¾ cups*
dark brown sugar	*½ cup*	*1 cup*	*1¾ cups*
lemons	*½*	*1*	*2*
eggs	*1½*	*4*	*7½*
flour	*1 cup*	*1⅔ cups*	*3 cups*
ground cinnamon	*¼ tsp*	*½ tsp*	*¾ tsp*
grated nutmeg	*¼ tsp*	*½ tsp*	*¾ tsp*
molasses	*1½ tsp*	*1 tbsp*	*2 tbsp*
ALMOND PASTE	*12 oz*	*1¼ lb*	*2¼ lb*
ICING FONDANT	*12 oz*	*1½ lb*	*2¼ lb*

To Decorate the Cake

The three-tiered cake is decorated with about 24 sugar-paste azaleas and 180 cut-out flowers. To make these you will need the following special equipment: a set of 3 blossom cutters, with ejector; small and medium 5-point calyx cutters; medium 8-petal daisy cutter; set of rose-petal cutters; a sponge block, a ball modeling tool, and fine paintbrushes.

MAKING SMALL FLOWERS
1 Break off a piece of sugar paste about the size of a large pea. (Keep the remaining paste tightly covered to prevent it from drying out.) Roll out the paste as thinly as possible using a little cornstarch or confectioners' sugar (the thinner it is, the better the flower).

3 Knead a little yellow dusting powder into some of the sugar paste. Repeat as above until you have about 180 flowers in all. When dry, pipe a small dot of royal icing into the center of each flower. Let dry.

2 Using the blossom, calyx, and daisy cutters, cut out flowers. The blossom cutters with ejector are easiest to use – depress the plunger over the sponge and the paste is automatically cupped in the shape of a flower. For the cutters without ejectors, use the ball modeling tool to cup the paste; let dry.

MAKING AZALEAS
4 Roll out a small piece of yellow sugar paste very thinly, keeping the rest well covered. Cut out 5 petals, using the large rose-petal cutter.

5 Gently mark the center vein of each petal with a toothpick and 2 veins on either side. Create the frilled edge by gently rolling a toothpick along the curved edge of the petal. Place the petal against a wooden spoon handle to curve into shape. Repeat with the remaining 4 petals.

6 Line 2–3 large pastry tubes with foil. Brush one side of the petal with water; place the next petal in position, overlapping the edges. Repeat until all 5 petals are in position, using the nozzles to hold in shape; dry. Repeat using various cutters until you have 12 large, 6 medium, and 6 small azaleas.

APPLYING DECORATIONS
8 Make the templates: Cut a strip of paper to fit around the side of each cake. Fold into 6 equal portions. Cut out a semi-circle, making sure the folds are linked. Transfer the outline using pin pricks.

7 Dust the outside of the flowers lightly with the lemon color. Dampen a fine brush with water and paint small spots of dust inside each azalea. Pipe a dot of royal icing into the center of each flower. Cut 3 stamens in half to give 6 heads, cut to size, and position in the icing. Let dry.

9 Using the pin pricks as a guide, attach the sugar-paste flowers with a dot of royal icing. Attach 1 or 2 azaleas on top of the cake where each loop forms a point. Attach 2 small cut-out flowers to neaten the back of the azaleas.

10 Using a star or rope tube, pipe shells of royal icing along the bottom edge of each cake.

To Assemble the Cake

You need 8 round 3-inch hollow cake pillars and 8 bamboo skewers for assembling – in situ, of course. Mark the position of the pillars on the bottom 2 tiers of the cake. Place in position and insert the skewers carefully into the cake until the point reaches the cake board. Mark the skewers ⅛ inch above the top of the pillar. Remove and cut to size. Replace skewers and assemble the cake. Finish with flowers.

❖ Butter Frosting ❖

MAKES 12 OZ	• 1 stick (½ cup) butter, softened	• few drops of vanilla extract
PREPARATION TIME 5 minutes	• 2 cups confectioners' sugar, sifted	• 1–2 tbsp milk
FREEZING Suitable		130 CALS/1 OZ

1 Cream the butter until soft. Gradually beat in the sugar, adding the vanilla and milk, to form a smooth frosting.

NOTE: This quantity is sufficient to coat the top and sides of an 8-inch cake.

Variations

ORANGE OR LEMON BUTTER FROSTING: Omit the vanilla and add a little finely grated orange or lemon rind and a little of the juice, beating well to avoid curdling the mixture.

COFFEE BUTTER FROSTING: Omit the vanilla and milk. Add 2 tsp instant coffee powder dissolved in 1–2 tbsp hot water; cool before adding.

CHOCOLATE BUTTER FROSTING: Flavor by adding 1–1½ oz melted chocolate, omitting 1 tbsp of the milk.

MOCHA BUTTER FROSTING: Dissolve 1 tsp unsweetened cocoa powder and 2 tsp instant coffee powder in a little hot water; cool before adding to the mixture.

❖ Buttercream ❖

MAKES 10 OZ	• ½ cup sugar	• 1½ sticks (¾ cup) butter, softened
PREPARATION TIME 15 minutes	• 2 egg yolks, beaten	
COOKING TIME 5 minutes		
FREEZING Not suitable		155 CALS/1 OZ

1 Place the sugar in a heavy-based saucepan with ¼ cup water and dissolve over low heat. When completely dissolved, bring to boiling point and boil steadily until a temperature of 225°F is registered on a candy thermometer, 2–3 minutes.
2 Put the egg yolks in a deep bowl and pour on the syrup in a thin stream, beating all the time. Continue to beat until the mixture is thick and cold.
3 In another bowl, cream the butter until very soft, then gradually beat in the egg yolk mixture to make a smooth frosting.

Variations

CHOCOLATE BUTTERCREAM: Melt 2 oz semisweet chocolate with 1 tbsp water. Cool slightly and beat into the buttercream.

ORANGE OR LEMON BUTTERCREAM: Add a little freshly grated citrus rind and a little juice to taste.

COFFEE BUTTERCREAM: Beat 1–2 tbsp coffee extract into the buttercream.

❖ Sugar or Glacé Icing ❖

MAKES 4–6 OZ	• 1–1½ cups confectioners' sugar	• flavoring (optional)
PREPARATION TIME 5 minutes		• coloring (optional)
FREEZING Not suitable		100 CALS/1 OZ

1 Sift the confectioners' sugar into a bowl, then gradually mix in 1–2 tbsp warm water until the icing is thick enough to coat the back of a spoon.
2 Stir in any flavoring. If necessary, add more sugar or water to obtain the correct consistency. Add a few drops of coloring, if required. Use at once.

NOTE: This quantity is sufficient to cover the top of an 8-inch cake or about 8 cupcakes.

Variations

EXTRA-SMOOTH SUGAR ICING: Place the sugar, water, flavoring, and coloring in a small pan and heat gently, stirring, until the mixture is warm; do not let it get too hot. The icing should coat the back of a wooden spoon and look smooth and glossy.

ORANGE OR LEMON SUGAR ICING: Substitute 1–2 tbsp strained orange or lemon juice for the water.

CHOCOLATE SUGAR ICING: Blend 2 tsp unsweetened cocoa powder in a little hot water and use to replace the same amount of measured water.

COFFEE SUGAR ICING: Flavor with either 1 tsp coffee extract or 2 tsp instant coffee powder dissolved in a little of the measured and heated water.

MOCHA SUGAR ICING: Flavor with 1 tsp unsweetened cocoa powder and 2 tsp instant coffee powder, dissolved in a little of the measured and heated water.

❖ Coffee Fudge Frosting ❖

MAKES 14 OZ	• 4 tbsp butter or margarine	• 2 tbsp cream or milk
PREPARATION TIME 5 minutes	• ½ cup packed light brown sugar	• 1¾ cups confectioners' sugar, sifted
COOKING TIME 5 minutes	• 3 tbsp coffee extract	
FREEZING Not suitable		105 CALS/1 OZ

1 Put the butter, brown sugar, coffee extract, and cream in a saucepan and heat gently until the sugar dissolves. Boil briskly 3 minutes.
2 Remove from the heat and gradually stir in the confectioners' sugar. Beat with a wooden spoon until smooth, then continue to beat until the frosting is thick enough to spread, about 2 minutes. Use immediately, spreading with a wet metal spatula.

Variation

CHOCOLATE FUDGE FROSTING: Replace the coffee extract with 3 oz semisweet chocolate.

❖ Boiled Frosting ❖

MAKES 8 OZ

PREPARATION TIME
15 minutes
COOKING TIME
5 minutes
FREEZING
Not suitable

- *1 egg white*
- *1 cup + 2 tbsp sugar*
- *pinch of cream of tartar*

225 CALS/1 OZ

1 Beat the egg white in a bowl until stiff. Put the sugar in a heavy-based saucepan with ¼ cup water and the cream of tartar. Heat gently, stirring until dissolved. Then without stirring, bring to a boil and boil to a temperature of 240°F, as registered on a candy thermometer.
2 Remove the syrup from the heat and, as soon as the bubbles subside, pour it onto the egg white in a thin stream, beating constantly. Let cool slightly.
3 When the mixture begins to appear dull around the edges and is almost cold, pour quickly over the cake and spread evenly with a metal spatula.

❖ Chocolate Ganache ❖

MAKES ABOUT 1 CUP

PREPARATION TIME
10 minutes, plus cooling
FREEZING
Suitable

- *¾ cup heavy whipping cream*
- *4 oz semisweet or milk chocolate, in pieces*

165 CALS/2 TBSP

1 Pour the cream into a small pan and bring to a boil. Remove from the heat and add the chocolate; stir gently until the chocolate has melted and the mixture is smooth.
2 Return the mixture to the heat. Bring to a boil, remove from the heat, and let cool. Use at room temperature: The mixture should be the consistency of softened butter.

❖ Apricot Glaze ❖

MAKES ½ CUP

PREPARATION TIME
5 minutes
COOKING TIME
2 minutes
FREEZING
Suitable

- *½ cup apricot jelly*

55 CALS/2 TBSP

1 Place the jelly and 2 tbsp water in a small pan. Heat gently, stirring, until the jelly begins to melt. Bring to a boil and simmer 1 minute.
2 Press the jelly through a nylon strainer. Use while warm.

❖ Almond Paste ❖

Almond paste or marzipan is applied to rich fruit cakes to create a smooth foundation for the icing. It is therefore important to apply it neatly.

You can either make your own almond paste, following the recipe below, or buy it ready-made. When buying ready-made choose the white variety, rather than the yellow one, as it is less likely to discolor the icing. The flavor of homemade almond paste is, however, better than either ready-made alternative.

If royal icing a cake, cover the cake with almond paste 1 week before applying the first coat of icing, to let the almond paste dry. Homemade almond paste takes longer to dry out than the ready-made variety.

MAKES ABOUT 1 LB

PREPARATION TIME
10 minutes
FREEZING
Suitable

- *2⅔ cups ground almonds*
- *⅔ cup granulated sugar*
- *1 cup confectioners' sugar*
- *1 egg*
- *1 tsp lemon juice*
- *1 tsp sherry*
- *1–2 drops vanilla extract*

135 CALS/1 OZ

1 Place the ground almonds and sugars in a bowl and mix together. In a separate bowl, whisk the egg with the remaining ingredients and add to the dry mixture.
2 Stir well to mix, pounding gently to release some of the oil from the almonds. Knead with your hands until smooth.

NOTE: If you wish to avoid using raw egg to bind the almond paste, mix the other liquid ingredients with a little water instead.

❖ Almond Paste Quantity Guide ❖

SQUARE PAN ❖	ROUND PAN ❖	ALMOND PASTE ❖
5-inch	6-inch	12 oz
6-inch	7-inch	1 lb
7-inch	8-inch	1¼ lb
8-inch	9-inch)	1¾ lb
9-inch	10-inch	2 lb
10-inch	11-inch	2¼ lb
11-inch	12-inch	2½ lb
12-inch	13-inch	3 lb
13-inch	14-inch	3½ lb

BREADS & YEAST BAKING

There really is nothing quite like the aroma and taste of homemade bread. Unfortunately bread-making is one of those traditional tasks that many believe to be difficult, but in fact it's never been easier. Rapid rise dry yeast is now readily available and simple to use; it speeds up bread-making dramatically. You will also find that many supermarkets and natural food shops now stock a good range of bread flours.

Once you've mastered the basic techniques there is nothing to stop you baking your own creations and imitations of commercially produced specialty breads at a fraction of the cost. Look to the recipes here for inspiration, but don't be shy of creating your own combinations: flavor savory doughs with cheese, fresh herbs, olives, or sun-dried tomatoes; sweet doughs with vanilla sugar or scented spices like cinnamon, as well as dried fruits and nuts.

Yeast

Yeast is one of those fantastic ingredients with unique properties. Although not difficult to use, it is a living organism and must be handled in the right way in order to work effectively. When you buy yeast it is alive, but inactive. Only when it is mixed with a warm liquid does it become active and release the gases that should make the dough rise. Yeast is available in a number of different forms that are interchangable in recipes, providing that the method is adjusted accordingly.

❖ COMPRESSED FRESH YEAST: Many supermarkets and natural food shops stock fresh yeast. When buying, check that the yeast is firm, moist, and creamy colored with a good "yeasty" smell. If it is dry and crumbly with discolored brown patches, it is probably stale and it won't work. Fresh yeast is easy to use – simply blend with a little of the liquid specified in the recipe, add the remaining liquid, then mix into the flour. It will only stay fresh about 3 days if stored in the refrigerator, but it freezes well – freeze in usable quantities up to 3 months. Thaw before using.

❖ RAPID RISE DRY: This product has revolutionized bread-making. It is sprinkled directly into the flour and the liquid is mixed in afterward. After kneading, the dough can be shaped right away and will normally rise in half the time required with other yeasts. However, for enriched doughs – particularly heavily fruited ones – the rising time will not be so dramatically reduced. Always make sure you adhere to the use-before date on the package – rapid rise dry yeast won't work if it's stale.

❖ ACTIVE DRY YEAST: The recipes in this chapter use rapid rise dry yeast. If, however, you want to substitute ordinary active dry yeast, blend it with the liquid (see below) and leave it in a warm place to prove about 15 minutes: A frothy head (similar to the

head on a pint of Guinness) should develop. This shows that the yeast is active. If it refuses to froth, then it is probably past its use-before date; discard and start again with a fresh package of yeast.

❖ SOURDOUGH STARTER: This is one of those old-fashioned methods that has never gone out of fashion. A mixture of yeast, flour, and water is left to ferment several days before it is added to the dough. It produces a close-textured loaf with a distinctive flavor. If you make bread regularly, a sourdough starter is a convenient way of leavening.

Simply blend a 0.6 oz cake compressed fresh yeast (or its equivalent) with 2 cups warm water and about 2 cups bread flour or enough to make a thick pourable batter. Cover the bowl with a damp cloth and let ferment at room temperature for 3–5 days, to develop the sourdough flavor. Use ½ cup of the starter to replace each 0.6 oz cake of fresh yeast called for in a recipe, then make the bread in the usual way. Providing the starter is nourished with a paste made from at least 3 tbsp bread flour mixed with water every 4 days, it will keep several weeks and always be on hand ready to use. Store it in the refrigerator.

❖ YEAST QUANTITIES: A 0.6 oz cake of compressed fresh yeast is equal to 1 package (¼ oz) of active dry yeast or rapid rise dry yeast. If you use more yeast than is required in a recipe, the dough will not rise any higher and the bread is likely to have an unpleasant yeasty taste. However, if the dough is enriched with fruit, sugar, butter, or nuts, the rise is more difficult and you will usually need more yeast – be guided by the recipes.

Liquid

Active dry yeast (not the rapid rise type) needs sugar to activate it. If using milk the natural sugars present in the milk will be enough; if using water add a pinch of sugar. For both active dry and fresh yeast, the liquid should be just warm or tepid: It should feel slightly warm to the fingertips. (Check manufacturer's instructions on packages of rapid rise dry yeast: Water temperatures may be different from those recommended for other yeast.) If liquid is too hot it could kill the yeast; if too cold the yeast will not begin to work. Always regard any quantity of liquid specified in a recipe as a guide because flour absorbency varies.

Flour

A variety of different flours is used for bread-making. Bread flours give the best results because they are high in gluten – the substance that stretches the dough and traps air in it as it cooks,

PRESERVING

There can be no finer or more satisfying sight than a pantry stacked full of homemade jams, jellies, chutneys, and pickles. These preserved delights can bring to life the most mundane or humble meal and they're infinitely superior to and cheaper than commercially prepared equivalents. Once you've mastered the basic principles, the recipes here can be adapted to cope with almost any produce, from a glut of fruit in the garden to a harvest picked from a local farm.

❖ Preserving Equipment ❖

If you make a lot of preserves, it's worth investing in a proper preserving kettle: The sloping sides help maintain a fast boil and reduce the chances of everything boiling over. Choose a kettle made from stainless steel, tin-lined copper, or lined aluminum. Don't use unlined aluminum, particularly when cooking acidic fruits or pickles, because aluminum has been linked with Alzheimer's disease and research suggests that acidic substances encourage transference.

If you don't have a preserving kettle use a large, heavy-based saucepan instead. Note that if you are using a saucepan rather than a preserving kettle the preserve will take much longer to reach the jell point owing to the reduced surface area.

For jelly making, you will need a jelly bag for straining the juice from the cooked fruit. Although you can improvise with a large piece of cheesecloth, a jelly bag is a worthwhile investment because it makes things easier. Whatever you use, it should be scalded with boiling water before use. If the jelly bag doesn't have a stand, suspend it from the legs of an upturned chair or stool. Leave until the dripping has stopped. Don't be tempted to squeeze the bag: If you do, the finished jelly will be cloudy.

❖ Preserving Ingredients ❖

❖ PECTIN is naturally present in fruit, and reacts with sugar and acid to set jams, jellies, marmalades, and preserves. Some fruits such as cooking apples, lemons, Seville oranges, gooseberries, and damsons are high in natural pectin and acid; eating apples, raspberries, blackberries, apricots, and plums have a medium pectin and acid content, while cherries, grapes, peaches, rhubarb, and strawberries score low on both counts.

Fruits with a low or medium pectin content should be cooked with a fruit high in pectin to achieve a set. Lemon juice is most commonly used since it is rich in both pectin and acid; 2 tbsp lemon juice to 4 lb fruit should be enough. Alternatively use "sugar with pectin" (see below) or commercially produced pectin to ensure a good set.

❖ SUGAR acts as a preservative as well as helping to achieve a set, so it is important to use the amount stated in the recipe. Granulated sugar – refined white cane or beet – is fine for most preserves. Brown sugar can also be used, but it will lend a

distinctive flavor and darker color that are more suited to chutneys and relishes. Some recipes substitute light corn syrup or honey for some of the sugar. "Sugar with pectin" contains apple pectin and tartaric acid. Preserves made with this should reach jell point in just 4 minutes (providing they are kept at a fast rolling boil).

❖ VINEGAR acts as a preservative in pickles and some chutneys. Virtually any vinegar is suitable – red, white, or flavored providing that the acetic acid content is 5 percent or more (as in most vinegars on the market today).

❖ Testing for Doneness ❖

Jams, jellies, marmalades, and preserves are cooked sufficiently when jell point is reached. There are various tests to determine this. Remove the pan from the heat while you are testing, to prevent overcooking.

❖ TEMPERATURE TEST: The jam, jelly, etc. is ready when the temperature registers 221°F on a jelly thermometer.

❖ SAUCER TEST: Drop a spoonful of the jam, jelly, etc. onto a chilled saucer and let cool. Push your finger through the jam: If the surface wrinkles, it is ready.

❖ SHEET TEST (FOR JELLY ONLY): Using a wooden spoon, lift a little of the jelly out of the pan. Let it cool slightly, then tip the spoon so that the jelly drops back into the pan; if the drips run together and fall from the spoon in a sheet rather than as drips, it is ready.

There is no accurate test for chutneys and pickles, because they are not cooked to a jell point. Instead, be guided by the consistency and cooking time specified in the recipe; they are ready when no excess liquid remains and the mixture is very thick.

❖ Yields and Processing ❖

It is difficult to give accurate yields since they vary from batch to batch. Jelly yields are particularly difficult to estimate since so much depends on the time allowed for draining and the quality and ripeness of the fruit. So that you can have enough jars prepared, we have given a rough guide wherever possible.

All preserves should be packed into hot sterile jars (canning jars for all preserves other than jellies). Ladle the hot jelly, jam, etc. into the jars, leaving ¼ inch of headroom. Wipe the rims with a clean towel dipped in boiling water, then put on the cap.

Put the canning jars in a deep pan and add enough boiling water to come 2 inches above the caps. Cover, bring back to the boil, and boil 5 minutes. Remove the jars and let cool.

Jellies can be sealed with melted paraffin wax, in a ⅛-inch layer, and then covered with a lid. Do not process in the boiling-water bath if sealing with paraffin.

❖ Raspberry Jam ❖

MAKES ABOUT 6½ LB	• 4 lb raspberries	• 1 tbsp butter
PREPARATION TIME 10 minutes	• 4 lb (9 cups) sugar	
COOKING TIME About 1 hour		40 CALS/1 TBSP

1 Put the fruit in a preserving kettle and simmer very gently in its own juice, stirring carefully from time to time, until the fruit is really soft, about 20 minutes.

2 Remove the kettle from the heat and add the sugar, stirring until dissolved, then add the butter.

3 Boil rapidly until jell point is reached, about 30 minutes.

4 Remove any scum with a slotted spoon, then pack, seal, and process.

❖ Gooseberry ❖ and Elderflower Jam

MAKES ABOUT 10 LB	• 6 lb gooseberries (slightly under-ripe)	• 1 tbsp butter
PREPARATION TIME 20 minutes	• 20 elderflower heads, cut close to the stem	
COOKING TIME 50 minutes	• 6 lb (13½ cups) sugar	
COLOR INDEX Page 87		40 CALS/1 TBSP

1 Trim the gooseberries. Wash the elderflowers and tie in a piece of cheesecloth. Put the gooseberries in a preserving kettle with 5 cups water and the elderflower bundle. Simmer gently until the fruit is really soft and reduced, about 30 minutes, mashing it to a pulp with a wooden spoon and stirring from time to time to prevent sticking.

2 Remove the pan from the heat, add the sugar, and stir until dissolved, then add the butter. Bring to a boil and boil rapidly until jell point is reached, about 10 minutes.

3 Remove any scum with a slotted spoon. Remove the cheesecloth bag, then pack, seal, and process.

NOTE: Elderflowers impart a delicious flavor, but they may be omitted if unavailable.

❖ Blackberry Jam ❖

MAKES ABOUT 3½ LB	• 2¼ lb blackberries (not over-ripe), washed	• 5 cups "sugar with pectin"
PREPARATION TIME 10 minutes	• juice of ½ lemon	• 1 tbsp butter
COOKING TIME About 35 minutes		40 CALS/1 TBSP

1 Put the blackberries in a preserving kettle with the lemon juice and ½ cup water. Simmer very gently until the blackberries are very soft and are well reduced, about 30 minutes.
2 Remove the pan from the heat, add the sugar, and stir until dissolved, then add the butter. Bring to a boil and boil rapidly for until jell point is reached, about 4 minutes.
3 Remove any scum with a slotted spoon, then pack, seal and process.

❖ Apricot Jam ❖

MAKES ABOUT 6½ LB	• 4 lb apricots	• 4 lb (9 cups) sugar
PREPARATION TIME 20 minutes	• juice of 1 lemon	• 1 tbsp butter
COOKING TIME About 40 minutes	40 CALS/1 TBSP	

1 Halve the apricots and remove the pits. Crack a few of the apricot pits with a pounder, nutcracker, or hammer; take out the kernels, blanch them in boiling water 1 minute, then drain.
2 Put the apricots, lemon juice, apricot kernels, and 2 cups water in a preserving kettle and simmer until the fruit is soft and the contents of the pan are well reduced, about 15 minutes.
3 Take the pan off the heat and add the sugar, stirring until dissolved. Add the butter and boil rapidly until setting point is reached, about 15 minutes.
4 Remove any scum with a slotted spoon, then pack, seal, and process.

❖ Strawberry Jam ❖

MAKES ABOUT 4 LB	• 2 lb strawberries, hulled	• juice of ½ lemon
PREPARATION TIME 10 minutes, plus standing	• 5 cups "sugar with pectin"	
COOKING TIME About 10 minutes		
COLOR INDEX Page 87	35 CALS/1 TBSP	

1 Put the strawberries in a preserving kettle with the sugar and lemon juice. Heat gently, stirring until the sugar has dissolved.
2 Bring to a boil and boil steadily until jell point is reached, about 4 minutes.
3 Remove from the heat and remove any scum with a slotted spoon. Let stand 15–20 minutes.
4 Stir the jam gently, then pack, seal, and process.

❖ Strawberry Preserve ❖

MAKES ABOUT 3 LB	• 3 lb strawberries, hulled	• 3 lb (6¼ cups) sugar
PREPARATION TIME 15 minutes, plus standing		
COOKING TIME About 20 minutes		
COLOR INDEX Page 87	65 CALS/1 TBSP	

1 Put the strawberries in a large bowl in layers with the sugar. Cover and leave 24 hours.

2 Put the strawberries and sugar in a preserving kettle. Heat gently, stirring until the sugar dissolves. Bring to a boil and boil rapidly 5 minutes.

3 Return the mixture to the bowl, cover, and leave in a cool place for a further 2 days. Return to the pan.

4 Boil rapidly 10 minutes. Let cool 15 minutes. Pack, seal, and process.

❖ Apple and Mint Jelly ❖

PREPARATION TIME
30 minutes, plus standing
COOKING TIME
About 1¼ hours
COLOR INDEX
Page 87

- 5 lb cooking apples
- few large mint sprigs
- 5 cups distilled white vinegar
- sugar (see method)
- ½ cup chopped mint

- few drops of green food coloring (optional)

`35–40 CALS/1 TBSP`

1 Remove any bruised parts from the apples, then roughly chop into chunks without peeling or coring. Put the apples in a preserving kettle with 5 cups water and the mint sprigs.

2 Bring to a boil, then simmer gently until soft and pulpy, about 45 minutes, stirring from time to time to prevent sticking. Add the vinegar and boil 5 minutes longer.

3 Spoon the apple pulp into a jelly bag suspended over a large bowl and leave to drip through at least 12 hours.

4 Discard pulp remaining in jelly bag. Measure extract and return to the preserving kettle with 2¼ cups sugar for each 2½ cups extract.

5 Heat gently, stirring, until the sugar has dissolved, then boil rapidly until jell point is reached, about 10 minutes. Remove any scum with a slotted spoon.

6 Stir in the chopped mint and coloring, if using. Cool slightly, then stir well to distribute the mint. Pack and seal (process if not using paraffin). Serve with roast lamb or pork.

❖ Rosehip Jelly ❖

PREPARATION TIME
25 minutes, plus standing
COOKING TIME
About 1¼ hours
COLOR INDEX
Page 87

- 2 lb cooking apples
- 1 lb ripe rosehips
- sugar (see method)

`35–40 CALS/1 TBSP`

1 Remove any bruised or damaged portions from the apples, then roughly chop without coring or peeling.
2 Put the apples and rosehips in a preserving kettle with just enough water to cover. Bring to a boil, then simmer gently until the fruit is soft and pulpy, about 45 minutes, stirring from time to time to prevent sticking.
3 Spoon the fruit pulp into a jelly bag suspended over a large bowl and leave to drip through at least 12 hours.
4 Discard the pulp remaining in the jelly bag. Measure the extract and return to the preserving kettle with 2¼ cups sugar for each 2½ cups extract.
5 Heat gently, stirring, until the sugar has dissolved, then bring to a boil and boil rapidly until jell point is reached, about 15 minutes. Remove any scum with a slotted spoon, then pack and seal (process if not using paraffin).

❖ Lime Marmalade ❖

`MAKES ABOUT 5 LB`

- 1½ lb limes
- 3 lb (6¾ cups) sugar

PREPARATION TIME
20 minutes, plus standing
COOKING TIME
2–2½ hours

`35 CALS/1 TBSP`

1 For this recipe, you need kitchen scales: Weigh the empty preserving kettle or large saucepan before you start.

2 Put the limes in the preserving kettle with 7½ cups water and bring to a boil. Cover with a tight-fitting lid and simmer until the fruit is very soft, 1½–2 hours.

3 Remove the fruit from the pan with a slotted spoon and slice very thinly (using a knife and fork), discarding the seeds and reserving any juice. Return the sliced fruit and juice to the pan and weigh it. If necessary, boil the mixture, uncovered, until reduced to about 2½ lb.

4 Add the sugar and stir until it has dissolved, then bring to a boil and boil rapidly until jell point is reached, about 15 minutes. Remove any scum with a slotted spoon. Let the marmalade stand about 15 minutes, then stir gently to distribute the fruit. Pack, seal, and process.

2 Simmer gently until the peel is really soft and the liquid reduced by about half, about 2 hours. Remove the cheesecloth bag, squeezing it well and letting the juice run back into the pan. Add the sugar. Heat gently, stirring until the sugar has dissolved.

3 Bring to a boil and boil rapidly until jell point is reached, about 15 minutes.

4 Remove any scum with a slotted spoon. Let stand 15 minutes, then stir to distribute the peel. Pack, seal and process.

❖ Seville Orange Marmalade ❖

MAKES ABOUT 10 LB	• 3 lb Seville oranges	• 6 lb (13½ cups) sugar
	• juice of 2 lemons	

PREPARATION TIME
30 minutes
COOKING TIME
About 2½ hours

`35 CALS/1 TBSP`

1 Halve the oranges and squeeze out the juice and seeds. Tie the seeds, and any membrane that has come away during squeezing, in a piece of cheesecloth. Slice the orange peel thinly or thickly, as preferred, and put it in a preserving kettle with the fruit juices, cheesecloth bag, and 3½ quarts water.

❖ Lemon Curd ❖

MAKES ABOUT 1¼ LB	• grated rind and juice of 4 medium ripe, juicy lemons	• 1 stick (½ cup) butter, cut in small pieces
	• 4 eggs, beaten	• 1¼ cups sugar

PREPARATION TIME
20 minutes
COOKING TIME
About 25 minutes
COLOR INDEX
Page 88

`55 CALS/1 TBSP`

1 Place all the ingredients in a heatproof bowl over a pan of simmering water. Stir until the sugar has dissolved. Heat gently, without boiling, until thick enough to coat the back of the spoon, about 20 minutes.

2 Strain the lemon curd and pour into jars. Cover in the usual way. Store in the refrigerator and use within 2–3 weeks.

Variation

LIME CURD: Replace the lemons with the grated rind and juice of 5 large ripe, juicy limes.

❖ Hot Mango Chutney ❖

MAKES ABOUT 3 LB

PREPARATION TIME
25 minutes
COOKING TIME
About 1 hour
COLOR INDEX
Page 88

- 2½ lb firm mangoes, just starting to ripen (about 2 large ones)
- 1-oz piece fresh gingerroot
- 2–3 small red or green hot chili peppers
- 1 large onion, peeled
- 1 garlic clove, peeled
- 1 lb cooking apples
- 1 tbsp salt
- 2½ cups white wine vinegar
- ½ tsp ground cinnamon
- 1½ cups coarse light brown sugar
- 1 cup + 2 tbsp granulated sugar

`30 CALS/1 TBSP`

1 Peel the mangoes and cut into 1-inch pieces. Peel and mince the ginger. Seed and mince the chilies, wearing rubber gloves to avoid skin irritation. Roughly chop the onion and garlic. Peel, core, and roughly chop the apples.

2 Put all the ingredients, except the sugars, in a preserving kettle. Bring to a boil and simmer gently until the fruits are beginning to soften, about 10 minutes.

3 Add the coarse and granulated sugars and heat gently, stirring until dissolved, then bring to a boil. Reduce the heat and simmer, uncovered, stirring occasionally, until thick, about 45 minutes. Cool the chutney slightly, then pack, seal, and process.

❖ Squash and Tomato Chutney ❖

MAKES 3½–4 LB

PREPARATION TIME
20 minutes
COOKING TIME
About 1 hour
COLOR INDEX
Page 88

- 3 lb summer squash
- 1 lb ripe tomatoes
- 2 onions, peeled
- 2 garlic cloves, peeled
- 2 tsp black peppercorns
- 2 tsp allspice berries
- 2 tbsp salt
- 2 tsp ground ginger
- 3½ cups sugar
- 3 cups cider vinegar

`30 CALS/1 TBSP`

1 Peel the squash, halve lengthwise, and remove the central seeds. Cut the flesh into ½-inch chunks. Peel and roughly chop the tomatoes. Roughly chop the onions and garlic.
2 Finely crush the peppercorns and allspice with a pestle and mortar, or use the end of a rolling pin in a bowl.
3 Put all the ingredients in a large saucepan. Heat gently, stirring until the sugar has dissolved. Bring to a boil and boil steadily, stirring occasionally to prevent sticking, until reduced by half, about 50 minutes. (This will be a little more liquid than most chutneys.)
4 Cool the chutney slightly, then pack, seal, and process.

❖ Green Tomato Chutney ❖

MAKES ABOUT 3 LB

PREPARATION TIME
20 minutes
COOKING TIME
About 2 hours

- 1 lb cooking apples
- 2 onions, peeled
- 3 lb green tomatoes
- 1⅓ cups golden raisins
- 1½ cups coarse light brown sugar
- 2 tsp salt
- 2 cups malt vinegar
- 4 small pieces dried gingerroot
- ½ tsp cayenne pepper
- 1 tsp mustard powder

`20 CALS/1 TBSP`

1 Peel, quarter, and core the apples. Finely grate the apples and onions. Thinly slice the tomatoes.
2 Place all the ingredients in a large saucepan. Bring to a boil, reduce the heat, and simmer gently, stirring occasionally, until the ingredients are tender and reduced to a thick consistency, and no excess liquid remains, about 2 hours. Discard ginger.
3 Spoon the chutney into jars, seal, and process.

FOOD SAFETY

Correct food storage and preparation is important for preventing food poisoning. It also helps extend the life of food and ensures that food remains as nutritious and flavorful as possible.

❖ General Kitchen Hygiene ❖

Following a few simple guidelines will help make your kitchen a safe and hygienic place for food preparation and storage:
- Wash down and dry surfaces regularly using a mild detergent solution or multi-surface cleaner.
- Use rubber gloves for dishwashing, so that water can be hotter than hands can bear. Let dishes drain, if possible: This is more hygienic than towel-drying.
- Change dish towels and cleaning cloths regularly.
- Use plastic chopping boards for preparing food. These are more hygienic than wooden ones as they can be washed in a dishwasher or in very hot water with a mild solution of bleach or sterilizing solution.
- Ideally, keep separate chopping boards for different foods, such as raw meat, fish, vegetables, and cooked foods. Wooden chopping boards cannot be cleaned as thoroughly as plastic ones; if you prefer to use them, scrub thoroughly after use and let dry thoroughly before storing.
- Always wash your hands before handling food and again between handling different types of food, such as raw and cooked meat where you could transfer bacteria from one to the other.
- Always wash knives and other kitchen utensils in between preparing raw and cooked foods.
- Never put cooked or ready-to-eat foods on a surface that has just had raw food on it.
- Use paper towels to wipe up spills from meat or poultry juices.
- Never handle food with an uncovered cut. Keep wounds covered with a clean, sterile bandage.
- Keep pets out of the kitchen, or at least discourage them from walking or sitting on work surfaces.

❖ Buying Food ❖

- When you are shopping, always be guided by the use-before date. It is illegal to sell food that is past its use-before date. Certain foods – such as salt, sugar, and alcoholic drinks – do not require a date mark. Date marks are only valid if the food is stored in accordance with the manufacturer's instructions; they do not apply once the packaging has been opened.

Apply the following guidelines whenever you are shopping for food:
- Shop at a reliable source; avoid stores that appear unclean.
- Avoid packs that are damaged or look dirty or dusty.
- Beware of chilled or frozen food display cabinets that are overfilled.
- Before you buy, look at the dates on the goods and make sure that they are still within their use-before date. Check that food will still be within this date when you are intending to use it.
- If you are buying chilled or frozen foods make sure they can be stored correctly right away. If you shop in your lunch hour, don't let chilled or frozen foods remain in a warm office or in the trunk of your car all afternoon.
- Pack all chilled or frozen foods together in an insulated cool bag or box at the checkout.
- Pack fresh food separately from cooked food.
- As soon as you get home, put perishable food in the refrigerator or freezer immediately.

❖ Safe Storage ❖

Always check the label to see if the manufacturer has given any storage advice; this is important even with familiar foods. As manufacturers have started to remove some of the additives from foods and reduce levels of sugar and salt, storage requirements may have changed. For instance, once opened, most jams need to be kept in the refrigerator.

Apply the following guidelines to food storage:
- keep your kitchen cabinets, refrigerator, and freezer clean. Spilt food, drips, and broken packages can spread bacteria and attract flies, ants, and mice.
- Cabinets or shelves used to store food should be cool, dry, and well ventilated.
- Use up staples efficiently, using older packs first.
- Do not use cans that are swollen, rusty, leaking, or badly dented.
- Once opened, canned foods should be treated as though they are fresh. Transfer contents to a clean container, cover, and keep in the refrigerator.
- Transfer dry goods such as sugar, rice, and pasta into moistureproof containers. Old supplies should be used up before new ones are started, and containers washed and dried thoroughly before refilling.

❖ Refrigerator Storage ❖

When choosing a refrigerator, make sure you buy one that is large enough for your needs. Most modern refrigerators have a separate freezer compartment, and the ratio of refrigerator space to freezer space varies from model to model. If you like to keep a lot of frozen food, choose a model that will give you adequate space. Or, buy a separate freezer, chest or upright. Note that the small